MIDDLE CLASS HOUSING IN BRITAIN

MIDDLE CLASS HOUSING IN BRITAIN

Edited by

M. A. Simpson and T. H. Lloyd

DAVID & CHARLES
Newton Abbot   London   Vancouver

ARCHON BOOKS
Hamden, Connecticut

This edition first published in 1977
in Great Britain by David & Charles (Publishers) Limited,
Brunel House, Newton Abbot, Devon,
in Canada by Douglas David & Charles Limited,
1875 Welch Street, North Vancouver, BC,
and in the United States of America by Archon Books,
an imprint of The Shoe String Press, Inc, Hamden,
Connecticut 06514

ISBN 0 7153 7273 4 (Great Britain)

Library of Congress Cataloging in Publication Data
Main entry under title:

Middle class housing in Britain.

Includes index.
1. Housing—Great Britain—History—Case studies.
2. Middle classes—Great Britain—History—Case studies.
3. Cities and towns—Great Britain—History—Case
studies. 4. Great Britain—Social conditions—19th
century. I. Simpson, Michael. II. Lloyd, Terrence H.
HD7333.A3S79   301.5′4′0941   76-12618
ISBN 0-208-01606-6

Printed in Great Britain

Contents

Introduction

M. A. Simpson and T. H. Lloyd

In his introduction to a symposium on the history of
working-class housing published in 1971, Dr Stanley
Chapman said: '... there has been nothing on housing
beyond an article or two in academic journals and a few
pages in more general works'. Yet the history of
middle-class housing is even more neglected, while there
has been some progress in the working-class housing field
since the publication of what might be termed our
companion volume.

Working-class housing has received some attention from
modern historians if only because it was of such great
concern to the Victorians. The housing of the working
class - both rural and urban - was perhaps the most
intractable social problem of the last century. Many of
the leading figures of the time wrote or spoke about it
or tried to improve it - Prince Albert, Lords Rosebery,
Salisbury, and Shaftesbury, Octavia Hill, John Burns and
others. It was discussed in novels and tracts, was
rarely out of the newspapers and journals of opinion,
several royal commissions touched upon it and one was
specifically devoted to it. It had a prominent place in
the exhaustive studies of working-class life by Booth
and Rowntree. Acts and bylaws were passed to improve it,
assisted by philanthropic endeavours. The result of a
century of concern for the housing of the less affluent
has been a massive accumulation of documentary material,
an apparently inexhaustible mine for historians,
probably frightening in its breadth and depth.

Middle-class families, on the other hand, generally
found satisfactory accommodation, at prices and rents
they could afford, through the operation of an unfettered
free market. Since the housing of the middle class was
not a social problem, neither contemporaries nor modern
scholars have paid it much attention, so that published
references are to be found chiefly in novels, memoirs
and architectural monographs. The middle class might

have been able to take care of itself, but, how it
took care of its own housing is surely a serious
historical question worthy of careful and scholarly
investigation. Moreover, even on the meanest definition
of the middle class, its numbers in Victorian times
certainly ran into millions. A visit to any major town
will show that it occupied considerable urban space.
Furthermore, in taking care of its own accommodation
problems, the middle class, and those who built for it,
often created works of art in domestic architecture and
urban planning, many of them serving as models for our
own times. However, what makes thorough and systematic
study of middle-class housing not only important but
urgent is the sad fact that much of the physical evidence
is fast disappearing - perhaps not as rapidly as the
greater mass of working-class housing, but as surely and
more regrettably. Urban redevelopment, inner city
blight, increasing institutional and commercial use of
suburban villas and terraces, all these take their toll.
Worse still, many of the relevant records are in private
hands, and, although scholars can often obtain access to
them, the archival ranks are being thinned as steadily
as the architectural ones.

Our object in this volume has been, first, to draw
attention to the unjust and increasingly disturbing
neglect of a major topic in modern social and cultural
history. Second, to stimulate further research,
especially by younger scholars. Representatives of
geography, architecture, economic history and various
branches of urban history have contributed essays on six
cities markedly different in size, location, function,
character and the nature of their middle class. We hope
that the range of places, periods, disciplines, methods,
source materials and problems included in this selection
will aid future workers in this rewarding and under-
developed field.

The cities chosen represent a wide spectrum of urban
types: Exeter, an old English county town, largely
unaffected by industrialisation; Royal Leamington Spa,
one of the leading resort towns of the first half of the
nineteenth century; Nottingham, also an old county town
but experiencing rapid growth in the nineteenth century,
based chiefly on light industries; Sheffield, the great
steel and metalworking city; Glasgow, the Scottish port
and industrial centre; and Hampstead, perhaps the most

distinctively middle-class borough in London. The period
on which each writer has concentrated also differs.
Exeter and Leamington enjoyed their heyday before
Victoria, or at least before mid-century, by which time
The Park at Nottingham was about to be developed, while
the best years of Hampstead, the western suburbs of
Sheffield and the West End of Glasgow were yet to come.
The periods chosen nevertheless overlap and between them
the essays cover what might be termed the 'classic'
period of British social and urban history, 1760-1914.
The source materials available also vary greatly in both
quantity and quality from one city to another. Among
those used are newspapers, magazines, guide books and
directories, reminiscences, antiquarian notes, novels,
diaries, title deeds, building leases and other estate
papers, builders' records, local government archives
and parliamentary papers, and contemporary maps, plans
and illustrations. Contributors have also made use of
their own observations while walking the bounds of their
areas.

Diversity in approach has been achieved but, nevertheless, several common themes can be distinguished. It is
clear that the inhabitants of all areas under discussion
were of the middling and upper middle class. In Exeter,
they were retired generals and admirals, East India
Company officers, clergy and 'persons of independent
means'; at Leamington, the same groups were represented,
both among the residents and the long-stay visitors;
in The Park, Sheffield and Glasgow, local industrialists,
professional men and merchants dominated. Hampstead
contained the whole spectrum of middle class groups though
the majority were of the middling bourgeoisie. In all
these places there were 'droves of widows' as Professor
Thompson terms them; in Glasgow, about a quarter of the
households were headed by widows or spinsters and the
proportion was similar in the other places.

Most of the capital for building the grand houses and
fine amenities of these communities came from local
sources - from Coventry and Warwick for Leamington, from
the lower Clyde valley for the West End of Glasgow.
Speculators were responsible for most of the developments
and while some were existing landowners and others
builders, perhaps the majority were lawyers and merchants.
The greater part of urban growth in places like Exeter,
Leamington, Hampstead, Glasgow and Sheffield was piece-

9

meal, developers operating on lots of less than 10 acres.
Only rarely was an estate developed as a whole, to a
coherent plan; comprehensive large-scale planning of this
kind took place on the Maryon Wilson estate in Hampstead,
in the Duke of Newcastle's Park at Nottingham and in
Kelvinside in Glasgow. The majority of builders, too,
were in a small way, probably erecting no more than ten
houses a year and often falling into bankruptcy, as
practically every builder in Leamington did in 1837.
Only a handful operated on a significantly greater scale
– the Hoopers in Exeter, the Buddles in Leamington and
Samuel Cuming, George Duncan and William Willett in
Hampstead. In view of the jigsaw of small-scale
developments which made up all these communities, it is
remarkable that they possess the unity which we see in
them today.

It is also clear from these essays that in talking
about the housing of the middle class, one has to
recognise the high degree of freedom of choice these
families exercised and the importance of the environment
to them. Because middle-class house-hunters could afford
to choose between several rival developments, it paid
those who catered for them to satisfy their requirements
beyond the provision of elegant and spacious housing.
As Dr Newton points out, 'the emphasis on the view was
an inevitable component of advertisements for new houses'.
This interest in scenery, trees, parks and landscaping
is echoed in all the contributions. Moreover, developers
were at pains to prohibit nuisances and maintain the
exclusively middle-class nature of their projects, as can
be seen from the restrictive covenants imposed on
building in the West End of Glasgow, The Park, the
corporation of Exeter's Southernhay scheme and in several
Hampstead properties. Provision of ancillary amenities
led to the preservation and extension of the Heath in
Hampstead, a trust to preserve the Castle and its grounds
in Nottingham, Jephson Gardens in Leamington and the
Botanic Gardens in Sheffield and Glasgow. The houses
themselves were designed to reflect the wealth, status
and high level of culture of the occupants. They were
great centres of entertainment – Mark Firth played host
to the Prince of Wales in Sheffield, and Leamington was
designed to provide entertainment and hospitality for
the great. It is remarkable how long the Classical
terrace and villa survived in these cities. It hung on
to the end of the century in Glasgow but Gothic and

10

Tudor forms began to replace it in Exeter, Leamington, Nottingham and Sheffield from mid-century. Characteristically, Hampstead evolved a bizarre collection of styles, both pure and hybrid. Whatever the stylistic pedigree of the houses in any given city, they all combined distinction and splendour with space and privacy. Their own attractions and that of their environment helped them to marry the best features of town and country without the drawbacks of either.

If this collection of essays opens the door to more systematic and comprehensive studies of the history of middle-class housing by students of the several relevant disciplines, it will have served its purpose.

M.A. Simpson
T.H. Lloyd

University College of Swansea

Chapter I

Exeter, 1770-1870

Robert Newton

In the history of the city of Exeter the century 1770-
1870 defines, with fortuitous chronological precision,
a distinct architectural period. With rather less
precision these dates mark the period when the city rose
to its peak, socially and culturally, as a provincial
capital, a time when bankers, lawyers, medical men and
clergy set the tone and constituted the governing class.
These professional classes supplied the initial demand
for the new houses of Exeter's Georgian and Regency
phases.

In 1769 Mackworth Praed, one of the proprietors of the
newly founded Exeter Bank, opened in the Cathedral Yard
an inn which, so far as is known, was the first English
inn to adopt the French style of hotel. (1) The opening
of the Clarence was regarded by a local historian as the
moment when 'the spirit of improvement now began to
manifest itself in the city'. (2) Almost simultaneously
the surgeon John Patch built his fine new residence
known as Rougemont House, a fitting inauguration of
Exeter's great period of domestic building by a member of
a profession acquiring status and influence in the city.
The construction of superior, or at least comfortable
and convenient, genteel houses, reached its peak in the
decade 1820-30, especially in the pleasant rural parishes
of Heavitree and St Leonard's which were later absorbed
within the municipal area of Exeter. (3) This development was singularly unaffected by the post-war economic
crises, including the severe deflation which followed the
government's monetary policy in 1820. The period ended
with a brief burst of residential building in St David's
parish, inspired by the construction of the Bristol to
Exeter railway which reached St David's station in 1844.

Architectural style throughout remained basically
classical in inspiration, though the 1840s also produced

some restrained early Victorian Gothic. The last
reflections of the classical tradition, as interpreted
by local architects and builders, lingered in the houses
constructed in St David's in 1868-69. About 1870 there
was a sharp change in materials and style. Henceforward
new houses were distinguished by shiny machine-made brick,
blue slates and red ornamental ridge-tiles. It was the
era of builders' catalogues, of new materials which were
sometimes an affront to the local landscape, of a
striving for individuality which too often replaced
harmony by discord. Architectural change coincided with
a loss of confidence in the city. It was no longer
claimed for Exeter that 'No reasonable being need seek
elsewhere a residence more salubrious, comfortable, polite
and friendly'. (4) Instead, the newspapers directed the
public's attention to a polluted Exe, a high death rate,
dirt and disease. In the sphere of local government it
had become only too obvious that the messianic visions
of the reformers of the 1830s had been followed by more
earthly realities.

For some seventy years Exeter regarded itself as moving
with the tide in 'the Age of Improvement'. Development
and improvement went hand in hand. Its citizens made
their own contribution to 'the daring flights of imagination' which, as Asa Briggs has pointed out, were
roused in that age. (5) Exeter had long had a reputation
for beauty, good society and a vigorous economic life.
Defoe had found Exeter remarkable for two things which,
he wrote, were unusual in the same town: '...A city full
of gentry and good company, yet full of trade and manu-
factures withal'. (6) When, 'from about 1688 to 1715,
the serge industry was the most important branch of the
national woollen manufacture ... Exeter was synonymous
in contemporary pamphlets with the serge trade'. (7)
At the end of the seventeenth century Exeter ranked
second only to Bristol among provincial ports. (8) But
technological change in the woollen industry led to the
decline of Exeter's major industry and this, together
with the long years of naval warfare in the second half
of the eighteenth century, reduced the once thriving
overseas trade to little more than coastwise activities.
Yet this period saw the 'take off' of Exeter's most
distinguished period of domestic architecture and a
vigorous expansion of good houses around the city.

Between 1801 and 1871 the population of Exeter within

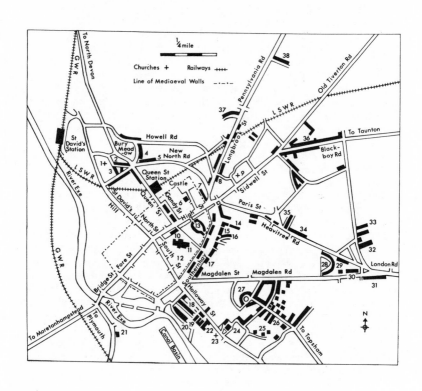

Fig 1 Middle class housing in Exeter, 1770-1870

Key to numbers in Fig 1

 1 St David's church
 2 Queen's Terrace
 3 Bystock Terrace
 4 Elm Grove
 5 Rougemont Terrace
 6 Rougemont House
 7 Northernhay Terrace
 8 Hampton Buildings
 9 St Sidwell's church
10 Royal Clarence hotel
11 Cathedral
12 Cathedral Yard
13 Bedford Circus
14 Dix's Field
15 Chichester Place
16 Barnfield Crescent
17 Southernhay Place
18 The Friars
19 Melbourne Place
20 Colleton Crescent
21 Sydney Place
22 Melbourne Street
23 St Leonard's church
24 Mount Radford House
25 Claremont Grove
26 Park Place
27 Radford Crescent
28 Baring Crescent
29 Midway Terrace
30 Baring Place
31 Salutary Mount
32 Mont Le Grand
33 Regent's Park
34 Higher Summerlands
35 Lower Summerlands
36 Hiram Place
37 Pennsylvania Crescent
38 Pennsylvania Park

GWR   Great Western Railway
LSWR London & South Western Railway

the municipal boundary rose from about 17,412 to 34,600,
the fastest rate of growth occurring between 1811 and 1831.
Exeter plainly was not in the main stream of the
contemporary expansion of urban England. Leicester,
starting from the same base, a population of 17,000 in
1801, had a population of 97,662 by 1871. The rate of
increase of inhabited houses was equally modest, the
best figures within the municipal area being 24.6 per
cent in 1821-31 and 23.5 per cent in the following
decade. Residential development, however, was primarily
in the three parishes of St Sidwell's, St David's and
Holy Trinity which lay wholly or in part outside the line
of the medieval walls, and more especially in the
adjacent rural parishes of Heavitree and St Leonard's. (9)
Inhabited houses in Heavitree increased by about 65 per cent
in 1821-31 and by nearly 52 per cent in 1831-41. Heavitree,
wrote the compiler of a directory in 1828, 'has, within
the last few years, felt extensively the exhilarating
hand of improvement. The vast number of genteel houses
and villas recently erected here far exceed our limits
of description'. (10) The growth rate for houses in St
Leonard's reached its peak of 187 per cent in the decade
1821-31; the population of the parish increased by nearly
126 per cent in 1821-31 and 163 per cent in 1831-41.
In absolute terms the numbers are small. In Heavitree
inhabited houses increased from 163 in 1801 to 725 in
1871, in St Leonard's from 26 to 295, the figures
referring solely to middle-class houses in St Leonard's
and predominantly to houses of that class in Heavitree.
  Building land was provided both by the development
of major estates and by the piecemeal development of
agricultural land, nurseries and market gardens, and
rack-yards of the decaying cloth industry, surrounding
Exeter. There was also much infilling of the relatively
large gardens in the older built-up areas as these
became less convenient, or less fashionable, for
prosperous citizens. Thus, in 1817, the bankruptcy of
a wine and brandy merchant provided 10 acres adjacent
to the Tiverton road with the requisite fine views:
'... A more desirable situation for building in the
vicinity of Exeter could not be found'. (11) By 1841
building and ancillary trades had become a major industry
in Exeter. The Militia List of 1803 suggests that close
on 8 per cent of the male population between the ages
of 17 and 55 were employed in building and related

16

activities: carpenters, masons, painters, plumbers and
glaziers. (12) In 1841 the proportion of males over the
age of 20 thus employed was 17.3 per cent, compared
with 9.3 per cent in York City and 7 per cent in Nottingham and Leicester. (13) In the early years of the
nineteenth century builders were usually house-agents
and auctioneers as well; but the demand encouraged
specialisation. The first house and land agent of the
modern type appeared in Exeter in 1822 when Robert
Dymond, land surveyor, informed the public that he had
established 'a general registry for lands, houses and
other property for sale or to let'. (14) In the same
year Mr O. Macdonald jr respectfully informed 'the
Nobility, Gentry, Land-Surveyors and Builders, who have
houses to let or sell, that ... he is induced to establish
an office for that purpose' in Exeter. Business prospects
attracted architects such as Andrew Patey, who was
responsible for the Exchange and Auction Mart at Plymouth
and the new Assembly Rooms at Teignmouth, as well as
various country houses, and who found it worth his while
to move to Exeter in 1826. Here he designed the new
and larger church of St Leonard's in the 1830s.
    The basic causes of the growth of Exeter were the
city's geographical position, its climate and, from the
late eighteenth century, the prosperity engendered
throughout the south-west by war. Since the Iron Age
Exeter's importance and prosperity had depended on the
city's position on the ridge-road above the crossing of
the Exe. Later all roads of importance converged at
this gateway of the Dumnonian peninsula; roads to the
garrison towns, naval bases and anchorages - Plymouth,
Devonport, Dartmouth and Falmouth, Tor Bay and Mount's
Bay. The vast improvement of the main roads of the
west in the second half of the eighteenth century
reaffirmed Exeter's key position as a centre of
communications and led to the rise of famous inns whose
proprietors became prosperous and respected figures in
local society. Through Exeter, itself a garrison town,
came royalty, English and foreign, admirals, generals,
members of the aristocracy, contractors and purveyors
for the forces, travelling between London, Plymouth and
Falmouth. For travellers such as these the Clarence
was redecorated in 1813 and the hotel was 'constantly
supplied with the choicest of wines and the best of
spirits ... with excellent venison and turtle'. (15)

17

Thirty-six coaches were advertised to leave Exeter daily
for major towns and cities - London, Bath, Bristol,
Liverpool, Plymouth, Portsmouth and Falmouth. In 1814
the Subscription coach reached Exeter from London in
seventeen hours.

The assizes, political and other business, brought the
county gentry and aristocracy into the city. Assemblies,
balls, concerts and theatrical performances were
provided for these visitors, for their families, and for
the naval and army officers on pleasure or business, or
as residents on retirement. Subscription balls could
boast of 'a very numerous assembly of nobility and
gentry' (16) to mingle with the leading professional
and business men of Exeter. In 1831 the city could
attract performances by Nicolo Paganini. In 1835 Richard
Ford, traveller, writer and man-of-the-world, could write:
'This Exeter is quite a capital, abounding in all that
London has except its fog and smoke. There is an
excellent institution here in which I take great pastime
and am beginning my education. There is a bookseller
who has some ten thousand old volumes'. (17)
Directories and local historians vied in eulogies of the
city and its neighbourhood:

'The richness of the soil, and fertility of the
country round Exeter, - the cheapness and plentiful supply of markets in the comparison with
other places, - the agreeable walks and rides
in the vicinity, - the numerous and genteel
society now found in the neighbourhood, - the
respectable schools for instruction, - and places
of divine worship for all denominations, together
with the most constant supply of amusements, -
the short distance from the sea and so many
fashionable watering places, render this city in
point of residence, one of the most healthy and
desirable in the kingdom'. (18)

Socially Exeter could not compete with Cheltenham, but
it was cheaper, if less fashionable, and the cost of
keeping up appearances was less demanding. The diary of
Lady Paterson, wife of General Sir William Paterson,
makes it clear that her husband preferred the society
of Cheltenham. (19)

War and expanding imperial commitments overseas provided

opportunities to acquire wealth which provided the means
for retirement in a mild climate with congenial society.
The directories (20) and the social columns of local
newspapers abound with evidence of the overseas connections of the city and its popularity with retired officers
in the early nineteenth century: men such as admirals
Cumberland, Raggett and Granger, and General Guard, all
living on Southernhay; Admiral Dilkes of Bedford Circus;
Admiral Swiney of Sydney Place in St Thomas's; Captain
Tanner, East India Company's Marine Service, of Summerland Place, who became mayor in 1858 after one of the
murkier episodes in Exeter's municipal history. Captain
Carter, also of the East India Company's Marine Service,
bought a recently constructed 'very tasteful and elegant
villa orné' in St David's in 1832. (21) Nabobs of the
old style did not retire to Exeter, and local society
would not have appealed to Joseph Sedley of Vanity Fair;
but retired members of the East India Company made a
major contribution to the demand for modern houses in the
city. Major Dowell, of the East India Company's Bengal
Establishment, financed the construction of some of the
new houses in Southernhay about 1816, (22) one of them
being the large house which in 1832 was sold to Colonel
Truscott, also of the East India Company, for £2,998.
Ten years later Truscott, by that time a general, sold
the house to another general for £3,200. The lure of
eastern empire led to an abortive proposal to convert
the former Baring (23) property, Mount Radford House,
into an Exeter public school on the lines of Haileybury
with special arrangements for the teaching of oriental
languages. Officers formed an important element in what
the bishop, in 1828, described as 'the fluctuating
nature of the population of Exeter'. Furniture sales
revealed the detritus of overseas service: '... A
collection of foreign shells and minerals, stuffed
crocodiles, birds of paradise and natural curiosities,
implements of war, brought from the South Seas', in one
of the new houses in Heavitree; lion and tiger skins,
'Zulu and Chinese curiosities' in a house in Radford
Crescent, St Leonard's in 1846. (24)
    The initial impetus for the expansion of middle-class
housing in the Age of Improvement, came from within the
city itself. It derived from the new tastes and
prosperity of the upper levels of Exeter's middle
classes who required houses with light and air and a
setting of natural beauty, though the picturesque was

19

expected to conform to correct standards of harmony and
composition. In Exeter almost every street offered some
glimpses of the city's unrivalled setting. Outside the
walls lay a wide landscape of orchards, fields and
gardens, the sea and the moorland heights of Haldon, the
farms and modest country houses which provided nature
with the requisite touch of human improvement. A country
house and an estate had always been the seal of success
for merchants and professional men; the new demand was
for Martial's <u>rus in urbe</u> within easy walking distance
of social and business centres. The concept was
essentially urban with the country confined to a small
garden and a view. This urbane and mannered union of
town and country was particularly evident in the growth
of the new residential areas of Pennsylvania and Heavitree
– Pennsylvania Building, Salutary Mount, Stafford Terrace,
Mont le Grand and Regent's Park – between about 1815 and
1840. Mont le Grand, completed in the 1830s with pilastered doors and elegant tympanum wreaths, in a spacious
setting, is a sophisticated development of the Georgian
terrace; the culmination of a process originated by the
Chamber (25) the old governing body of the city, in the
1770s.

The difficulty of attempting any definition of the
middle classes is notorious:

'In nineteenth century Britain there were landowners and people occupying land, who might, or
might not, be conceived to be gentlemen. There
were rich men graduating into gentility. There
were the professional classes – lawyers, doctors,
the clergy, army and naval officers, and later
such people as architects, civil engineers and
civil servants – who might be conceived to be
gentlemen by reason of function. All these groups
might in some analyses be called middle classes,
in others not.' (26)

'Rich men graduating into gentility', lawyers, doctors,
newspaper proprietors, bankers, the Anglican clergy,
these were the groups within the city itself which set
social and cultural standards and exercised local power.
They were the guardians of a respectability conferred by
Toryism and membership of the Church of England. At the
top Exeter's middle classes merged with county society.

Some bankers and clergy undoubtedly had county connections; so did an occasional attorney. Other members of the legal and medical professions, and Anglican clergy, were brought into close association with the county and aristocracy professionally and socially without necessarily being accepted as gentlemen by social purists of the day. Sir Walter Elliott of Kellynch was misled by the application of the term gentleman to a curate; Lady Catherine de Burgh, while accepting the gentility of Mr Bennett, dismissed his wife as merely an attorney's daughter. (27) This attitude would undoubtedly have been shared by the 'gentleman of rank' who advertised for a bride in one of the Exeter newspapers in 1834 and was at pains to emphasise that 'he could not, of course, contract any inferior alliance. His wishes, therefore, would incline him towards respectable county families and the junior branches of the nobility'. (28) Among those who lived in the new houses of Exeter some were certainly members of county families or the aristocracy; but The Times in 1857 regarded the EICS - so well represented in early nineteenth-century Exeter - as essentially middle-class, claiming in a leading article that it was 'the business-like talent, the energy, the will, the sobriety, the justice of this class which has conquered India'. (29) By the strictest social standards of the time, Exeter society as a whole, and its ruling groups, may be regarded as middle class with some connecting links with county society.

W.G. Hoskins has drawn attention to evidence of a cleavage in early eighteenth-century Exeter between merchants and professional men. (30) By the end of the century the professional classes dominated most aspects of local life (especially if they were Anglican and Tory) and set the pattern of cultural standards and taste. The prominence of the medical profession was remarkable. In 1835 the Chamber, with a total membership of twenty-five, included no less than nine doctors or surgeons, including the mayor. Medicine was a road to prosperity; thus Dr Miller, who charged a guinea for prescribing a change of air to General Paterson's daughter, lived in one of the fine new houses in Southernhay Place and left £35,000 in personal estate. (31) The lawyers were ubiquitous on both sides in city and parliamentary politics, especially after the reforms of 1832-5. Only one lawyer was a member of the Chamber in 1835; there were five in the reformed corporation in 1837 and eleven

in 1838. At the top of the social structure stood the
bankers; they provided influential members of the Chamber
but their overt participation in local government dimin-
ished after the Municipal Corporations Act. As a group
the Anglican clergy shared the social status, and much of
the political influence, of the leading medical men and
lawyers; the voting lists show that they were staunchly
Tory. Local clerical society was reinforced by other
clergy, who, like laymen, found Exeter an agreeable place
for retirement.

As a provincial capital, and a centre of distribution
and communications, Exeter provided goods, especially
luxury goods, and financial, professional and political
services, for a wide area. The prosperous business
element included inn proprietors, licensed victuallers,
brewers, goldsmiths and silversmiths, drapers, haber-
dashers, hatters, ironmongers, auctioneers and builders.
Communications in its various aspects amounted to a
major industry. Grocers, wine merchants and tea merchants
did business with the well-to-do visitors attracted by the
neighbouring seaside resorts. In the first half of the
eighteenth century, when Exeter was still largely confined
within the circuit of the old walls, businessmen custom-
arily lived above shops and offices which were often
substantial premises, such as those of a grocer at 248
High Street which in 1828 comprised two large cellars,
a large shop and warehouse, store-rooms, two kitchens,
dining-room, drawing-room, six bedrooms, two dressing-
rooms and two water-closets. (32) A cabinet maker's
house in Fore Street at this period comprised a large
cellar, on the ground floor the shop, parlour, kitchen
and two pumps, on the first floor a drawing-room 22ft
square. There were eight 'lodging rooms' (ie bedrooms)
on the second and third floors, those on the third floor
being converted into workshops. Even a watchmaker's
house in the West Quarter, a working-class area of the
city in the vicinity of the river and the church of
St Mary Steps, included a shop, parlour, kitchen,
drawing-room and six bedrooms, but this must have been
the decayed shell of a former merchant's dwelling.

As in all ancient cities much vacant space existed
side by side with such congestion. The former properties
of Tudor merchants within the walls provided relatively
extensive gardens and small orchards which, as already
mentioned, became available for building development.
But despite these open spaces, its famed beauty of situation,

its salubrious air and polite society, old Exeter was
dirty and smelly, with an inadequate water supply.
Streets were heaped with ordure and offal. It was not
until after the cholera epidemic of 1832 that vigorous
attempts were made to remedy the insanitary condition of
the city; by that time road widening and construction
had been in progress for some sixty years.

   The new middle-class houses of the early nineteenth
century were intended to provide comfort, space for
entertainment and a suitable setting for the wealth and
status of the owner. The dining-room was particularly
important both for entertainment and display, and in
middle-class homes it was often the family room, the
drawing-room being used only on important occasions.
To allow freedom of movement for the servants a minimum
width of 14ft was regarded as essential, and 18ft was
preferable. In a superior house such as 4 Baring Place,
built by the Hoopers and occupied by General Paterson
in the 1830s, the dining-room measured 26ft x 17ft. (33)
It was a common practice to provide a folding or sliding
door between the dining-room and the drawing-room so that
the two could be used as one. Smaller houses, such as
Hampton Buildings completed in the 1820s in Longbrook
Street, retained the parlour as dining-room and family
room, though there was also a drawing-room. Larger
houses contained a breakfast-parlour, housekeeper's room
and butler's pantry. Houses in Stafford Terrace,
Heavitree, completed for 'the reception of genteel
families in 1826' included a dining-room and drawing-room,
each measuring 22ft x 14ft, three sitting-rooms, six
bedrooms and water-closets fitted with hydraulic pumps.
Furniture of a high quality - rosewood couches, loo and
card tables, and rosewood chairs covered in damask -
were provided by local craftsmen.

   The water-closet was coming into use by the end of the
eighteenth century but evidently was still worthy of
specific mention in advertisements of new houses in the
early decades of the nineteenth. The pumps in Stafford
Terrace seem to have been those advertised in 1815
'on the Oxford plan', comprising a 'brass hydraulic pump
fixed on a plank with handle power, completely mounted
... to fill cisterns in mansions and serving for common
use as well'. (34) In 1815 the cost was 9 guineas.
The large old-fashioned house of Thomas Mack, stationer
of Fore Street hill, with the shop on the ground floor,

contained in the cellar a pump of hard water which also
supplied the wc as well as a tank holding 30 hogsheads
of rain-water. Domestic water supply in Exeter remained
unsatisfactory until the end of the nineteenth century
and most of the new houses had pumps for both soft and
hard water.

Gas street-lighting was introduced into Exeter in 1817;
cooking by gas was demonstrated in the 1830s. By 1833
G. and J. Garton, smiths and brass-founders, were
offering to heat houses by hot water, hot air or steam.

Emphasis on the view was an inevitable component of
the advertisements for new houses. Supreme in this
respect were Pennsylvania Buildings, built by Joseph
Rower for the Quaker banker Joseph Sparkes and completed
by 1823. Standing on a height of over 300ft 'on the
ascent of an easy hill' they commanded a justly famous
view from Exeter to the sea, the subject of many paintings
and engravings. A stucco terrace elegantly classic in
style, the houses, one of which was occupied by Joseph
Sparkes himself, contained dining- and breakfast-rooms,
drawing-room, library, five family and four servants'
bedrooms, and had a water-closet. Near at hand were
sites for stables and coach houses. (35) Even the
modest contemporary houses of Hiram Place, off Blackboy
Road, with only a parlour, drawing-room, three bedrooms
and two attics, were offered with the inducement of 'a
delightful view'. Their occupants in 1828 included a
tea-dealer and a builder.

The opening stage of Exeter's expansion beyond the
walls was pre-eminently the period of the Georgian
terrace; well-proportioned and unadorned rows of houses
constructed in the soft local brick. The first such
extensive project for the construction of 'large,
convenient dwelling houses fit for the reception of
genteel families' was undertaken by the Chamber in
Southernhay, the south hay or enclosure outside the
city walls. Though now marred by a multiplicity of
traffic signs and unsympathetic modern buildings in the
vicinity, Southernhay remains today one of the outstanding architectural attractions of Exeter and a fine example
of provincial Georgian planning. House-building in the
area lasted some thirty years, from the simple houses of
a Georgian terrace to the more imposing Southernhay House
of the Regency period with a Doric colonnaded portico,
and the Doric columns and stucco of Chichester Place,

built by William Hooper in about 1825. Southernhay House
has been described as 'representative of the large type of
middle-class house of its period'. (36) The appeal of the
new houses, as expressed by an advertisement for two
offered for sale by the builder Matthew Nosworthy in 1819,
lay in 'the respectability of their neighbourhood, their
extreme pleasantness, the salubrity of their situation and
their internal conveniences'. (37) They were suitable both
as private residences and as 'genteel lodging houses' for
the visitors coming to Exeter at a time of improving
communications and more extensive travel.

The development of Southernhay residential area originated with a decision of the Chamber on 24 October, 1774:
'... Ordered that Mr Receiver do employ Mr Stowey Esq.
and Mr Jones, Builder of this city, to draw a proper plan
for buildings as soon as possible and to lay the same
before this body'. In November of the same year the
Chamber reaffirmed that 'it is the opinion of this Body
that Building upon Southernhay will be beneficial to the
publick'. (38) No effective action appears to have been
taken and in 1787 Jones was still being pressed to produce
his plan. In the meantime local builders had apparently
become impressed by the area's potentialities. Development
began in April, 1792 when Chamber Minute Books record that:

'The Southernhay Committee having reported that several
Builders had made proposals for Buildings and Houses
on Southernhay according to the plan and elevation
produced and such proposals being read the same
were approved of, and the Committee with the assist-
ance of the Town Clerk are empowered to contract
with such builders that they may proceed forthwith
in such building and also to contract with any other
Builders who are willing to undertake for Buildings
or any other Houses on Southernhay.' (39)

Progress was slow. It was not till 1796 that the Chamber
ordered arrangements to be made for drawing up the formal
leases. In 1803, presumably encouraged by the response
to the first stage of development, and faced with new
applications, the Chamber ordered the surveyor to draw
up a plan of an additional area on which it was proposed
to build new houses, and also to provide plans and
elevations of the proposed buildings for inspection by the
Chamber at its next meeting. The leases granted by the

Chamber all followed the same pattern, a term of three
lives with no fine and a covenant to add an additional
life on payment of a fine.

William Hicks, an Exeter builder about whom little is
known, was prominent in the construction of Southernhay.
Two houses were leased to him on completion in 1798.
In 1810 his proposals for 'additional houses on Southernhay' were referred to the Southernhay Committee and, after
his death in 1822, No 29 was leased to his executors.
Many other Exeter builders took part in the development
and erected houses in small groups or singly for individual clients. John Brown was building at least one house
in this area in 1804 before undertaking, in 1818, the
construction of the houses for which he is best known
today, Baring Crescent. Thomas Cole, later the builder
of Northernhay Terrace and the Devon and Exeter Subscription Rooms, built several houses on Southernhay; Joseph
Rowe, builder of Pennsylvania Buildings and of many other
lesser houses in the first two decades of the nineteenth
century, was also involved. In 1822 the Chamber approved
Rowe's application for a further area 'to build two more
additional houses, in all six on the same terms as before'.
(40) In that year James Green, architect and land surveyor,
submitted plans for finishing buildings and enclosing the
ground at the 'upper end' of Southernhay and for houses in
the 'lower part'. The Chamber noted that the iron railings
were offered by Samuel Kingdon, ironmonger and future mayor,
who was resident on Southernhay. 'Iron Sam' offered to wait
for payment until the houses were built.

The Chamber maintained close control. No trees were to be
cut down without an express order. The ground in front of
the new houses was levelled and laid out by the occupiers
at their own expense under the Chamber's supervision.
Alterations and additions were carefully scrutinised.
In 1810 the Chamber rejected a proposal by the rector of
St Martin's and St Pancras to build a room at the back of
his house on Southernhay of larger dimensions than was
originally proposed. (41) Messrs Hicks and Cornish,
appearing to 'have deviated from the original plan in
erecting the offices of a house on Southernhay in the
occupation of Mrs Dacres', were called upon to explain. (42)
And in the 1820s, when Southernhay was virtually completed,
an order was made for the inspection of 'the houses on
Southernhay now building by Mr James Chapple with reference
to the materials used and the manner of building.' Chapple

was called upon to complete two houses for which he had contracted or to give up his contract. Later he was fined £10, about £100 in modern terms, 'for having deviated from his contract', and was not to be granted a lease of the house under construction until the £10 had been paid. (43)

Though the Chamber's original policy was development by building leases, some leases at least were converted into virtually outright sale. In 1816 the banker William Nation paid £350 for 'the sale of his house, coach house and stable on a site to erect the same thereon for 1000 years'. (44)

The occupiers of Southernhay included representatives of county families, such as Samuel Kekewich, or those with county connections: Major Dowell's son-in-law was Sir Edwin Stanhope of Holme Lacy, Herefordshire. Prominent and more indisputably middle-class were the members of the medical profession: Dr John Blackall and Dr Patrick Miller; Samuel Walkey, surgeon, apothecary and coroner. Samuel Luscombe of Luscombe & Edge, surgeons and apothecaries, sold his 'convenient family house at the corner of Gandy Street' in about 1817 and moved his residence and consulting room to Southernhay. (45) In 1827 H.M. Jones, surgeon dentist, announced that he would see his patients at his residence there. Their neighbours included Shirley Woolmer, proprietor of The Exeter and Plymouth Gazette; Robert Trewman, proprietor of The Flying Post; and James Paddon, cathedral organist and music master, whose house was 'very centrally situated for a professional gentleman' with kitchens, housekeeper's room, larders and cellars in the basement, a large dining-room and a main bedroom on the principal floor (and probably a drawing-room, too), three bedrooms and attics above. The house of course had its own well, and river water was available. (46) Houses were available for letting to appropriate tenants on suitable conditions: '... Fit for the reception of a genteel family except where there are many children, which would be objectionable'. (47)

Southernhay houses were commodious in an age when domestic service was cheap and abundant and hospitality carefully related to status. The residence of the rector of the city parishes of St Martin's and St Pancras contained a basement with two kitchens, a servants' hall, the usual domestic offices, three cellars and pump. On the principal floor were the dining-room and breakfast-parlours. The drawing-room and one bedroom were situated on the first floor and above were three other bedrooms and three garrets. (48) Another clergyman living on Southernhay had a similar house with the addition of a housekeeper's room and a butler's pantry. Horrell & Son, builders and auctioneers, had several houses on Southernhay for lease or sale in 1817: one of these 'situate at the Higher Part of Southernhay with an extensive view over the River Exe and surrounding country' contained a dining-parlour 22ft x 10ft 6in, with a drawing-room above and 'a handsome balcony' on the floor above. There was a breakfast-parlour measuring 18ft x 12ft 6in, six good bedrooms, two dressing-rooms, two large garrets and storerooms, a servants' hall and a butler's pantry, a wash-house, well, a tank and pump for supplying the house with soft water and a 2-stall stable and coach house. (49) Its neighbour, 'a new built and very substantial brick dwelling' contained much the same accommodation but the dimensions of the rooms were slightly smaller.

The rateable value of houses such as these was necessarily high; the majority in 1838 ranged from £58 pa to the £104 of the corner house and offices owned by the young solicitor Mark Kennaway, and the £129 of Colonel Truscott's large dwelling-house, stables, coach house and large garden. These figures compare with the £8 rateable value of the new houses occupied by superior artisans and members of the lower middle class in St David's parish. (50) Southernhay was never a purely residential area; it began and remained as a stronghold of the professional classes.

A more provincial contemporary version of the Southernhay terraces still exists in Sydney Place, by the Alphington road across the river in St Thomas's. Completed in about 1815 in an unfashionable neighbourhood, Sydney Place was yet constructed for the retired officers and professional men whose tastes fostered so much of the demand for new houses at this period. The new terrace was occupied by a retired admiral, a naval lieutenant, and a prosperous surgeon whose effects sold by auction in 1817 included much mahogany furniture, dining-tables, side-tables, chairs, a writing-desk and 'a handsome blue-and-white dinner service consisting of 214 pieces'. The accommodation was moderate by the standards of the time; it included a dining-parlour and dining-room, four bedrooms, one of which could be converted into a breakfast-room, a drawing-room, two dressing-rooms and two servants' bedrooms. There was also a courtyard with the inevitable pump. (51)

The climax of the terraced house of this early period of building outside the walls is Colleton Crescent,

completed in 1805. Viewed from the west the crescent
stands high and dominant on its bluff above the Exe;
an imposing line of brick houses four storeys high with
wrought-iron balconies and Coade stone ornament framing
the doorways. Colleton Crescent is a confident, self-
assured structure, constructed to be seen against a wide
background of the river and its meadows. It was a fitting
stronghold for members of Exeter's ruling society. In the
early nineteenth century it was the home of the bankers
Charles Sanders and Joseph Barnes Sanders, of the Exeter
City Bank; Ralph Sanders the attorney; Samuel White,
brewer, member of the Chamber and twice mayor of pre-
Reform Exeter; Captain Bond, RN, Tory alderman in 1837;
a prosperous tanner, fellmonger and woolstapler; and a
retired general. For these local magnates Colleton
Crescent provided, on the ground floor, kitchens, butler's
pantry, housekeeper's room, servants' bedrooms, storerooms,
larder, cellars and wash-house and pump; on the first floor,
breakfast-parlour and dining-room, laundry and storerooms.
Two drawing-rooms occupied the second floor and there were
three bedrooms on both the third and fourth floors.
Situated at a discreet distance were 3-stalled stable,
coach house and harness room. (52)
   Simultaneously with the development of Southernhay the
Duke of Bedford's property in the centre of the city was
being transformed into 'one of the best examples of
unified urban architecture in England ... the quintessence
of the 18th-century philosophy of civic design'. (53)
Bedford Circus was largely destroyed by enemy action in
1942. (54) In May 1773 the Exeter builders Robert Stribling and Giles Painter contracted with the Duchess of
Bedford and others to pay £530 for the buildings and
materials of Bedford House, the Exeter town house of the
Russells. (55) The ground was to be cleared and, upon
'the Southern Moiety of the East side of a new circus
intended to be built', the contractors were to construct
within five years 'seven brick houses with vaults, areas,
stables, coach houses and garden walls upon substantial
and workmanlike manner'. They were also responsible for
drainage, walls and the erection of iron railings. After
completion the houses were to be leased to Stribling and
Painter for sixty-one years at an annual rent of £28.
A similar contract provided for the construction of a
further seven houses on the same terms. The original plan
provided for the construction of twenty-five houses, but

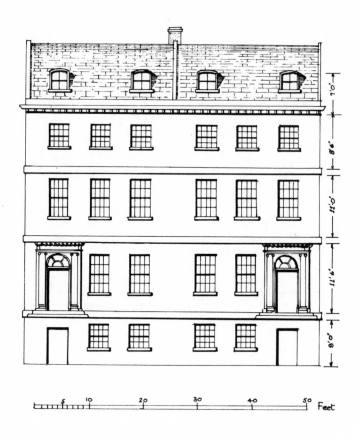

Fig 2 Elevation of houses in the centre of Bedford
        Circus from the plan of 1773. Reproduced by
        kind permission of the Bedford Estates, Bedford
        Office, London

30

it was not fully executed until 1825 when the builder
Thomas Wills Horrell undertook the construction of a
further thirteen houses, thus making a total of twenty
seven. Care was taken to ensure that the new 'full-sized,
first-rate houses' should conform with the houses already
built and that Horrell should provide adequate drainage
and pavements. The houses were to be completed within
three years from 25 March 1825; they were leased to Horrell
at a peppercorn rent for the first three years of a 63-
year lease, and thereafter at £28 yearly. (56)

Bedford Circus, well proportioned and harmonious, was a
fine example of the urban architecture of its period and
could invite comparison with any contemporary group of
buildings in England. Two of the houses available for
sale or lease after completion in 1827 contained on the
ground floor dining-room, breakfast-room, a 'small book-
room' and water closets. On the first floor were two
large drawing-rooms communicating by folding doors. The
upper floors contained eight bedrooms. In the basement
were the kitchens, housekeeper's room, larder, china
closets, wine and other cellars. There was also said to
be 'an excellent supply of spring and river water'. (57)
From its early years Bedford Circus was attractive to
Exeter's professional classes, especially lawyers. Its
inhabitants in the early nineteenth century included men
like Thomas Flood, banker and twice mayor before Reform;
Paul Measor, postmaster, mayor in 1830-1 and later a
member of the reformed corporation; John Gidley, town
clerk 1836-65, with his corner front dwelling, solicitor's
offices and garden rated at £96 in 1838. The large houses
were amply large enough for private schools such as the
preparatory school where Mr and Mrs Hake developed 'the
mental faculties of young children and ... habits of
kindness and forebearance'. (58) Houses used for residential purposes only were rated at £62.

Bedford Circus was followed closely by some of the last
terraced houses in the grand manner, Matthew Nosworthy's
Barnfield Crescent, just to the east of Southernhay, begun
in 1792 and for some reason never completed. Barnfield
Crescent is 'domestic building of the most civilised
refinement and beauty', (59) a combination of the urban
and the urbane which is the hallmark of Georgian building,
designed and constructed by a local builder-architect.
Constructed, as were the others, of the soft handmade
local brick, with cast-iron balconies, its curve is both

emphasised and disciplined by the cream plat-bands at the upper-floor levels. There was some justification for the claim of a local historian in 1806 that, when completed, Barnfield Crescent would 'scarcely be excelled by any pile of brick buildings in the kingdom, even at the capital itself'. (60) No 1 Barnfield Crescent, built for Dr Thomas Shapter, comprised a large drawing-room, dining-room and breakfast-parlour, nine bedrooms and 'every kind of office requisite for a gentleman's residence', together with coach house and stable. There were commodious cellars, such as those of a neighbouring house which yielded '100 dozen very fine old port' for sale in 1825. (61) In 1838 two of the houses were owned by Samuel Barnes, a member of Exeter's élite as a prosperous surgeon with family connections in banking and ecclesiastical circles.

Nosworthy's last achievement was the construction, begun in 1806, of the twelve terraced houses known as Dix's Field in the neighbourhood of Barnfield and similarly situated on the edge of open country. Again built of brick, these houses were designed for the same class of society as Barnfield Crescent; occupants included Sir Henry Carew, Bt, and John Were Fox the dentist. These houses contained ample space for entertaining people in county society or on the fringe of it; Henry Blackhall, three times mayor, for example, entertained a county MP and the recorder in 1832. The house occupied by Joseph Palmer, dean of Cashel in Ireland, contained housekeeper's and servants' rooms, kitchen, wine and beer cellars in the basement; on the ground floor two breakfast-parlours, storerooms and butler's pantry; on the first floor two drawing-rooms connected by folding doors, and a library; on the second floor four bedrooms, with attics above. A neighbouring house built under the instructions of the proprietor, a Miss Wyatt, contained a drawing-room on both the first and second floors. The first floor contained a conservatory and there were only two main bedrooms. (62) Nosworthy evidently kept Dix's Field in his own hands. He himself lived there and, after his death in 1831, ten houses were sold by his executors.

The last of the terraces of the early period, architect-urally and socially the least important, was situated under the ruins of the castle in an area long famed for its elms and promenades. Northernhay Terrace, designed by the local architect John Lethbridge, was begun in 1821 by the builder Thomas Cole who went bankrupt in 1827. Two houses were

ready for sale in 1821 'in every respect calculated for
the residence of genteel families'. (63) They were
brick-built, with study, breakfast-room and dining-room
on the ground floor, drawing-room and lodging-room on
the first floor, five rooms on the two upper floors and
in the basement the kitchen, housekeeper's room and
cellars. Six completed houses, one occupied by James
Leakey the artist, and another occupied by Charles
Brutton, a prominent attorney, after 1837 a member of the
city council and mayor 1845-6, together with one completed
but empty house and another unfinished, were sold after
Cole's bankruptcy. Nine of these houses were bought by
Brutton. (64)
   By the time Northernhay Terrace was under construction
the brick terrace characteristic of eighteenth-century
urban architecture was giving way to the stucco villa.
'Beauty and strength' proclaimed an advertisement for
stucco colouring in 1819; one peck, costing 2s 6d could,
it was claimed, give brilliance to the front of a moderate
sized house and 'a whole village might be beautified by
one cask'. (65) The Georgian style was replaced by the
Regency and the latter, as an architectural style, remained
dominant until the 1840s. The new villas, or cottages
according to the conventions of the day, carried Exeter's
housing development further into the countryside, an
expansion made possible by the sale to speculative builders
of substantial estates outside the city.
   In 1827 the Colleton family sold by auction the whole of
their property on the south-western edge of Exeter,
primarily a large compact area lying between Holloway
Street and the Exe, much of it consisting of gardens and
ground occupied by the decaying rack-yards of the old
woollen industry. The ninety-two lots included Colleton
Crescent itself. (66) The sale of the Colleton property
was followed by the construction of provincial Regency-
type houses, such as still remain in Melbourne Place,
Melbourne Street and the Friars. Much of this development
was undertaken by John Mitchell, a builder who went bankrupt in 1837 leaving for sale eleven new houses, five
unfinished and a number of building sites. The area had
a bad start. In 1838 there were eleven empty houses out
of twenty-two in Colleton Buildings, and seven out of
nine in Lower Melbourne Street. (67) The 'superior
houses' of Friar's Terrace were owned at this time by the
solicitors John Laidman and Charles Brutton. Their rateable values ranged from £35 to £46 and their occupants

33

included William Kennaway, wine merchant, and mayor in
1832; the French academy of Monsieur Duval; an attorney;
a road surveyor; a writing-master; an accountant; and a
business agent.

Far more successful was the development of the Baring
estate which led to the creation of nineteenth-century
St Leonard's. John Baring, MP for Exeter from 1776 to
1803, added to the accumulated purchases of his father by
acquiring through marriage the house known as Mount Radford with its extensive grounds in the parish of St
Leonard's. In 1770 he purchased the manor of Heavitree
and thus owned a wide belt of rural property forming the
south and south-east boundary of Exeter. The bulk of
this property was sold by his eldest son to his cousin
Sir Thomas Baring.

Some housing development on the Baring estate was
instituted in the early years of the nineteenth century
contemporaneously with the development of Southernhay
and Bedford Circus. In 1804 John Baring leased to John
Hooper, shopkeeper of Exeter, a parcel of land occupied
by three recently burnt houses. Hooper undertook to
construct 'two good and substantial dwelling houses' to
cost not less than £400. (68) About this time William
Hooper, of St Sidwell's, built the pleasant group of
stucco houses known as Midway Terrace, now Nos 138-56
Heavitree Road, much altered though still distinguished
by trellis porches. Here Hooper himself lived in his
latter years. In the same neighbourhood, in 1812, John
Baring leased to William Hooper a 'dwelling house lately
erected by the said William Hooper ... between the two
roads from Paris Street and Heavitree and being number
ten of an intended row of houses now building by the said
William Hooper on the ... said piece of ground distinguished by the name of Baring Place'. (69) Now 151-63
Magdalen Road, these houses form a fine group of modest
provincial Regency buildings, brick-built with Doric
porticoes and graceful semi-circular fanlights, iron
balconies and tall, narrow first-floor windows with
delicate glazing-bars. After completion they were popular
with senior retired members of the services, such as Sir
William Paterson, and their dependants.

The construction of superior houses on Baring property
in the same neighbourhood was continued in 1818 by the
lease to John Brown of three fields, comprising about
11 acres, for sixty-six years at an annual rent of £94 12s.

34

Brown undertook to complete, within six years, twelve
houses to be known as Baring Crescent. The specifications
were meticulous. There was to be a balcony 'with a fence
or guard of iron net'; a handsome flight of stone steps
with iron guard-rails was to lead to the balcony and
entrance door; the main rooms were to be not less than
9ft 6in from floor to ceiling and the basement rooms not
less than 8ft 6in. The exterior walls were to be
'plastered in a handsome and durable manner' and the
building was 'to be crowned with a projecting boss or
cantilever with moulded cornice'. The painting was to be
not less than three coats thick, and decorations were not
to reduce the value of each house below £1,000. Each
building was to have stables and a coach house constructed
at the back and was to be leased to John Brown at £5 a
year. (70) In the phraseology of a generation accustomed
to the often gigantic scale of aristocratic or plutocratic
building, the announcement that the first stone of the
new houses of Baring Crescent was to be laid on 1 October
1818 described tham as 'superior cottages'. (71) They
comprised a basement with kitchen, scullery and housekeeper's room, pantry, beer and wine cellars; on the
ground floor the dining-room and drawing-room, breakfast-
room and butler's pantry; on the upper floors a second
drawing-room and eight bedrooms. By 1828 one was occupied
by Edward Adams, goldsmith of Exeter High Street, three by
Church of England clergy, and one by a naval captain whose
widow remained in occupation until about 1845. In 1835
four were in the occupation of army officers.

The Hoopers, William Hooper (1757-1831) and his sons
William, Junior and Henry Hooper (1794-1868), whose
association with the development of the Baring Estate
began in the early years of the nineteenth century, were
the most prominent, if not the most eminent, of the Exeter
builders of their generation. (72) William Hooper Senior
lacked the touch of genius which Nosworthy displayed but,
if obituary notices can be accepted as a standard of
measurement, he made the most impression on his contemporaries. 'Towards the improvement of this city he has
largely contributed', commented the Flying Post on his
death in 1831, 'and the numerous public buildings raised
by him will long form a monument of his public usefulness'. (73)

In the vicinity of Exeter William Hooper had built
(c.1820-30) the great house of Silverton Park, now demolished,
for Lord Egremont. Within the city's adjacent parishes
he built between 1804 and about 1816 the two rows of brick

35

houses known as Higher and Lower Summerlands; the former
originally named Hooper's Buildings. Constructed under
the terms of a building lease on two fields belonging to
the Corporation of the Poor, Higher Summerlands (damaged
by bombing and now demolished) was a row of eight
detached houses on the site of the modern police station
facing Heavitree Road - elegant Georgian brick structures
of three storeys with small formal gardens in front behind
iron railings. In 1838 they were rated at from £62 to £88.
The houses of Lower Summerland, a terrace which survives
today, were smaller. Both were occupied, and largely
owned, by the upper levels of retired society: officers,
clergy, widows, unmarried ladies and, for a time, E.L.
Sanders, the banker.

In 1823 the Barings sold to the Hoopers for £1,500 some
4 acres of land on which the six houses of Baring Crescent
had recently been erected. (74) In 1825 arrangements were
made to sell by auction the furniture of Mount Radford
House, the advowson of St Leonard's rectory and also three
walled gardens with hothouses, a peach house and greenhouse.
The gardens were each recommended as suitable for the
building of a 'gentleman's residence' or as a desirable
investment for a gardener or nurseryman. (75) Presumably
there were no suitable offers since it was not till March
1827 that the Hoopers purchased for the very substantial
sum of £16,730 10s the whole of the Mount Radford property,
technically 'the capital messuage and hereditaments called
Larkbeare'. (76) Much of the original purchase was speedily
resold. In October 1829 the Hoopers recouped over one-
quarter of the purchase price by the sale to Samuel Haydon
of Heavitree of an area together with a right of way
adjoining the gardens of Mount Radford for £4,350. They
also appear to have sold to the same purchaser the field
called the Grove, on which substantial villas called
Claremont Grove were erected in the 1830s. Samuel Haydon,
appearing as esquire or gentleman in the directories, seems
to have been a heavy investor in property in St Leonard's.
In 1831 he was involved in the sale of Mount Radford Gardens
and by 1835 he had moved from Heavitree to No 1 Mount
Radford Terrace.

Several local builders and architects took part in the
development of St Leonard's but the Hoopers were regarded
as the creators of this late Georgian suburb and were
responsible for the main lines of its layout; these lines
themselves being determined by the external and internal

36

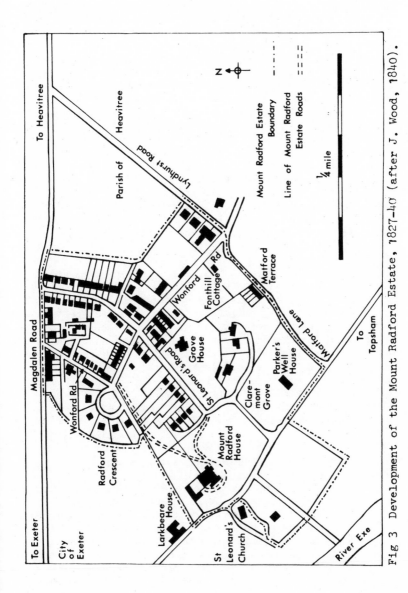

Fig 3 Development of the Mount Radford Estate, 1827–40 (after J. Wood, 1840).

boundaries of the estate. (77) St Leonard's Road,
originally known as Upper and Lower Mount Radford Terrace,
was laid out along the main carriage-drive from Mount
Radford to Magdalen Road, while Wonford Road, from Radford
Crescent to the future Lyndhurst Road on the eastern edge
of the estate, was based on a hedge boundary. Radford
Crescent was fitted into the curve formed by the north-
western boundary of the estate, its base formed by a track
running from the Magdalen Road to Larkbeare. The upper
or northern end of the modern Wonford Road bisects the
area formerly occupied by Mount Radford Gardens. Construction began on 1 September, 1828, with the first stone of
'a line of cottages' which inaugurated Mount Radford
Terrace, now St Leonard's Road. By 1831 there were already
a few occupied houses and a long-enduring social atmosphere
was already suggested by their first occupants: Mrs Clarke's
Ladies Academy; the Classical Academy of the Reverend Edwin
Houlditch; a captain, RE. Elsewhere on the estate Charles
Force, Exeter builder and auctioneer, had completed two
houses for sale to anyone 'having from four to five hundred
pounds to invest'. (78)

The development of the three walled gardens presented
difficulties. After the failure in 1830 of an attempt to
sell the area in one block they were again on offer in 1831,
this time laid out in building plots by the architect Charles
Hedgeland, together with the plants, trees, shrubs and
bricks from demolished walls and hothouses. At the end of
1832 Hedgeland had an area available as 'small sites for
the erection of genteel cottages ... not to exceed £25-£30
in rent'. Two years later six plots at £50 each or £280
for the six were still on offer. (79)

Some of the new houses on the estate were ambitious.
Grove House, completed by John Gill of Heavitree in 1829,
was described as 'a capital new-built freehold residence'
with gardens and shrubberies and a 'substantial portico
hall'. This house contained a dining-room and drawing-
room, each 20ft x 17ft, a breakfast-parlour almost as
spacious, and a small library. On the second floor there
were five good bedrooms and two dressing-rooms. Above
were the attics. The basement contained the usual complement
of pantry, storeroom, wine, beer and coal cellars. (80)
A similar house, No 1 Claremont Grove, was completed by
1834 and leased for seven years at a rent of £135 a year,
the owner undertaking to build a coach house and stable,
and to install grates, bells, chimney pieces and water-

closets. The lessee had the right of purchase for £3,200. Evidently the offer was not taken up since the house was again to let in 1838 at a reduced rent of £115. The garden inventory was impressive; it included silver firs, poplars, acacias, horse chestnuts, beeches, mountain ash, a cedar of Lebanon, arbutus, ilex and the locally famous Luccombe oak. (81) Gardening was an interest which the more prosperous citizens of Exeter shared with their county neighbours; both provided members for the Exeter Botanical and Horticultural Society and bought the Dutch bulbs imported by Exeter nurserymen. Also characteristic of the larger residence was the house on sale in Mount Radford Terrace in 1838; this contained a parlour, a drawing-room with windows opening on to a verandah, three good bedrooms, two attics, two kitchens, including a back kitchen with a stone floor, wine cellar, larder, pantries and water-closet, the inevitable pump, small garden in front and a larger walled garden behind. (82) A neighbouring house included a drawing-room, dining-room, breakfast-parlour, four bedrooms, three 'good garrets', as well as the usual scullery, pantries and cellars.

Though some of the houses on the former Baring property were large and pretentious, the typical house which gave the area its social and architectural character was modest. One of the first of the new houses offered for sale in 1830 contained only two parlours, kitchen, pantry, four bedrooms and had a small walled garden. This was let at £32 a year and was offered for sale at not less than £260. (83) A small house known as East Cottage, designed by Charles Hedgeland and built by Henry Hooper, contained a good sitting-room, kitchen, pantry and three main bedrooms; in 1836 this house was offered for sale at £440 or for lease at £26 a year. It was purchased by a clergyman, one of several who found comfortable but modest homes in St Leonard's. One of the new houses in Park Place occupied by an accountant contained only a parlour, a second-floor drawing-room, two bedrooms and an attic said to be capable of conversion into two more bedrooms. Houses such as these made no effort to compete with the large dining-rooms, drawing-rooms, butler's pantries and housekeeper's rooms such as were found in Southernhay or Bedford Circus.

By 1835 at least thirty houses had been completed in Upper and Lower Mount Radford Terrace, five of them occupied by service officers. Though much changed since World War II and harassed by the motor car, St Leonard's still retains

today something of the atmosphere of the time of William
IV. The parish was long noted as a staunch 'Church and
State' area, its politics not unfairly epitomised by the
large prints of George IV, William IV, the Duke of York
and the Duke of Wellington, property of the Reverend
Robert Hall of East Cottage, in 1838. The villas with
their iron balconies and verandahs, their shuttered windows,
their small compact gardens with fruit trees and an occasional ilex or magnolia, were the homes of modest retirement,
of professional men and tradesmen who sought quiet respectability. The new houses in the 1830s provided homes for
the widows of a major in the 20th Dragoons and of John
Gullett, barrister at law; for Joseph Brutton of the
Exeter Brewery; for Mr Parmenas Mudge, music master; for
Elizabeth Mary, 'daughter of the late Major Waller, of
Jamaica', who died at sixteen of a decline; as well as for
unmarried ladies and clergy as exemplified by the Ladies
Academy of the Misses Kendall and the already-mentioned
Classical Academy of the Reverend Edwin Houlditch.

The construction of 'Regency' St Leonard's was completed
by 1840, coinciding with evidence of decline in Exeter's
position as a provincial capital. The parish had been
developed 'as a place of residence for people of independent means' (84) and Exeter was to remain popular with this
class. The standards of the neighbouring county society
and the educated professional men remained dominant but,
in comparison with 1770-1840, there was now a perceptible
decline in the quality and extent of social life. Housing
development after 1840 was stimulated more by the hopes
of economic growth, and less by Exeter's attractions for
genteel retirement; by the completion of Queen Street in
1838 and by the arrival of the railway in 1844 when the
locomotive City of Exeter steamed into the new St David's
station built by Henry Hooper. Both events focussed
interest on St David's as a potential development area,
and the houses built in the parish at this time form a
postscript, socially and architecturally, to the preceding
seventy years. Though much of the classical tradition
remained, Exeter for a time came under the influence of
'early English Gothic'. In St David's the battle of the
styles in the early Railway Age has left its memorial in
Queen's Terrace, half modestly classical, half with ornamental barge-boards and gables. Close at hand Bystock
Terrace, now a hotel, completed about 1845 with castell-
ations, 'Tudor' doorways, steeply pitched roofs and gables,

is a more adventurous essay in the style popularised by
J.C. Loudon and A.J. Downing. The houses in Bystock
Terrace contained dining-room and breakfast-room on the
first floor; on the second floor a drawing-room, principal
bedroom and water-closet; on the third floor, two bedrooms
and storerooms. On completion they were offered on lease
at £40-£45 a year. (85) To the east the tall stucco houses,
originally known as Carlton Terrace and Rougemont Terrace,
were built on the New North Road in anticipation of the
arrival of the LSWR at Queen Street in 1860.

The whole of this corner of Exeter owes its creation to
the stimulus of the railways and although it is now marred
by some of the more obtrusive examples of modern construction,
it is still an area of simplicity and good taste, the classical
and Gothic blended in 'an easy commerce of the old and the
new'. It was not completed till the end of the 1860s but
it preserves something of the atmosphere of a country town
of the 1840s. The development was largely the work of John
and Charles Ware, builder and architect, who were also zealous
promoters of road improvements in the neighbourhood.
With the construction by the Wares of the houses in Elm
Grove Road and Velwell Villas, now Howell Road, in about
1860-9, the continuity of an architectural tradition that
had lasted one hundred years was broken.

The northern end of Queen Street was developed at a time
of high hopes that the railways would restore Exeter's
ancient economic importance and status. But it was not
till towards the end of the nineteenth century that the
influence of the railways became effective and the new
houses and terraces in St David's never acquired social
status. Many were used as lodgings. None was intended
to enshrine the 2,000oz of silver plate, the 250 dozen
of 'choice bottled wines' such as J.J. Tanner, leather
dresser, glove merchant and city councillor, left in his
house on Southernhay on his death in 1850. (86) John and
Charles Ware lived in their own houses in Velwell Villas.
Their neighbours included Henry Norrington, merchant in
agricultural implements and manures, and a Liberal member
of the city council; Walter Trehane, wine and spirit
merchant, also a Liberal; a music master; and the rector
of the small parish church of St John's. This later
development in St David's marks the last significant area
to be developed in Exeter in the years 1770-1870. It is
fitting that the story should end with a note on what
little is known of the builders themselves and how they

financed their projects.

Exeter's surge of house construction in the second half of the eighteenth century was, as we have seen, broadly financed by the share of the south-west in eighteenth-century economic growth, and by the profits of war and conquest overseas. The Exeter bread riots of 1796 are a reminder that prosperity in the south-west was not universal; but the landed gentry and their tenant farmers, and the Anglican clergy as members of the landed interest, shared in the economic benefits of a wet harvest and a bloody war, as did the naval officers who survived to enjoy prize money, the officers of John Company from Bengal and the Carnatic, the war contractors and purveyors. Professional men, merchants and retailers of the provincial capital took their due proportion of this accumulating wealth.

The evidence, though sparse, suggests that many of the houses constructed towards the end of the eighteenth century and later were built to meet the specific require-ments of clients who helped to finance the construction. Thus, according to a conveyance of 1795, one Edmund Walker had agreed 'many years ago' to buy a house in the still unconstructed Bedford Circus. Alterations costing more than £180 were made at Walker's request and Walker had also made a payment of £280 by the time he finally acquired the property for £441 12s. (87) One of the Hoopers' new houses in Southernhay Place was constructed by contract for a surgeon, J.H. James, in 1824 at a cost of £1,381 payable by instalments at certain agreed stages of construct-ion; and one of Nosworthy's houses in Dix's Field was built according to the instructions of a Miss Wyatt. More humble builders obtained working capital through mortgages. In 1827, for instance, Robert Fisher, joiner, acquired the site of King William Terrace for £550. Fisher then borrowed £380 from William Luke, grocer, to finance the construction of a row of houses intended for the lower levels of the middle classes and superior artisans. For this purpose Fisher mortgaged to Luke 'all the dwelling houses and buildings to be erected'. (88) Similar houses in Russell Street were mortgaged in advance to a pawnbroker for £700. Advertisements by solicitors seeking investments for sometimes substantial sums in house property abounded, and this method of financing building would explain why so much of the large blocks of lower-middle-class and artisans' houses was shown by the Exeter Survey of 1838 to have been in single ownership. John Bussell, attorney,

owned nineteen houses in St David's parish; John Terrell,
another attorney, owned twenty-six in St Olave's in the
centre of the city; and the builder Henry Johns twenty-
one in St Sidwell's.

No detailed accounts of the Exeter builders of this
period appear to have survived. Of their lives, too,
little is known. Some were active as technical advisers
of the council and the improvement commissioners, and the
proceedings of the latter were sometimes brought to a
standstill by acrimonious clashes of competing interests.
They were not deemed worthy of obituary notices. Even
when Matthew Nosworthy died in 1831, aged eighty, it was
merely recorded that he had 'formerly carried on extensive
business in this city as builder'. (89) Much more was
written of Henry Hooper, when he died in 1865, but this
interest was due to Hooper's stormy and sometimes dis-
creditable career as Conservative city boss. (90) Their
achievements survive in what remains, or is recorded, of
their work. They gave to Exeter 'Georgian and Regency
quarters as extensive (in proportion to the size of the
city) as those of any town in the country, excepting only
Bath; and they were of a singular grace and beauty'. (91)
Since they were above all craftsmen they might be content
with that epitaph.

Chapter 2

The West End of Glasgow 1830-1914
M. A. Simpson

Victorian and Edwardian Glasgow liked to think of itself
as the 'Second City of the Empire'. In terms of population,
wealth, industrial might, commercial importance and municipal enterprise, it had a good case. Between 1750 and
1811, it grew from a modest provincial town of about
25,000 people to a city of over 100,000; in the following
century the population of the city and its environs rose
to about a million. (1) Victorian Glasgow became a major
seaport, the principal shipbuilding centre in Britain,
the main focus of the Scottish railway and canal networks
and the home of important textile and engineering industries.
By the last quarter of the nineteenth century it had also
become the distributive, financial, cultural and professional
services centre for much of Scotland. As one local novelist
expressed it, by 1912 'the city was at a zenith', having
developed a fierce local pride and an aggressive self-
confidence. (2) Although it had immense social problems,
chiefly related to the poor housing conditions endured by
most of its citizens and ultimately to their desperately
low wages, the municipality felt that it had done all it
could to relieve them within the confines of Victorian
political economy. (3) It enjoyed a fine range of cultural
activities, a splendid park system, excellent water, cheap
gas and a surprisingly extensive and inexpensive transport
network. It was, for all its infamous slums, a strikingly
handsome Victorian city - probably the best we have, with
as great a collection of public buildings and fine houses
as any city in the western world. (4)
  One consequence of Glasgow's economic progress between
1750 and 1914 was a substantial increase in the upper
middle class. Victorian Glasgow's haute bourgeoisie
would have fallen into the Registrar-General's present
Social Classes I and II: wholesale merchants, shipowners,
shipbuilders, chain and department store executives,

44

manufacturers, lawyers, doctors, teachers in higher
education and school principals, higher civil servants
and senior local government officers, the clergy, army
and navy officers, senior ocean-going merchant navy
officers, company directors and managers, landowners and
other rentiers, brokers, senior insurance executives,
bank managers, accountants, house factors, surveyors,
architects, professional engineers, leading journalists
and authors. (5)

Before the opening of the nineteenth century, these
people had lived in the old town, to the west of Glasgow
Cross and often above their counting houses. However,
the onset of industrialisation rendered this central
business district uninhabitable. Their dwellings were
in demand for business premises and a massive influx of
Highland and Irish workers led to the overcrowding of the
vennels and wynds of the west end. Industrialisation also
led to serious pollution of the air, water and streets.
The great increase in population multiplied the problems
of drunkenness, vagrancy, crime, vice and disease. As
the city authorities were initially incapable of combatting
the evil effects of rapid industrialisation and urbanisation,
the wealthier citizens felt compelled to leave the town
and 'domiciles which last century formed the cozy retreats
of city clergymen, physicians, lawyers, and merchants are
now often tenanted by the pickpocket and prostitute'. (6)

Changes in fashion and improvements in transportation
provided the upper middle class with more positive induce-
ments to leave the central business district. Their
counterparts in London and Edinburgh had begun to settle
respectively in the ducal estates of the West End and in
the New Town about Prince's Street. From about 1780, many
of Glasgow's leading families also began to separate home
and work. Dr Cleland, the celebrated local statistician,
noted in 1837 that 'Families, who were formerly content
to live in a flat of a house in the old, have now handsome
self-contained houses in the new parts of the town'. (7)
The opening after 1800 of several local turnpikes, together
with the coming of the horse buses, light cabs and private
carriages also enabled those who could afford to do so to
escape the confines of the old walking city. At first,
they moved in all directions. Speculators built elegant
terraces just south of the Clyde in the Gorbals, others
built quiet tree-lined squares north-east of the city centre,
while to the east and fronting on to Glasgow Green stood

Monteith Row (1803), 'built to be the most exclusive
terrace of Regency Glasgow, overlooking Glasgow's Hyde
Park'. (8) To the west of the old town lay the 479-acre
Blythswood estate of the Campbells, who in about 1790
judged that it was ready for development. A succession
of speculators, many of whom bankrupted themselves,
participated in its transformation into an exclusive and
attractive suburb, rather severely classical in style and
laid out on a grid pattern; without deference to contours,
the streets strode up and down the low but steep conical
hills of boulder clay, known as drumlins, which dot the
northern shore of the lower Clyde. Blythswood, plainly
imitative of Edinburgh's New Town (1767-1835), was often
called 'the New Town' by Glaswegians. It absorbed by far
the largest proportion of the haute bourgeoisie but its
days as the city's premier suburb were short. (9)

Even before the completion of building in 1837, Blythswood
was largely a western extension of the central business
area. The Gorbals, one of Blythswood's rivals, and then
a separate burgh, was rapidly overrun by the working class,
which found the area convenient for its places of employment on the riverside and just across the bridge in the
old city. Monteith Row, still fashionable up to the reign
of William IV, decayed as the industrialists began to
leave in the forties, 'escaping from the smoke of these,
their own factory chimneys'. Grafton Place, which stood
directly above the city centre to the north-east, was
quickly surrounded by industry and warehousing, and Ure
Place, a little farther down the hill, was redeveloped. (10)
Most of Glasgow's industry and commerce was concentrated
along the Clyde or to the north and east of the city,
close to the canals and railways which brought in coal
and iron from Lanarkshire. Since the working class was
still compelled to live within walking distance of its
employment, Monteith Row, Ure Place and Grafton Place
were increasingly surrounded by alien social groups.
A last attempt to maintain a middle-class presence in the
east end was the new suburb of Dennistoun, created about
1860 but still adversely affected by air pollution and the
proximity of the 'lower orders'; in general, it only
attracted the petit bourgeoisie and skilled artisans.
One or two lower-middle-class suburbs south of the river
flourished in the late nineteenth century - for example,
Queen's Park and Langside, and one relatively small
upper-middle-class suburb, the Maxwell estate of Pollok-

46

shields West. Far enough south of the Clyde to escape
pollution and the masses, they were laid out with care
and elegance by the leading architects of the day; this
was particularly true of Pollokshields West. (11) However,
they suffered from an awkward position in relation to the
central business district. Commuters had to approach the
city via dock and slum areas and cross the Clyde over
crowded bridges. The arrival of the railways led to
attempts to develop villages lying several miles beyond
Glasgow's built-up area; as early as 1850, for example,
106 acres at Viewpark, Uddingston, 'near the Railway',
were offered for sale for villa building. At Bothwell
in 1860, a landlord had ground to feu 'near the station
and in a favourable locality' with 'Railway Villa tickets
at half-price'. However, Glasgow's middle class was unwilling to leap-frog beyond the built-up area until the
mid-eighties, by which time commuter services had been
improved and new lines built. Most of the stone villas
in the commuter suburbs of Bearsden, Milngavie, Lenzie,
Kirkintilloch, Bothwell and Uddingston date from the
period 1885-1914. (12)

By 1830, there was need of another suburb to house the
bulk of Glasgow's expanding upper middle class, so that
those who built for it were compelled to turn to the area
beyond Blythswood, further to the west. What later became
the new West End was an irregularly-shaped wedge of ground,
about 3 miles long and up to a mile wide, totalling some
1,250 acres distributed among twenty-three estates and
consisting of several drumlins and the gorge of the Kelvin,
which bisected it from north to south.

Legal documents and the elaborate and calculated advertisements of property developers suggest that by 1830 this
élite had a clearly-defined set of criteria by which to
judge a potential suburb. First of all, it had to be
exclusive to the upper middle class. The developing landlords of the West End assured the social élite that their
proposals satisfied this requirement. The proprietors
of the largest estate, Kelvinside, declared that 'the whole
of these 450 acres are to be occupied solely by Dwelling-
houses of a superior description'. (13) The same decision
was made independently by the owners of all twenty-three
West End properties, thus ensuring a solid block of entirely
middle-class territory on Glasgow's western flank. There
is no satisfactory explanation for this remarkable
unanimity. There were then no statutory planning controls;

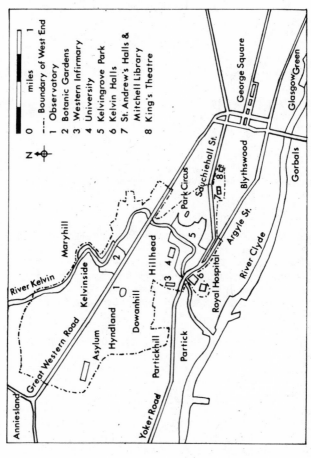

Fig 4 The West End of Glasgow, 1914.

the estates were all rich in coal, iron, brick clay,
building sand and freestone - which could have led to
industrial and working-class development; the terrain,
though hilly, presented no insuperable difficulties to
any kind of urbanisation. The most likely reason was
that Blythswood had begun the tradition of building for
the middle class west of the city centre and when it began
to turn into an adjunct of the central business district,
estates immediately to the west began to cater for disposs-
essed middle-class families, leading to a chain reaction.
South of the West End, the Clyde shore was already committed
to industrial and dockland uses, while northwards lay the
Forth and Clyde Canal, a natural attraction for industry.

This exclusiveness had to be protected by distinct
boundaries and preferably buffer zones separating the
suburb from inferior neighbouring areas. The West End
met this demand, too, for on the east it adjoined the clean,
well-maintained business area of Blythswood. On the south
Sauchiehall Street and Dumbarton Road - broad, four-lane
highways - parted it from dockland Anderston and shipbuilding Partick. The Kelvingrove or West End Park became
a buffer zone for the southern fringes, just as the Botanic
Gardens did for the northern border, assisted by the River
Kelvin. To the west lay sweet meadowland, undeveloped
until the twentieth century.

Within the West End itself, the exclusiveness was maintained by restrictive clauses in feu charters and ground
annuals (leaseholds) and dispositions (freeholds) in which
'the amenity of the area is thoroughly secured'. Land was
leased or sold on very strict conditions. A typical feu
charter (the most common form of land tenure) was that
granted in 1850 by the Kelvinside Estate Company to John
Christie jr, a builder, for five steadings (plots) to
form part of Kew Terrace on Great Western Road. Christie
was permitted to excavate the freestone and brick clay on
site for use in the construction of the terrace. Each
occupier was to enter individually with the company;
Christie was not allowed to sub-feu, as that might weaken
the force of the feuing restrictions. He was prohibited
in great detail from carrying on any occupation likely
to create a nuisance. Hotels and flats were restricted
to one at each end and one in the middle of the terrace
(options almost never exercised). The houses themselves
were to have polished ashlar fronts and coursed rubble
backs, with slate roofs and outhouses strictly limited

49

in height. The building line was to be at least 70ft
from the south-west side of Great Western Road and each
house was to be provided with iron gates and railings
atop a 3ft stone wall. Christie was obliged to construct
a mews lane 20ft in width, a carriage drive of 21ft 6in,
a common shrubbery, footpaths, and sewers corresponding
to the diameter of the main estate system. The feudal
superiors (the company) undertook to meet half the cost
of these operations. Occupiers were bound to maintain
their houses in good repair. When three houses had been
occupied, the householders were to form a 'Board of
Management' to arrange for drainage, the disposal of
refuse and the lighting of the terrace and its portion
of Great Western Road. Gas lamps 'of a superior design'
to be approved by the company were to be erected at intervals of 28yds. Feuars were also made responsible for the
upkeep of the common shrubbery, the mews lane and the
carriage drive. On their part, the superiors bound
themselves to insist on similar conditions in neighbouring
feus. They reserved the right to seek the inclusion of
Kelvinside in any unit of local government of their choice,
or even to petition for a separate burghal authority for
the estate; their feuars were forbidden to oppose them. (14)

Later feu contracts differed only in detail from the one
signed by Christie. One new clause laid down a minimum
market price for a given house, for which it must be insured.
Other additions prohibited dormer windows and limited the
number of storeys. Footpaths had to be of best quality
Caithness stone - whinstone or granite being specified
for kerbs. The general oversight of building operations
and the subsequent maintenance of the property was placed
in the hands of the estate surveyor, who had powers of
entry at all times. Thus, throughout the West End's period
of development, speculators, builders and householders had
to sign agreements in much the same terms as Christie's. (15)
It was this stringent application of the feudal superior's
ancient rights which ensured success for the West End as
an exclusively upper-middle-class suburb. The amenity of
the area being secured in perpetuity, the grand houses
were spared the fate of those in the Gorbals and elsewhere
which had degenerated through failure to control the
environment in which the houses were situated.

The middle class was also extremely appreciative of fine
views, trees and open country; one of the features of the
Romantic era of the late eighteenth and early nineteenth

centuries had been the discovery of scenery. The West End
in its natural state was full of beauty. It was based on
several wooded drumlins which raised it to heights of up
to 200ft above the Clyde, offering breathtaking prospects.
Developers made a conscious appeal to this middle-class
obsession with scenery. The local builder, David Clow,
trying to sell 14-roomed terrace houses in Westbourne
Terrace, just off Great Western Road, in 1870, typified
their approach:

'The surface is varied, mostly elevated, commanding
fine views, and securing good air ... embracing a
view of the Vale of Clyde and the valley of the Cart,
skirted by the Braes o' Gleniffer and the bold
outline of the Grampians ... the country between is
undulating and beautifully wooded, presenting a
landscape truly picturesque, seldom obtained in
Suburban Dwellings.' (16)

Even where West Enders could not obtain views of the
Firth of Clyde or its enclosing hills, they were offered
a prospect of the communal pleasure gardens in front of
their terrace, or well-laid out and extensive villa
grounds, or a sight of the Botanic Gardens or Kelvingrove
Park, usually from an oriel window on the first-floor
drawing-room - a real 'room with a view'. Developers
retained and planted trees, some of the pleasure grounds
were laid out with imagination and roads often wound
uphill along contours.

Another requirement of the nineteenth-century bourgeois
in search of a suburb was a salubrious climate. The
elevation of the West End which helped to isolate it from
its less fashionable neighbours also lifted it well above
their smoke. More important, lying to the west of the
city and its industries and with no major industrial centre
downstream of it, the prevailing westerlies, which blew
in from the Atlantic on three days out of every five,
brought clear, fresh air - 'ozone', as the Victorians
preferred to call it. Developers frequently pointed out
how 'healthful' and 'well-aired' the West End was, in
distinct contrast to the notoriously unhealthy old town.
Public health statistics reinforced their claims and the
Glasgow Herald referred to the 'establishment of the
Observatory in this quarter, on account of the purity of
the atmosphere, and of the Botanic Gardens, on account of

its salubrity, which speaks volumes for its desirableness as a healthy locality'. (17)

The vast majority of Glasgow's leading citizens worked in the central business district and in the days of horse-drawn transport required their suburban residences to be within a few minutes of their business premises, especially since it long remained a local middle-class tradition to lunch at home. (18) The West End was only between 2 and 5 miles from the city centre but this area of outstanding natural beauty and planned exclusiveness was largely inaccessible before 1840. Until about 1800 the country estates of what was to become the West End were connected to the city only by parish lanes and drove roads - not fit for driving a cow according to one contemporary. (19) Then came the opening of the Yoker Turnpike (now Argyle Street and Dumbarton Road), skirting the southern boundary of the West End on its way westwards from Glasgow across the floodplain of the Clyde. (20) But it only tapped the southernmost fringe of the West End - a more centrally placed, direct, all-weather highway to town was needed before development could really be stimulated. The main agent in opening up the West End was the Great Western Road - a broad, straight shaft from the north-west corner of the business district at St George's Cross to the far western frontier of the West End at Anniesland Cross, a distance of 2 miles. Organised by a group of Yoker Road Trustees and authorised by an Act of 1836, it was opened for traffic in 1841. It cleft the West End almost exactly in half. In doing so, it promoted feuing up to half-a-mile deep on either side and acted as an axis round which building was planned. (21) The Great Western Road's connection with the city centre made the West End 'the only district from which access to town can be obtained without passing through an inferior district'. (22) With some of the parish roads macadamised and straightened to act as feeders, the Yoker and Great Western Turnpikes drew the West End into Glasgow's orbit and brought its natural attractions within reach of the city's upper middle class, which could afford to maintain private carriages and was soon offered the alternatives of hire cabs and several competing horse-bus services. From 1870, there were horse trams, electrified and extended after 1900. Suburban railways and a subway also served the West End from the late nineteenth century. It must be emphasised, however, that while the contribution of the Great Western

Road was crucial to the development of the West End, later additions to the transport network never ran ahead of the suburban frontier and indeed tram and railway lines served established and highly-populous quarters of the West End. Although the West End was provided with an incredibly lavish and extremely cheap transport system by 1914 (by which time everyone was within five minutes walk of trams or trains), neither the five tram routes nor the four suburban railways contributed much more to urban growth than the filling in of a handful of vacant spots; transport followed settlement and not the other way round. (23)

Improved communications also permitted West Enders to partake of the cultural and social life of the city and to meet their shopping requirements by means of the famous 'carriage trade' to the great department stores on Sauchiehall Street. In the middle of town were gentlemen's clubs, music halls, theatres and meeting rooms. But the middle class also wanted a full range of amenities in their chosen suburb and so most of Glasgow's cultural life eventually came to the West End, for by 1914 it contained a loosely-arranged and somewhat fortuitous cultural centre. (24) Early settlers in the West End were the Royal Botanic Gardens (1841) and the Glasgow Observatory (1841). The Botanic Gardens later acquired the Kibble Palace (1873), a glazed public hall which was used for religious revivals, political rallies, education and concerts. Open-air band concerts were an important feature of the summer in both the Botanic Gardens and Kelvingrove Park. The latter was the site of three great exhibitions (when it became 'Bagdad on the Kelvin') and there was always a museum there, joined in 1905 by an art gallery. (25) Opposite the park were the Kelvin Exhibition Halls (1910) and within a few minutes' walk the King's Theatre (1910), St Andrew's Concert Halls (1878), Mitchell Reference Library (1906) and the Royal Hospital for Sick Children (1911). North of the park lay the Western Infirmary (1872) and the University of Glasgow (1870), while to the east were the Queen's Rooms for concerts and dancing (1857) and the Free Church College (1857). The great middle-class cultural centres of the day, however, were the churches; by 1914, there were twenty-nine (mostly Presbyterian) in the West End - roughly one to every thousand people. (26) Almost every amenity and.service of the times was available in the West End - except public bars, which were vigorously opposed as they would lower the tone of the district and encourage the entry of ruffians. There were curling and skating ponds, cricket and rugby grounds, bowling greens, tennis courts, two major public day schools and a number of board schools. (27)

The West End amply satisfied the most stringent requirements and became a truly sub-urban neighbourhood, successfully combining the advantages of town and country without the disadvantages of either. Its natural advantages together with those conferred by development, enabled the West End to become 'par excellence, the fashionable suburb' of Victorian Glasgow. The disadvantages suffered by potential rivals and the loss of Blythswood to commerce left it virtually unchallenged during Victoria's reign. (28)

On the eve of development in 1830, the West End's twenty-three pastoral estates ranged from properties of 2 acres to the 472 acres of Kelvinside, though most were in the 10-30 acre category. They were held by the local gentry like the Stirling Crawfords of Hyndland and the Buchanans of Dowanhill, or by Glasgow lawyers and merchants such as the West Indiaman Robert Bogle of Gilmourhill, the East Indiaman John Fleming of Claremont and the banker and accountant Henry Paul of North Woodside. In most cases these were not the people responsible for development; on the whole, they preferred to enjoy their properties as country homes. (29)

However, some of them made spasmodic attempts to feu all or part of their ground before mid-century. Sensing the steady approach of the building frontier, anticipating benefits from the Great Western Road and other improvements in communications, and drawing attention to their rich mineral deposits, they lured builders with 'liberal pecuniary accommodation'. A few like Walter Gibson of Hillhead (about 100 acres) even went to the length of preparing a feuing plan though most advertisements were vague about the proposed form of development. Most of them emphasised the natural beauty of their properties, a ploy typified by the Mowbray family's notice of 1830, offering four portions of Kelvinside totalling 100 acres:

'The beauty of the situations, their proximity to Glasgow, the almost certainty that in a few years the whole of these Grounds will be in demand as Building Ground, and withal, the very moderate price at present asked, render the purchase of them a most promising speculation ... it will soon be

'in contact with the principal streets of the
West End of the town.' (30)

This invitation explained its own failure, for in 1830
the edge of the built-up area was still 1-2 miles east of
these properties, hazily visible across rolling meadows.
Until the intervening fields were covered by bricks and
mortar, cautious homeseekers and homebuilders were unwilling to pioneer that far west. No-one saw any advantage
in tying up capital in ground which would not be built over
for perhaps ten or twenty years and, in almost all cases,
these early efforts to transform the West End were complete
failures. Where estates did change hands, as did Kelvingrove
(28 acres), owned by William Dennistoun, a local merchant,
since 1806; and North Woodside (28 acres), owned by Bailie
Henry Paul, the first manager of the City of Glasgow Bank,
they went to a further generation of 'country gentry' owners
- Kelvingrove to Colin MacNaughtan, another merchant, in
1841, and North Woodside to John Bain of Morriston in 1845. (31)
  The only properties to be successfully transformed by
their original owners were, significantly, those in immediate contact with the leading edge of the built-up area
in 1830 - South Woodside and Claremont (both about 30
acres). These estates were adjacent to Blythswood and
fronted on to Sauchiehall Street. The proprietors of
South Woodside, Allan Fullarton and James McHardy,
exploited this propinquity, pointing out that their lands
were 'in contact with the newest and most fashionable
part of Glasgow'. They paid assiduous attention to middle-
class residential demands:

  'The lands of South Woodside are, from the state of
  the surrounding property, effectively secured against
  any kind of nuisance, while the form into which the
  pleasure grounds, and openings of the lands has been
  thrown, is such as to exclude the possibility of
  disturbance from carting, carriage-drawing, or any
  foreign intrusion whatever. And as neither pains
  nor expense have been spared to give those who may
  choose to fix their residence here the combined
  advantages of town and country, they trust the
  public will support them in their undertaking.' (32)

Everything the middle class, and the builders who catered
for it, wanted to see in a suburb was there - a firm link

55

with the existing built-up area, tight planning controls, scenic beauty and a truly suburban environment. Their neighbour Fleming had Claremont laid out in harmony with South Woodside.

For most of the West End estates, success came only after mid-century and a change of ownership. Between 1840 and 1867, nearly all of them changed hands, and it was these new owners who really began the process of development. On the transfer of their estates to the developers, the country gentlemen - both genuine and ersatz - moved deeper into the countryside. The new owners were often from the same background as those they replaced. There were lawyers like Mathew Montgomerie and John Park Fleming of Kelvinside and merchants like Thomas Lucas Paterson of Dowanhill and Robert Malcolm Kerr of Hillhead. Some were from newer fields of industry and commerce, like James Beaumont Neilson, the inventor, and a partner in the Kelvinside venture; Thomas Russell, a partner in Walter MacFarlane's famous Saracen Foundry; James Whitelaw Anderson, a shirtmaker; and John Ewing Walker, the horse-bus king - all of them purchasers of sections of Kelvinside. (33) Some properties went to institutional buyers. Gilmourhill and Donaldshill (48 acres), acquired by Robert Bogle for £8,500 in 1802, was sold for an undisclosed sum in 1845; the purchaser then was the Great Western Cemetery Company, which hoped to create on this commanding height a western rival to the necropolis near the cathedral, then a popular promenade. By 1856, it was evident that no-one wanted to walk over or be buried under Gilmourhill and the cemetery company became a speculator, asking £59,750 for its land. It was ultimately bought by the university in 1864 for £81,000.(34) Another institutional speculator was the City of Glasgow Bank, which acquired North Woodside in 1867; but the greatest institutional purchases were made by the Corporation of Glasgow. The city bought about 100 acres between 1852 and 1867, mostly the remaining vacant ground east of the Kelvin. Most of it was turned into the Kelvingrove Park, the cost of which was partly offset by 18 acres of housing development. (35) The financing of this extensive transfer of land (over 1,200 acres in twenty-seven years) is a matter of almost as much speculation as the enterprise itself. Apart from the corporation's various deals and those concerning Kelvinside, only scattered information is available, either on the prices paid for the properties or the sources of capital.

56

Kelvinside, the most fully documented estate, changed hands several times between 1760 and 1840. A prominent local merchant family, the Dunmoores, bought it in 1760 and sold it for £7,750 in 1785 to Thomas Lithan, a Bengal nabob. After his death, his wife remarried in 1807, her new husband being a local lawyer, Archibald Cuthill, who was a speculator in Blythswood during the early twenties. He kept Kelvinside as a country home until his death about 1826 and, on his widow's death about 1830, the lands passed to her brothers and nephews, the legal and mercantile Mowbray family of Edinburgh and Leith. Their attempts to feu parcels of ground in the thirties having failed, they sold the 472-acre estate to their local agents, the already mentioned lawyers Mathew Montgomerie and John Park Fleming, and their associate J.B. Neilson, in 1840. Neilson, related to Montgomerie by marriage, was probably attracted by a band of Garibaldi ironstone made commercially viable by his hot-blast smelting process. The three partners, forming the Kelvinside Estate Company, paid £52,495 for the ground, of which £22,000 was borrowed from the trustees of Lieutenant-General Sir Thomas Munro (replaced by a Standard Life Assurance bond in 1856). Neilson probably contributed some of his business profits but Montgomerie and Fleming were not wealthy men. Since feu charters down to 1869 were granted 'with the consent of the British Linen Company' (a bank), they probably took out a substantial bank loan in addition. In 1845, they added the 104-acre Gartnavel estate, formerly a part of Kelvinside, for £10,450. At a total cost of £62,945, they had obtained 576 acres, almost half of the West End, in six years. (36)

Though little is known about most other transactions, rather more is known about the money market upon which speculators were able to draw. Though most Scottish banks were proud of their canny conservatism, the country's banking system was well developed by 1830 and two or three new banks opened up in the following decade to intensify an already fierce competition for clients. Even Montgomerie Fleming, in association with the lawyers Mowbray Howden of Edinburgh, tried to form a joint-stock bank in 1840 with a capital of £1 million to be raised in £20 shares; nothing seems to have come of it. (37) The most adventurous banks, the Western and the City of Glasgow, were said to have invested heavily in property. Both ultimately collapsed, the Western Bank in 1857; and the City Bank, in a spectacular crash which ruined many local businesses, in 1878.

Their commitments in the land and housing market, however,
do not appear to have been major causes of their failures. (3
Although the other banks were ready enough to lend money
to institutions and authorities in the West End apart from
the British Linen Bank's probable loan to Kelvinside, the
part they played in other deals is unknown. (39) Similarly,
the only known intervention of an insurance company is
Standard Life's grant of bonds totalling £202,000 to
Kelvinside between 1856 and 1898; all but one of these
were for undisclosed purposes and were not finally redeemed
until 1957. However, insurance companies were generally
ready to lend upon the security of land. (40)

The building society movement, though not as widespread
in Scotland as in England, seems to have fallen into two
parts. (41) In the first place, there were small subscription societies which seem to have existed for artisans and
tradesmen to buy their own houses and which held regular
auctions of their funds, generally not exceeding £1,000,
sold to the highest bidder among their members. (42)
The second type was more of an investment association,
which was organised on a subscription share basis for
lending to house buyers, builders and land speculators.
There was a rash of these during the housing boom of the
seventies. They were usually headed by local people of
substance. The Western Provident and Building Society,
for example, formed in 1870 to lend on 'good heritable
security', promised to pay 4 per cent on its £25 shares
and included among its trustees a Glasgow councillor as
deputy chairman, an ironfounder who was also Provost of
Helensburgh, the Lord Dean of Guild (head of the city's
mercantile fraternity), and a coalmaster. The Scottish
Prudential Investment Association, founded in 1876, was
led by a cotton spinner, an advocate, a leather merchant,
an architect and a builder. Its capital was £150,000 in
£5 shares and it hoped for a gross profit of 20 per cent
and a dividend of 7 per cent. An advertisement described
it as 'recently formed for the purchase, holding and
selling of heritable securities in Scotland, and other
kindred purposes'. An example of one of these institutions at work is contained in the Kelvinside estate
papers. The Heritable Securities Investment Association
Ltd, lent £19,262 to the Victoria Park Feuing Company in
1868 for the purchase of 34.85 acres. The terms are
unknown but the Victoria Park company was itself a skill-
ful combination of expertise and resources, its directors

consisting of a builder, a house factor, an accountant, a lawyer and two merchants. (43)

The local money market was further supplied by charities, friendly societies, successful tradesmen and 'persons of independent means', although it is likely that these channels contributed only modest amounts. House factors were important, for they had contacts among lawyers and accountants and often acted as agents for building societies and insurance companies. They frequently offered mortgages in conjunction with fire or life policies. Though the term of years was rarely stated, most mortgages were for no more than a half or three-quarters of the purchase prices of the properties on offer. As with all forms of money, interest rates ranged only from 3 per cent to 5 per cent throughout the period 1830-1914. (44)

Probably the largest single source of development capital and mortgages were the trust funds (marriage settlements, charities, dependants' allowances and bequests) managed by accountants and lawyers and regularly advertised for lending on 'first-class heritable securities'. Trust funds entered Glasgow from all over Scotland - from Oban, Rothesay and Aberdeen - though most of them came from Edinburgh or the Clyde valley. Individual amounts varied greatly, from £100 to £10,000, but the supply was seemingly unaffected by changing economic circumstances. Glasgow's developers and house buyers were never short of cheap and ready money. The total amount from all sources on offer in the press on a given day was usually a five-figure sum, frequently over £100,000 and, on at least one occasion, £500,000. Most of it 'could remain on loan for a term of years'. (45)

Once having acquired their properties, developing land-lords employed surveyors or architects to draw up feuing plans, design the houses or at least vet the designs of others, and supervise building operations and the subsequent enforcement of feuing regulations. Some of these feuing plans were minor works of art and since the models for Glasgow's West End were London's West End and Edinburgh's New Town, it is not surprising that among the first plans were two prepared by designers from London and Edinburgh. The owners of South Woodside, the first estate to be opened up, commissioned George Smith, fresh from work in the New Town of Edinburgh, to lay it out, while the neighbouring proprietor, John Fleming of Claremont, retained John Baird I, a leading Glasgow architect, to draw up a feuing plan in harmony with Smith's design. The combined scheme was for terraces lying along the

contours of the steeply rising ground and fronted by
pleasure gardens. It set a happy precedent, followed
throughout the West End, for elegant classical terraces
and pleasant communal gardens. (46)

Kelvinside, the largest estate, was also the grandest
in conception. The most dynamic of the three partners,
Mathew Montgomerie, had a clear and magnificent vision of
its future. His nephew, James Brown Fleming, the son of
the second partner, John Park Fleming, who inherited his
uncle's rather than his father's personality, described
this vision in 1894, when it had been largely realised:
'From the first it was resolved ... to make the suburb of
Kelvinside the best residential district of the city'.
Montgomerie had 'an implicit belief that the best class
of houses in the rapidly expanding suburbs of Glasgow must
ultimately come to be built on the line of Great Western
Road'. It was 'by far the handsomest thoroughfare in
Glasgow', a bold, broad swathe driving through the heart
of the West End and lined with trees. To carry out its
grand design, the partnership appointed Decimus Burton
as estate architect immediately after the acquisition of
the lands in 1840. Burton, regarded as 'the most eminent
man in his profession', had been active in the Regent's
Park scheme and other suburban projects in the London area
His 'admirably conceived' plan envisaged terraces standing
proudly above Great Western Road with villas widely dis-
persed in sylvan glades behind the great turnpike. The
Burton design was expensive on land, however, and his
scheme was revised and extended in 1858 by the local
architect James Salmon, who also designed Dennistoun. (47)

There were four estates of around 100 acres each -
Partickhill (which may have been composed of several
properties), Downhill, Hillhead and Hyndland. Hillhead
was platted on a grid system in about 1850 (when R.M. Kerr
probably became owner) and Hyndland, feued out between
1890 and 1914, was similarly straightforward. The other
two were both planned with more regard for the physiography
of the area. When T.L. Paterson acquired Dowanhill in 1850
from the family of the late James Buchanan, MP, who died
in 1844, he appointed a local architect, James Thomson,
to prepare a feuing plan. Thomson, like most of his
contemporaries a convinced classicist, had one of the
largest practices in Glasgow. Dowanhill centres round a
drumlin with its southern and lower flanks in industrial
Partick. Thomson divided the property into two sections,

the one adjoining Partick becoming Dowanvale, described
as 'very favourably situated for tradesmen's houses, which
are in great demand at remunerative rents'. The line
dividing it from Dowanhill proper runs along Highburgh
Road, where a churchyard and a recreation ground create
a buffer zone. The bourgeois half, 'as laid out for
tenements of a superior class, and for self-contained
lodgings', is clustered about the hill, tenements giving
way to terraces and villas as the summit is neared. Tree-
lined roads sweep up the hill in wide curves and the upper
middle class could feel comfortably isolated from the rest
of the world in Dowanhill, described in 1901 as 'the
quietest district imaginable'. (48) The neighbouring
drumlin to Dowanhill is Partickhill, just to the west and
a district about which little is known. Most of it appears
to have been laid out in the thirties and forties to one
design, probably by the local architect Alexander Taylor,
agent for the scheme and designer of Royal Crescent, Sauchiehall Street (1839). Partickhill also is rich in trees and
has extensive views down the Clyde. Its uninterrupted view,
its proximity to the Yoker Road and the the independent and
burgeoning community of Partick led to its early feuing.
Laid out in gentle curves principally for villas, it is
separated from Partick proper by the steepness of its
drumlin; indeed, it was so well isolated that as late as
1892 'the gardens up here were still rural and unsullied'. (49)
Most of the other estates were too small to allow of any
plan other than one which maximised the use of their limited
space consonant with meeting the requirements of their
middle class clientele. They have pleasure-grounds and
trees and one or two small squares, but there was general
difficulty in avoiding straight roads.

The finest piece of planning in the West End was that
carried out for the Corporation of Glasgow between 1852
and 1860 by Charles Wilson, the leading local architect
of the day. Following agitation in 1850 by residents on
and about Sauchiehall Street for 'a Queen's Park in the
West', Wilson prepared and offered to the corporation a
scheme for a park in the valley of the Kelvin, the cost
of which, as already mentioned, would be defrayed in part
by an upper-middle-class housing development on the hill
above it. The corporation approved the project in 1851
and by 1860 the scheme was complete and the park open.
Wilson, who was assisted in laying out the park by Sir
Joseph Paxton, also designed houses on Woodlands Hill and

the Free Church College with its three brilliant towers
in a highly personal style. The mansard roofs, classical
proportions and grand porches of the houses, with the
soaring towers of the college and equally idiosyncratic
Gothic revival tower of the Park Church (J.T. Rochead,
1858), seen from the park below offer the finest skyline
in Glasgow, indeed one of the finest anywhere. Wilson
had a confident grasp of scale and perspective, a mastery
of detail and a bold imagination. From the summit, there
is a superb view of the hills enclosing the Clyde, the
river's lower course, and most of Glasgow. (50)

The next stage in the development process was to feu,
lease or sell building plots or steadings. Landowners
trying to woo builders and house buyers had to demonstrate
the excellence of their sites, the strictness of their
planning regulations and the extent to which they were
prepared to aid builders. For example, the Kelvinside
Estate Company advised the public that:

'The whole of this ground is situated at the Western
end of the city, in a direction rapidly taking up
for genteel residences. The surface is varied,
mostly elevated, commanding fine views, and securing
good air. From the great extent of the Property,
and regulations in the Feuing rights, entire freedom
from nuisances is secured; the Public may believe
with confidence that full omnibus accommodation will
be provided, so as to render a residence on these
grounds in every way suitable.' (51)

The proprietors subsidised a horse-bus service to town
via Great Western Road from 1847. It was provided by
John Ewing Walker, the leading local liveryman, to reward
the brave who had gone out to Kelvinside then 'considered
quite in the country', and to encourage the timid. (52)

The West End being well endowed with building materials,
builders were offered the free use of what was found on
site. North Woodside, for example, advertised in 1840,
was 'full of freestone, close to the surface, and there
is also clay suitable for brick-making'. The whole area
was dotted with quarries and brick pits. (53) Most landowners also tempted builders with 'advances given to
approved builders'. This 'liberal pecuniary accommodation'
took various forms. Burnbank offered a two-thirds mortgage
or 'every facility to a builder'. For 6 acres on Great

Western Road, up for roup (auction) in 1856, 'the price
will be converted to a ground annual if required'. Land
on either side of Kelvinbridge, advertised in 1870, was
offered with advances to builders and as a further inducement the proprietors undertook to pay all road, drainage
and pleasure ground expenses. (54)

When builders began the lengthy task of construction,
they sometimes commissioned an architect, but in many cases
they worked from plans already drawn up by an estate
architect, as in Dowanhill:

'The Proprietors of Dowanhill are prepared to feu
certain parts of their ground for the erection of
self-contained houses of a value of about £1600,
which are presently much wanted in the locality.
The ground is very advantageously situated for such
houses, and they would command a speedy sale, if
well built, according to plans which have been
prepared and will be submitted to intending feuars.' (55)

Construction took about twelve to eighteen months in the
case of villas and terrace houses, rather longer in the
case of four-storey tenements. All materials were readied
on site, only the best quality stone, timber, marble and
fittings were used and a high standard of finish was
demanded in these large 10-14 roomed houses and tenement
blocks of up to fifty apartments.

Since almost all West End houses were speculations,
building them was a hazardous venture. Most firms were
small, undercapitalised, short of management skills and
survived only for one generation, many ending in the
bankruptcy court. Hedged about with so many limitations,
it is not surprising that West End builders proceeded
with extreme caution. John Christie's policy in Kew
Terrace is typical. Christie feued five steadings in 1850,
erected the houses and then began to sell them. With
returns on capital coming in, he could afford to feu six
more in 1851, then, having sold or rented one or two,
reinvest the proceeds, coming back for five more in 1852
and a final four in 1853. Other builders were equally
circumspect. William Young feued a fresh steading every
few months in Montgomerie (now Cleveden) Crescent between
1873 and 1878. John Renwick, at work just round the corner
in Montgomerie Quadrant, took five steadings in 1881, five
in 1882, four in 1883, two in 1885 and a final four in 1886.

The largest builders in Kelvinside were William and Peter
Miller of Partick, who were active in almost every year
between 1877 and 1903, yet their total production came to
only forty-three villas, semi-detached pairs and terrace
houses. However, they were building elsewhere in the West
End over the same period, putting up Nos 28-41 Westbourne
Gardens South in 1876-82, for example. Similarly, William
Young seems to have built extensively in Victoria Park
between 1875 and 1890. (56) Most West End builders, however,
were probably incapable of erecting more than half-a-dozen
houses a year. There were one or two large firms at work,
though little is known about them. The largest seems to
have been J.A. McTaggart & Co, still in existence, who
built a good deal of working-class housing between 1890
and 1914 and at the same time constructed numerous huge
red-sandstone tenements for the middle class on the Hyndland estate. John Lindsay and William Benzie of Byres
Road, Partick, put up about £200,000 worth of housing in
Dowanhill, Kelvinside and Hillhead between about 1870 and
1910. William Stobo, the pioneer builder in Hillhead, who
had been in business since about 1845, was said to be worth
about £30,000 in 1878. Otherwise, little information has
come to light on the builders of the West End. (57)

On completion, both houses (about two-thirds of the West
End's homes) and apartments (the remaining third) were
generally placed in the hands of house factors for selling
and letting. Sales were fairly evenly divided between
roup (auction) and private bargains. Before 1914, apartments were universally for letting, while houses were
normally sold. Occasionally builders, lawyers, accountants and businessmen dealt in house property but house
factors were a well-organised profession by 1860, publishing
monthly lists and advertising daily in the local press,
which had by then classified property advertisements.
There was also a Glasgow Advertiser between 1856 and 1860,
specialising in property, a Glasgow Property Circular
between 1893 and 1900, and an annual Property Index
between 1898 and 1900.

Once properties were sold or let, the development process
was over. The period from the transfer of a country estate
to a developing landlord, through the preparation of a
feuing plan, the attraction of builders and the building
operations themselves, to the final disposal of the
properties could be very long indeed, perhaps a generation,
punctuated by false starts, bankruptcies and depressions.

1. Exeter: Barnfield Crescent, begun about 1792 (*Exeter City Council*)

2. Exeter: Southernhay, early nineteenth century (*Exeter City Council*)

3. Glasgow: the grand terrace, Great Western Terrace, 1870 (*M. A. Simpson*)

4. Glasgow: the average terrace, Westbourne Gardens North, about 1870 (*M. A. Simpson*)

Three distinct sticking points in the development process -
the search for a developer, his search for builders, their
searches for tenants or buyers - helped to explain the
relatively slow growth of the West End (about 1,000 acres
in eighty-five years).

Development proceeded roughly from south-east to north-
west, starting from the solid block of South Woodside and
Claremont but quickly producing outliers of settlement
with which the general frontier was slow to catch up.
Beginning in 1830, the terrace building in South Woodside,
Claremont and on Sauchiehall Street proceeded steadily
according to the plans, which were completed by the mid-
fifties, by which time the corporation was feuing out
Woodlands Hill. Partickhill was an early if isolated
middle-class outpost; although substantially complete by
mid-century, there were vacant steadings as late as 1870. (58)

The Great Western Road, open fully by 1841, spurred urban
growth at its eastern end, where it joined another turnpike
from Maryhill, and encouraged landowners along its flanks
to offer their land for building. In Hillhead, the first
half-dozen terraces began to go up in the late forties,
with two more on the Great Western Road frontage of Northpark; but it was not until about 1860 that the land west
of the Kelvin began to develop with any speed. By that
time the urban frontier had reached the river in several
places and within a decade the properties north of the
turnpike - North Woodside, Burnbank and Northpark,
totalling over 60 acres - were covered with houses. Hillhead had over 3,000 people by 1869, and was sufficiently
urbanised to be granted burgh status. Its street plan
was virtually complete, although there were many vacant
lots, filled in by 1891 when the burgh, with a population
of 9,000, was annexed to Glasgow. (59)

Byres Road, which linked the Great Western and Yoker
turnpikes, also separated Hillhead from Dowanhill. Like
Hillhead, Dowanhill passed in 1850 to a landlord intent
upon development. Crown Circus and Victoria Crescent were
built in the fifties but the heart of the estate was
developed for villas and terraces in the sixties. Little
was done in the seventies (the peak building years for
the West End) or the eighties, but most of the remaining
land was filled in between 1890 and 1914, mostly by
tenements adjacent to new tram routes. (60) Hyndland,
similarly tenemented, was first offered for sale in 1877
but was not built over until 1890-1914, when it was able

65

to exploit the North British suburban branch line which
terminated there (1886) and the two tram routes which
passed by it. (61) Villa and terrace residents took cabs
or ran their own coaches, but tenement people (outside of
Hillhead) were generally a shade lower down the social and
economic scale and relied much more on public transport.
The little properties on the periphery of Hillhead, like
Ashfield, Cliff House and Westbank (all of them about 3
acres), generally succumbed to development at about the
same time as their larger neighbour, though two, Saughfield
and Lilybank (each 10 acres), survived in sylvan splendour
until the late eighties. (62)

The development of Kelvinside is chequered, less obviously
east-to-west than its neighbours. Soon after Burton's plan
was produced, land was feued to the Botanic Gardens (less
a disinterested public service in giving the Glasgow Royal
Botanic Institution a permanent home than a shrewd move to
provide Kelvinside with a park run and paid for by some-
one else); the Observatory, glad to escape city smoke; and
the proposed Free Church College (the three partners in the
Kelvinside development were 'Wee Frees' who had 'come out'
at the Disruption of 1843), though this feuing was later
renounced when the college set itself up on Woodlands Hill.
The partnership then built the first half of Windsor (now
Kirklee) Terrace, adjacent to the Botanic Gardens, between
1845 and 1848, undertaking it themselves to encourage
builders to invest in Kelvinside. Although Fleming and
Neilson themselves went to live there (Montgomerie, the
master planner of the trio, lived in Kelvinside House),
the last house of the twenty does not seem to have been
sold until 1864 - about twenty years after the terrace
was begun. In the 1850s, two terraces facing the Botanic
Gardens were erected and two more in the sixties. But the
Kelvinside venture was hardly successful in its first
thirty years: the struggling Great Western Turnpike, so
crucial to Kelvinside's success, was bailed out to the
extent of over £3,000 in its early days; Walker's horse
bus had to be subsidised for several years; the Botanic
Gardens failed to meet its annual feu duty payments.
Neilson left the partnership in 1851 and had to be bought
out. Kew Terrace (1850-5) was almost as slow in selling
as Windsor Terrace. J.B. Fleming said later that his
uncle and his father hung on to Kelvinside during the
1850s despite great financial difficulties and only sixty-
eight feus had been given off by 1868. (63)

By the end of the 1860s, however, the building frontier
had reached Kelvinside and within a few years, 1868-73,
during which both Montgomerie and Fleming died, leaving
the estate in the shrewd and aggressive hands of J.B.
Fleming, its fortunes dramatically improved. Some 187
acres, nearly a third of the estate, were given off in
feus and dispositions. The boom began with James Whitelaw Anderson's acquisition of 16.65 acres for £15,556 in
1868; he went bankrupt in 1870 but continued the development of his property until it was completed in about 1882.
In 1869, John Ewing Walker, having sold his horse buses to
the new Glasgow Tramways Company, bought 93.42 acres in
the 156-acre Maryhill section for £33,647. Most of the
remainder of the Maryhill land was feued out for industry
or working class tenements by 1876. The Victoria Park
Feuing Company, backed by the Heritable Securities Investment Association, Ltd, obtained 34.85 acres in 1868 for
£19,262. James B. Mirrlees, a marine engineer, bought
23.86 acres (the projected site of the Free Church College)
for £9,703 in 1869. Thomas Russell, who lived at Meikle
Ascog in Bute, acquired 11.20 acres for £13,249 in 1873.
Also in 1873, Thomas Johnston Smillie, a lawyer, and
Andrew Goodall, a builder, took 6.96 acres for an annual
feu duty of £421. Despite these large-scale transactions,
most of Kelvinside was developed on a piecemeal basis, a
few steadings at a time. Victoria Park became terraces
arranged round squares. Walker's property was devoted
mainly to working-class and industrial use with a few
middle-class terraces and tenements stretching along the
Kelvin. Russell's land was for villas in ½-acre steadings.
Smillie and Goodall built semi-detached pairs. Mirrlees's
land ultimately became terraces, after his death about 1900.
Almost 200 acres were still vacant in 1914, mostly in the
extreme north-west. (64)

Development of the West End, steady but unspectacular
before 1870, was at its most rapid in the seventies, when
a quarter of the area was covered. There was a decline
in the eighties but building still went on at a faster
rate than before 1870 and there was no noticeable slacken-
ing until about 1903, when the building industry throughout Glasgow fell into a malaise from which it had not
recovered by 1914.

The principal determinants of house prices and apartment
rents were both temporal and spatial. The housing market
reflected cyclical fluctuations in the local economy,

usually lagging on both the upswing and the downswing by
a year or more. Prices also responded to the rate of growth
of the local social élite. There is no evidence that money
was ever short or dear for buying houses though some builder
may have suffered in these respects for, as Cairncross has
expressed it, 'It was the prosperity of the Dakotas, so to
speak, that brought building to a standstill in Dalmarnock'.
In good times, money stayed at home and went into construction, particularly industrial- and working-class building;
in bad times, this money fled abroad. It is likely, however
that the middle-class market was much less affected by
cyclical swings and the consequent ebb and flow of capital
and population. (65)

The spatial influences centred mainly around size and
its concomitants. Generally speaking, the larger the house,
the higher the price. With greater size went more and
better fittings and a more imposing façade. Position, too,
was an important determinant - main-road locations and
convenience for transport, shops and other facilities raised
values by hundreds of pounds. In Hillhead in 1850, for
example, building land along Great Western Road was advertised at 5s 9d per square yard but the price slipped with
every step away from the turnpike until a quarter of a mile
away, it had slumped to only 1s 6d. (66) Proximity to
Kelvingrove Park or the Botanic Gardens or the presence of
a pleasure ground reserved for residents also boosted prices
and rents. The terraces of Claremont and South Woodside,
adjacent to Sauchiehall Street and Charing Cross, held
their prices extremely well throughout the period, becoming
Glasgow's 'Harley Street'. Not only were the large receptio
rooms ideal for surgeries but the houses were also convenien
for the University, the associated Western Infirmary, the
Royal Hospital and the city centre a mile or so away.
Identical houses could also vary in price substantially
at any given time, depending on condition, interior fittings
and the different pressures on each vendor; for example,
financial exigency or death often lead to a desire for a
quick sale at a low price.

Given these temporal and spatial influences on rents and
prices, houses and apartments have been divided into groups
and studied at several points over the period 1830-1914.
A total sample of 650 house prices (mostly asking prices)
and 300 apartment rents has been built up from the property
pages of the Glasgow Herald, scanned at 10-yearly intervals
from 1830 to 1900. Supplementary information has been

obtained from the Herald for 1876-7 (the peak of the building boom), 1878-9 (the period of the City Bank crash), and 1914; the Glasgow Advertiser and Property Circular (available for 1856-7 and 1860); the Glasgow Property Circular (available for 1893-4 and 1897-9); and the Glasgow Property Index (1898-1900). In addition, the feu charters of Kelvinside often contain minimum selling prices.

The houses of the West End fall into five groups - grand villas, semi-detached, best terraces, average terraces, and small terraces and lesser villas. The grand villas before 1850 were almost entirely mansion houses erected before 1830 and since overtaken by development and left with an acre or so around them. In the fifties, the first 'purpose-built' suburban villas went up on the Dowanhill estate around the crest of Observatory Hill, and in the period 1873-93 another concentration grew up in Kelvinside north of Great Western Road.(67) The semi-detached houses were often as large as the free-standing villas and were frequently mixed in with them. They were a solely Kelvinside phenomenon, built in two groups, one north of Great Western Road in the middle of the estate (1872-90), the other in the Gartnavel section, between the south side of Great Western Road and the Royal Asylum, on the western extremity (1893-1910). Both villas and semi-detached houses had grand halls, 3-4 large reception rooms, 6-10 bedrooms, with kitchen, basement, dressing-rooms and bathrooms and extensive offices and outbuildings. (68) The superior and average terraces usually had an imposing hall, 2-3 reception rooms and 6-10 bedrooms, with kitchen, basement, dressing-rooms, bathrooms and outbuildings; they differed only in that the dozen best terraces - at the summit of Dowanhill, along the Kelvinside section of Great Western Road and around Park Circus - possessed more favourable locations, more majestic façades and better fittings. The average terraces, the commonest form of housing in the West End, were built in all parts of the district. The small terraces and cottages had 2-3 reception rooms and 3-5 bedrooms, with fewer of the 'usual offices'. The cottages were sometimes survivals from pre-development days but a number of new ones were built before mid-century on Partickhill and others late in the century in North Kelvinside. The small terraces were mostly situated in Hillhead but there were others around Partickhill.

Table 1

House Prices in the West End, 1830-1914

Year	Villas	Semi-detached	Best terraces	Average terraces	Small terraces
To					
1860	£2,175	--	£2,475	--	£925
1870	3,100	--	3,300	£1,550	1,100
1876	3,500	£2,150	4,700	2,700	--
1877	--	--	--	2,550	1,300
1878	--	--	--	2,425	--
1879	--	--	--	2,075	--
1880	3,750	2,400*	4,100	2,375	--
1890	2,900*	2,075*	3,350	2,075	1,125
1893	--	--	3,075	1,575	875
1894	--	--	3,125	1,650	900
1897	--	--	3,425	1,600	1,050
1898	--	--	3,550	1,625	1,050
1899	--	--	3,150	1,650	925
1900	--	2,350*	3,750	1,750	1,100
1914	--	--	--	700	--

*Average for the whole decade

SOURCES: Property advertisements, Glasgow Herald,
decennial intervals, 1830-1900 and 1876-9, 1914;
Glasgow Advertiser and Property Circular, 1856-7, 1860;
Glasgow Property Circular, 1893-4, 1897-9;
Glasgow Property Index, 1898-1900; Kelvinside Estate
Papers .

Average prices are only given for years in which there
is a large enough sample, i.e., at least 6 prices for
a given category.

Groupings are necessarily somewhat arbitrary and samples
for each group in a given year are generally small - an
average of ten prices for each group. However, these
limitations notwithstanding, the prices give some indic-
ations of the trends in the housing market.

Before 1860, it was not usual to list prices and the
first sample includes prices from 1830. There were only
one or two prices for average terraces and there were no
semi-detached houses before 1876. By 1870 the West End
was an area of general development. The Dowanhill villas
were almost all completed and, being purpose-built suburban residences, helped to push the average price over
£3,000. Most of the best terraces were also occupied by
1870, while the average terraces were growing rapidly.
Quite a large number of the small terraces had been built
in the sixties. The early seventies were a time of booming
prices, reaching a ceiling in 1876. The economy was already
in the downswing of the business cycle and the housing
market eventually began to reflect this, prices dropping
in 1877-8 (and before the City Bank crashed in October
1878) and continuing to fall in 1879. The continuing
increase in villa prices was a consequence of the building
of very large villas on Russell's feu in Kelvinside (1873-
93). The semi-detached houses nearby consisted of several
types, varying in price from £1,800 to £3,000; the periodic
predominance of one type over another, rather than market
forces, seems to account for the fluctuations in semi-
detached house prices. (69) The apparently sharp recovery
in average terrace prices in 1880 was due to a heavy predominance of the larger houses in the property lists. The
local economy continued to be depressed throughout the
eighties and West End building seems to have been down by
about a third compared with the seventies. Nevertheless,
the population of Hillhead and Kelvinside, representing
the greater part of the West End, increased by a third
between 1881 and 1891, while in the same decade Hillhead's
gross rental climbed by 15 per cent compared with the
neighbouring working-class burghs of Partick and Maryhill,
where the overall valuation stagnated. (70) The local
professional and mercantile groups probably continued to
expand as Glasgow developed its regional service functions
and as commerce profited from falling commodity prices and
rising real incomes.

Economic recovery had set in by about 1890 but house prices,
as always, were slow to reflect this improvement. The 1890

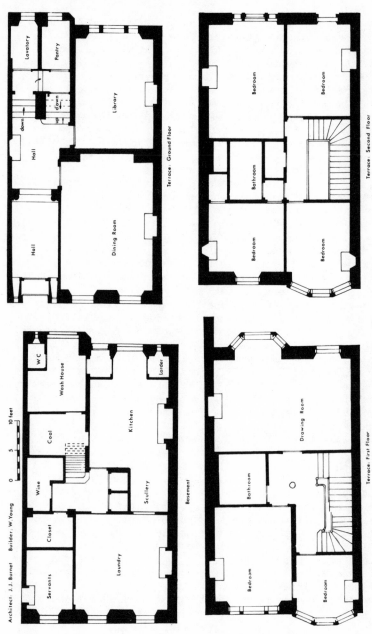

Fig 5 Terrace House, Saughfield Terrace (now University Gardens), Hillhead, 1886.

prices show sharp falls over the preceding decade, only
the smallest houses hanging on to their boom-time gains,
probably because of increasing lower-middle-class demand
for suburban residences. During the nineties, the oldest
villas - the survivors of pastoral days and the Partickhill group - dropped in price, but the Dowanhill and Kelvinside properties maintained their prestige and went on the
market at around £4,000-6,000 and even above that. The
semi-detached houses spread to the Gartnavel section of
Kelvinside but they were somewhat smaller than the earlier
group, hence the fall in price. The best terraces, though
sharply reduced in price since 1880, kept above £3,000 for
the whole decade, helped by their evident grandeur and the
completeness of their accommodation, together with the
continued attraction for the medical profession of those
in the south-eastern quarter. Although the average terrace
continued to dip steeply even after 1890, it staged a
modest recovery late in the decade. The small terrace and
lesser villa prices apparently fluctuated a good deal -
the higher prices in 1897-8 reflecting a higher proportion
of small villas in the samples. Very few prices are
available for 1914, by which time the bottom had dropped
out of the market to such an extent that building in the
West End had ceased and house factors were offering 3 per
cent of sale prices to individuals who found purchasers
for houses on their lists. (71) The two villas advertised
in 1900 were Dunard in Dowanhill (at £6,500) and Averley
in Kelvinside (at £5,000, reduced to £4,750), while in 1914
only Southpark House in Hillhead was listed (at £3,600; it
had been on offer at £3,500 in 1893). A lesser villa,
Edradour on Partickhill, was listed at £700 in 1914 whereas
it would have gone on the market at twice that figure in
1900. (72) The average terrace was a notable casualty of
the catastrophe which struck the local housing market,
falling over £1,000 between 1900 and 1914, with some dipping
below the £700 average to as low as £250. (73) The trend
in building for the middle classes from about 1885 was to
smaller, two-storey, semi-detached properties, with private
gardens and without basements, located mainly in rival
suburbs south of the Clyde, or in Jordanhill to the west
or Bearsden to the north-west; the large West End terrace
house may therefore have suffered from a change in taste,
a drop in family size and a declining number of domestic
servants as much as from market difficulties. Prices in
other parts of Glasgow were usually below those for average

West End terraces throughout the period except in Pollokshields, where prices rivalled those of the best West End
terraces and villas. (74)

Apartments (Table 2) have been divided into three groups
though, as with houses, the divisions are not watertight.
A handful of apartments constituted a superior group,
usually consisting of 6-8 rooms plus kitchen and bathroom,
generally purpose-built in a tenement block but occasionally
converted from a self-contained terrace house. While most
of them were in the area east of the Kelvin, there were a
few in Dowanhill, Partickhill, Hyndland and Hillhead. The
majority of apartments, situated in Dowanhill, Hillhead and
neighbouring smaller development properties, consisted of
4-6 rooms plus kitchen and bathroom. The third group,
marginal properties for middle-class occupation, were located
on the fringes of the West End and contained 3-5 rooms plus
a kitchen and bathroom. Most apartments were in four-storey
tenements which were usually in separate streets from houses.
The most favoured and generally most expensive apartments
were those which had a separate or 'main door' street
entrance; all other apartments were entered off an open
stairway. This was common to both working-class and middle-
class tenements. Legend has it that Glaswegians told the
difference between the two by asking if the stairway was
tiled; if so, it was middle-class, for working-class stair-
ways had only painted plaster. Two apartments were situated
on each 'flat' or floor. The first-floor apartments were
popular, for they possessed a view (especially if they had
an oriel window) without too much stair climbing. Top-floor
apartments often had the use of attics and ground-floor
occupants sometimes had basements. All occupants had equal
rights in the rear 'bleaching green'. Whatever their group,
all apartments were designed around a common plan - a
vestibule (generally including a large wall cupboard), a
kitchen (with a draped bed recess for a maid or a child),
a bathroom, a dining-room and a sitting-room (though the
two were sometimes combined), and from one to eight bedrooms (including a maid's room in some of the larger apartments). (75) There is no indication that apartments were
for sale before 1914; renting seems to have been universal.
Furnished accommodation was rare but, when available, it
led to a doubling of the rent.

Tenement blocks were frequently for sale but advertisement details were normally too skimpy to permit any analysis
of trends; prices ranged from £1,000 to £20,000. (76)

74

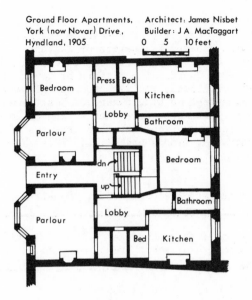

Ground Floor Apartments, York (now Novar) Drive, Hyndland, 1905

Architect: James Nisbet
Builder: J A MacTaggart

0   5   10 feet

Bedroom

Press | Bed

Kitchen

Lobby

Bathroom

Parlour

Entry

dn

up

Bedroom

Bathroom

Parlour

Lobby

Bed | Kitchen

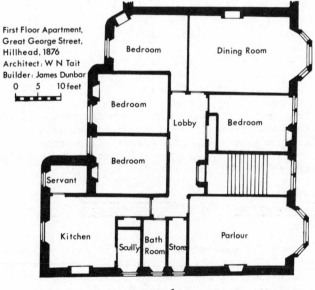

First Floor Apartment,
Great George Street,
Hillhead, 1876
Architect: W N Tait
Builder: James Dunbar

0   5   10 feet

Bedroom

Dining Room

Bedroom

Lobby

Bedroom

Bedroom

Servant

Kitchen

Scull'y

Bath Room

Store

Parlour

Fig 6

Tenements were often owned by absentee landlords who lived
in other parts of the city or elsewhere in Britain; their
properties were managed by lawyers or factors. Other
tenements were owned by property companies, such as the
St Mungo Property Co Ltd, proprietors of No 176 Great
George Street, Hillhead, in 1914; and the Glasgow & District
Heritable Investment Co Ltd, owners of Nos 14 and 16 Great
George Street. Tenements were thus a form of investment
for local businessmen, rentiers, and trustees of charities,
marriage contracts, minors and wills. (77)

Table 2

Apartments: Sizes and Rents, 1860-1914

Year	Superior rooms	rent	Average rooms	rent	Marginal rooms	rent
1860	8	£50	6	£35	5	£21
1870	7	£62	6	£54 10s	-	-
1876	-	-	4	£35	4	£26
1878	-	-	4-5	£34 10s	3	£23
1879	-	-	5	£40 10s	3	£26
1880	-	-	4-5	£34	5	£25
1890	-	-	6	£36	5	£25 10s
1893-8	-	-	6	£31	-	-
1900	-	-	5	£40	5	£30
1914	-	-	5	£42	5	£31

Note: All rents are annual sums. Average rents are only
given for those years in which there are at least 6
examples in a given catgory. Almost all apartments were
inclusive of bathroom, kitchen and vestibule; 'rooms'
therefore only refers to reception rooms and bedrooms.

Sources: Property columns, Glasgow Herald, 1860-1914;
Glasgow Advertiser, 1860; Glasgow Property Circular,
1893-8.

There were few apartments before 1850 and even by 1860
they were still a rarity confined to Hillhead and the area
round Sauchiehall Street. In the sixties, the average class
grew significantly in Hillhead. Furnished superior apart-

ments were available in Hillhead in 1870 with 6-8 rooms
for £108-£144 per annum. (78) The one or two marginal
apartments listed were offered at £20-£25 for 4-5 rooms. (79)
By 1876, Hillhead was growing rapidly and the lower slopes
of Dowanhill were being covered with average tenements.
The meaner sort were being built extensively north and east
of the Kelvin. The two superior apartments listed in 1876
were in Royal Terrace (5 rooms, £65) and Claremont Street
(6 rooms, £70), both adjacent to Park Circus and its
superior terraces. (80) The decline in the house-purchase
market does not seem to have affected rents. These
remained reasonably constant throughout the rest of the
period. Superior apartments continued to be unusual but
when they did appear, rents averaged around £10 per room. (81)
Hillhead became the chief apartment district and by 1888,
by which time it was almost fully built-up, there were
1,528 apartments and only 439 houses. (82) After Hillhead
ceased to offer scope to the tenement builders, they
continued to build in Dowanhill and also opened up Hyndland
and North Kelvinside. These districts were developed
chiefly for average tenements, causing an enormous rise in
the stock of this class of apartment. A few of the smaller,
poorer variety continued to be built but they were still
confined to the frayed edges of the West End where they
merged almost imperceptibly into lower-middle-class and
artisan streets. By 1914 the most stylish apartments were
in the new red-sandstone tenements of Hyndland, with
electricity and (in the 4-5 room versions) a maid's room.
They all averaged £10 per room, even the 2-3 room types. (83)
Despite the calamitous fall in house prices, rents held up
- evidence, perhaps, of an influx of lower-middle-class people
into the suburbs and of a general trend towards smaller homes.
    One of the chief attractions of the West End is its
architecture. It was fortunate in being built at a time
when Glasgow had one of the ablest groups of architects
of any western city, with a highly traditional and pleasing
basic style and notable personal idiosyncracies. Glasgow's
classicism, rather plain in Regency times, became more
flamboyant in the Victorian era and, towards the end of
the century, died out in the face of the so-called 'art
nouveau', and the influence of Norman Shaw, Chicago and
the École des Beaux Arts. For most of the century, however, Glasgow's middle class was conservative in its taste.
Jealously proud of its independence of mind, it knew the
town's architects socially and was rather better educated

than the Victorian bourgeoisie is generally reckoned to be. (84)

The houses of the West End have certain features in common. Whether villas, tenements or terraces, they are invariably of stone; either the warm, creamy-brown limestone of the West End itself, or, increasingly after 1880, the red Ayrshire sandstone. Courses are often banded, particularly in the lower storeys. The lines of most houses and tenements are almost unadorned, though some have inventive detail. Some villas and late terraces were given extravagant flourishes and where there are dormers, they are in many cases late additions and regrettable. Bays or oriels became almost universal after 1870, replacing the straight-fronted Regency style. Invariably, the grandest single feature of the terraces and villas is the main entrance, which is porched, pedimented and pillared in most instances. The average terrace was built to three storeys and a basement. Except for villas, gardens were unusual at the front, though rear 'bleaching greens' were universal; the few late terraces have front gardens and the more modern tenements provided 'postage stamp' strips for ground-floor apartments.

Although there are some attractive villas on Partickhill and No 996 Great Western Road is a nicely-proportioned essay in the Italian palatial style, the most memorable features of the majority are their imposing sites, their bulk and their opulence. It is difficult to categorise them according to accepted styles but the choice for clients was normally between a fussy Italianate and that strange romanticism, Scottish baronial. (85) The huge tenements are, by contrast, quite plain and uniform. There is the occasional pedimented or scrollwork doorway or window, but they are notable chiefly for straight fronts broken only by oriels or bays, massive proportions and a sense of brooding solidity.

It is in the terraces that architecture becomes more than neat, conventional and competent. Even here, the best work was finished by 1870. The West End terrace was given a good start by George Smith's massive but somewhat sombre and daunting series in South Woodside (1830-45). John Baird I was a little more adventurous in neighbouring Claremont, but it was Charles Wilson who really demonstrated the potential of the terrace as a study in composition, balance, mass, detail and elegance. (86) He began with an ambitious Italianate commission in Windsor (now Kirklee) Terrace in Kelvinside (1845-8). This gains inestimably from its elevated position above Great Western Road and behind a pleasure ground, and has distinctive hooded windows, hefty balconies, imposing square-columned porches and enhanced centre and end houses. His outer terraces on Woodlands Hill (1852-60) are bay-windowed with great pilastered doorways and steep mansard roofs, while his finest composition, Park Circus (1855-7), is extremely subtle in its novel detail and in the grouping of the individual components of the great oval. (87) J.T. Rochead, one of Wilson's contemporaries, whose work is often juxta-posed with the master's, designed Buckingham, Ruskin and St James's Terraces on the north side of Great Western Road in Hillhead in the fifties and Kew Terrace, on the south side of Kelvinside, opposite the Botanic Gardens, in 1850. All were in the conventional Glasgow idiom - attractive, well-proportioned but rather restrained. However, his Grosvenor Terrace (1855-7), also opposite the Botanic Gardens, is a complete contrast. Built with 'a view of the brilliant parterres of the Botanic Gardens, with the umbrageous woods of Kelvinside beyond', it was exposed to the north winds. Rochead boldly fronted it as much as he could with glass; indeed there was so much glass on the north-facing terrace that the proprietors of Kelvinside feared the houses would be rejected by potential buyers as too cold. But they sold relatively quickly, and for better prices than their neighbours, throughout the nine-teenth century. The repetitive Romanesque windows, separated only by slim columns, present a striking façade of opulent grandeur which has been likened to a Venetian palace. (88) The man who best understood middle-class tastes and who designed most if not all the houses in Dowanhill, where he was estate architect, and many in Kelvinside, too, was James Thomson. His best work was his earliest, Crown Circus (1858-60), a perfect piece of summitry as its convex crescent effectively crowns the hill on the south side of Dowanhill, which rises steeply out of Partick. His two Belhaven Terraces (1860 and 1866-70) on Great Western Road, Kelvinside, follow Rochead's neighbour-ing Kew Terrace in their general lines - restrained, dignified and pleasant. He probably designed several of the terraces in the Victoria Park section of Kelvinside and in Westbourne Gardens, where his familiar hallmark, the first-floor oriel on the drawing-room, is easily visible. As late as 1900, he laid out the late J.B. Mirrlees's Redlands estate and may have been responsible for some of the houses. (89)

The greatest Glasgow architect of the nineteenth century and probably of all time was Alexander 'Greek' Thomson. He was no more Greek than his fellows and fits into no category save a personal one. The general lines of earlier Glasgow terraces survive in his work and there is a distinctive Graeco-Egyptian detail in all his buildings. Thomson's flair, apart from his unique detailing, was his ability to handle massed compositions and yet meet middle-class demands without conceding his own principles of design. This skill in satisfying the market while creating a work of art is best seen in his Westbourne Terrace on Hyndland Road (1870-81). Here he incorporated the currently fashionable first-floor bay window with an impressive porch by projecting the ground-floor building line to the extent of the bay, which thus rests on the porch and dining-room. His own style of frieze work adds to a range of houses which, standing back from and above the road, is enhanced by larger end houses. Just round the corner on Great Western Road is an even more impressive example of Thomson's gift for handling large compositions. This is Great Western Terrace (1869-70), with perhaps less flourish in its detail than other Thomson works but magnificent in its grouping of very large terrace houses, the two taller sections of the terrace being placed skillfully neither at the ends nor in the centre but a little way in from the ends. There is some nice external ironwork and there are typical Thomson touches inside. Otherwise, the terrace's appeal rests on its restraint, massing and elevated position – the last a characteristic Thomson device, seen also in his three brilliant city churches (at St Vincent St, Caledonia Road and Alexandra Park). Other works by Thomson in the West End outshine their neighbours without rising to the excellence of Westbourne and Great Western Terraces. They include additions to Lilybank House, Hillhead; Oakfield Terrace nearby, designed about 1865 and a West End approx-imation of his Moray Place in Pollokshields West, with its pedimented end houses and his inimitable personal detailing; and Northpark Terrace of 1866, also in Hillhead, a terrace impressive for its careful balance and relative severity, though there is a doubt about its authorship. (90)

Most late-nineteenth and early twentieth-century terraces are smaller versions of the huge tenements with fussier details and less evidence of classical influence. The best of the later terraces is Montgomerie (now Cleveden)

5. Glasgow: the tenement block, York (now Novar) Drive, 1905 (*M. A. Simpson*)

6. Glasgow: the grand villa, Great Western Road, about 1880 (*M. A. Simpson*)

7. Leamington: three houses by W. Buddle & Son, 1830s, west side of Clarendon Square (*T. H. Lloyd*)

8. Leamington: centre of terrace, Waterloo Place, 1830s (*T. H. Lloyd*)

Crescent by John Burnet sr (1873-6), with elements of the classical past in its banding, plain first floor and cornice, but hints of modernity in that the terrace is less of a unity than earlier ones, the bay windows are on the ground floor and there is no basement. (91) The younger Burnet (1887-96) and J. Gaff Gillespie (1900) between them designed University Gardens with a varied façade and almost no classicism. After the turn of the century came J.A. Campbell's pleasant Kirklee Road terrace (1900-3), more like a row of English semi-detached houses with long front gardens (seen also in contemporary Kensington Gate in Kelvinside, a red-brick novelty with Queen Anne details); and the bizarre trio Nos 8-10 Lowther Terrace by James Millar and A.G.S. Mitchell (1904). (92) At its best the architecture of the West End is superb; at its worst, it is competent but unexciting. More than most suburbs, however, it creates excellent townscapes and exhibits a high degree of continuity of design.

The front door of a typical West End house opened on to a high broad hall given dignity by a pair of Greek columns, carefully draped in damask or velvet, for which deep rich colours were preferred. (93) Carpeted in the local Turkey Red or Brussels tapestry weave, the hall was furnished in heavy oak, with a large mirror, sundry ornaments and one or two engravings - 'Wellington and his Generals' or 'The Death of Lord Nelson' were widely favoured. The wax fruit on a pedestal, common until the 1890s, was gradually replaced by a potted aspidistra. Artificial lighting was by gas chandeliers; electricity was not a rival until the nineties. The principal ground-floor room was the dining-room, often 30ft x 20ft, usually furnished in mahogany, though oak was becoming popular from the eighties when Axminsters and Wiltons were beginning to replace Turkey Red and Brussels carpets. The centrepiece was the fine white Carrara marble fireplace, surmounted by a gilt mirror (90in x 60in) and crammed with ornaments. Small japanned or marquetry tables abounded and the personal contribution of mother and daughters was a handsewn banner firescreen. Watercolours of Scottish scenes lined the walls. The remainder of the ground floor was given over to a dressing-room and another reception room at the rear known variously as a billiards room, library, study, parlour, music room, smoking-room or breakfast-room; from the end of the century it became fashionable to have the kitchen in this position.

The grandest room of all was the first-floor drawing-room,

approached by a fine staircase with a landing on which the lady of the house received guests. The drawing-room, frequently even larger than the dining-room, was even more crammed with furniture and ornaments, laid out above its Minton-tiled fireplace or on the innumerable occasional tables. A settee and six or twelve leather or velvet high-backed devotional chairs in rosewood occupied the centre of the room, surrounded by music Canterburys, Pembrokes, whatnots, napery presses and hassocks. A harmonium or baby grand piano was universal and late in the century a Singer sewing machine occupied one of the alcoves. Edwardian households dispensed with stuffed birds, antlers and engravings in favour of family photographs. West End drawing-rooms were the homes of many celebrated art collect-ions - roup sales listed works by Watteau, Old Crome, Lely, Wouvermans, Raeburn, Leickhardt and contemporary masters such as the Nasmyths, Landseer and Sidney Cooper. (94) The upper-middle-class bookshelf was rather limited in its range with bibles, hymn books, Travels in the Holy Land and collected sermons by Spurgeon and Drummond. Novels were restricted to the classics: Dickens, Scott, Eliot, Thackeray, Goldsmith, with Mrs Henry Wood for the ladies. Until the end of the century children were confined to 'morally improving ' works but then came Stevenson, Henty and Ballanty (95) This reading matter may have been sober, but it is also evident from sale catalogues that West Enders kept remarkably good cellars. (96)

Also on the first floor were the two main bedrooms, furnished in mahogany until oak took over in the 1880s, when the four-poster with its bedsteps was finally replaced by an iron and brass bedstead. Dressing-rooms and a bath-room completed the first floor and there was usually a bath-room on the second floor, which contained from 2-4 secondary bedrooms, furnished in birch or fir with iron or wooden bedsteads. Flush toilets were standard from the sixties and mains water a generation earlier. Some of the largest houses had a servants' attic and a top-lit billiard room. However, servants normally lived in tiny rooms in the basement, which they shared with a great kitchen and several storerooms. Their furniture was sparse and cheap and handed down from upstairs; the floors were covered in oilcloth. The kitchen was handsomely equipped, contrasting with the meanness of the servants' accommodation, in which bars were placed over the windows allegedly to prevent midnight assignations with lovers. At the end of the rear 'bleaching green' stood a wash-house (with one of Walter MacFarlane's patent iron mangles) and often a stable with a coachman's flat above it. Most of the furniture for these great houses was made locally and generally to order. To present-day taste, the houses seem stuffy and overcrowded; elegance in furniture tended to fade in favour of massiveness after Victoria's accession. (97)

The West End's grand houses were products of the upper middle class's highly disproportionate share of Glasgow's income and the operation of an almost totally free market. The houses of the élite played a large part in their lives. They were an important factor in the West End's excellent health record, together with the bourgeoisie's ability to pay for medical care, a good diet, suitable clothing, lengthy holidays and clean air. (98) Their generous dimensions allowed the separation of domestic functions and of generations and the sick. Moreover, the tasks of keeping clean a huge house packed with furniture and occupied by five to eight people, feeding them, washing clothes and preparing for guests, were undertaken by domestic servants. The average household had a resident cook and from one to three housemaids. In addition to their keep and uniforms, cooks were paid between £20 and £50 a year, wages remaining fairly constant from the 1870s down to 1914, with only slight increases at the top of the scale; wages depended on one's range of abilities and experience and were higher if one had been trained in an aristocratic household. Scullery, kitchen and general maids were often very young - in their early teens - and their annual incomes ranged from £12 to £26; house- and table-maids had higher ceilings, around £30; general nurses earned from £17 to £26 a year, but well-qualified and experienced nurses could double this range. Apart from coachmen, few men were employed; coachmen generally had free accommodation above the coach-house and stables. Domestics, mainly girls from the Highlands and Ireland, were recruited from local agencies. Their employers acted in loco parentis and instilled the virtues of hard work, thrift, church attendance, daily prayers and bible reading. (99) The size of the houses reduced social tensions and improved family health, while the presence of domestics freed the family from drudgery and released their energies and time for a busy social life.

Houses were also centres of entertainment and culture. Social gatherings were common occurences and the drawing-room was often filled with family parties, business hospitality, charitable activities and formal visits (the visitors preceded by their printed cards borne before them on a silver tray). Dinner parties and soirées were occasions for the display of possessions and the high degree of formality which marked the social behaviour of the middle class. (100) Some West Enders, like the shipowner Sir William Burrell, the noted collector of Impressionists and stained glass, and Bailie McClellan, whose collection of paintings forms the basis of the city's art gallery, were genuine patrons of the arts; others, like the mangle-maker Walter MacFarlane, filled their houses with art treasures for the sake of prestige and from a notion that such behaviour was expected of the social élite. (101)

The houses and what was crammed into them were so valuable that the upper middle class was greatly concerned for their safety. It agitated constantly for increases in police patrols, fearing total destruction by the mob rather than the selective depredations of the burglar. Indeed, this fear of the mob was a major factor in the attempts of West Enders to secure the annexation by Glasgow of the three-quarters of the West End which lay outside the city boundaries, in the belief that it would lead to better police protection. The Hillhead and Kelvinside residents who promoted the annexation bill of 1886 asserted that the local county police had 'only a handful of men to protect life and property in the event of a disturbance arising in the district or what is more probable the incursion of a mob from the neighbouring police districts' The owner of the largest house in Kelvinside, Bailie James Morrison, a city councillor and magistrate, told the parliamentary select committee which was hearing evidence on the bill that 'on Saturday nights we're really sometimes a little alarmed when they (the miners from Skaterigg) are making their way home after they have been indulging too freely'. The pitmen were said to sing lustily on their way along Great Western Road - perhaps Mr Will Fyfe's 'Glasgow Belongs to Me' originated with these merry gentlemen. (102) This fear for their worldly goods persisted throughout the Victorian period but in general the West End's attractiveness, quietness and exclusiveness, combined with their spacious, comfortable and well-staffed homes, gave the upper middle class a firm base from which to control the local economy and polity, to press their values upon it and enjoy life to the full.

Between 1830 and 1914, the West End housed a remarkable

collection of figures of local, national and even international importance: Lister; Kelvin; Charles Rennie Mackintosh; J.B. Neilson; Hugh Foulis ('Neil Munro'); the Blackie, Collins (publishing), Teacher (whisky) and Stewart (iron and steel) families; Dübs the locomotive engineer; Alexander Stephen the shipbuilder; Sir William Bilsland the master baker; Sir James Marwick the great Victorian town clerk; nearly all the city's lord provosts; most of its MPs; QCs, assorted knights and the odd peer. (103) Apart from the distinction lent it by its residents, the West End was one of the finest, richest, healthiest, busiest and most exclusive Victorian suburbs in Britain, remarkably well-equipped to provide the upper middle class with the 'good life' as they conceived of it.

Chapter 3

Hampstead, 1830-1914

F. M. L. Thompson

In the public eye Hampstead has a double image. There is
'Happy Hampstead', thronged, bustling, boisterous - the
Hampstead of roundabouts, ice-creams, sticky fingers, kite-
flying, donkey rides, lovers, and dogs with their mistresses;
this is the Heath. And there is intellectual Hampstead,
Hampstead of the aesthetes, artists, authors, theatrefolk,
journalists, academics, nests of politicians, and pavement
exhibitions - this is the Village and its overgrown satellite,
the Garden Suburb. Each a truth of a sort, but between
them they make for a double vision that fails to distinguish
the great middle ground of solid, respectable and anonymous
families for whom Hampstead was chiefly created. Hampstead
was not only what came to be a highly prized address in the
NW3 postal district which marked possession of a desirable
middle-class home, for this postal district overstepped both
class and parish boundaries at its eastern extremity of
Gospel Oak. Beyond the western frontier of NW3, into NW8
where the land north of Boundary Road belonged to Hampstead,
over the Finchley Road deep into NW6 territory in Swiss
Cottage, in much of West Hampstead, in Fortune Green, even
in NW2 towards Cricklewood, the roads, avenues, gardens,
and drives were also part of middle-class Hampstead.

Just as the postal authorities did a moderately good job,
though not a perfect one, in delineating the most eligible
parts of Hampstead, so the speculative builders of the
nineteenth century did a reasonably thorough, but not
entirely complete, job of making the parish and borough
of Hampstead into one continuous solidly middle-class suburb.
The Heath escaped the builders, thus allowing an aristocratic element in property values and large-estate scenery,
as well as a whiff of the masses at play. There was room
on the edges of the Heath and around the old town for the
equivalent of stately homes for upper-class and élitist

elements, patricians or celebrities who lived on a grander
level than that of the undistinguished middle class; and
there was considerably more room, over towards Kilburn and
in the Fleet Road district, for numerous artisans and
poorer workers living on a very much humbler, if not poverty
stricken, level. But by 1914 the Hampstead prospect was
overwhelmingly one of leafy suburban roads lined with
housing for the prosperous middle classes. It was, perhaps,
more through-and-through middle-class than any other metropolitan borough, for rivals like Wimbledon at the higher
end of the middle-class bracket or Hammersmith at the lower
end were high-class districts of boroughs with substantial
lower-class quarters. It was solidly respectable, solidly
conservative, harbouring a leaven of radicals who never
seemed to succeed in making any headway against the sheer
weight of numbers of business and professional men, rentiers
and men of property, and it was utterly safe. It had just
the right blend of assured social position with a dash of
picquant romance - 'suit family where three servants are
kept', 'wanted, single gentleman taking late dinners' - to
make it an estate agent's dream. It was, in Charles Booth's
words, simply 'one of the largest and most prosperous of
the well-to-do residential suburbs of London'. (1)

Hampstead provides as good a parade as any of the different
ways in which the well-heeled Victorian middle-class Londoner
was housed, and as near-perfect a working model of single-
class residential zoning as one can expect to encounter over
such a large area as 2,250 acres, particularly when those
acres have never been in single ownership and control. It
is an example, however, which does not conform too strictly
with theories of urban structure, whether concentric or
sectoral, but which suggests that within the high level of
generalisation of theoretical urban sociology or geography,
the actual determinants of the class and character of
development in any particular locality are less a matter
of distance from the city centre (whether that be reckoned
in miles, journey time, or decades) or of the reputation
of older inner neighbours (whether high-class unblemished,
or lower-class suspect) and more a question of local
topography and above all of local property arrangements. (2)
It might seem that local topography predestined Hampstead
for high-value housing as soon as it should come within
the metropolitan orbit, for the land rises fairly steeply
from the 100ft contour at Chalk Farm station, by way of
Haverstock Hill and Rosslyn Hill, to 442ft at Jack Straw's

Castle. There are of course large areas of low-lying ground
within the parish, for both Edgware Road and Finchley Road
follow relatively easy gradients. Nevertheless the rise
to the northern heights is the dominating physical feature,
and urban hills generally confer high social status.
Industry, and hence jobs, prefers to avoid hills because
there both sites and transport are difficult and expensive;
workers shun hills because jobs are few and transport is
difficult and expensive; the well-to-do take to the hills
because the situation is healthy and pleasant, is well
removed from the smell and dirt of the city, and has its
exclusiveness protected by difficult and expensive transport
from interference by undesirables. This points to gradient
analysis as the key to urban social morphology, though the
gradients are those of the civil engineer not the social
scientist.

Hills, however, even London hills, have not enjoyed
uniform treatment at the hands of society and the builder.
Highgate, Blackheath or Dulwich, for example, may conform
to the Hampstead physical-social elevation equation; but
the slopes of Muswell Hill, Dollis Hill, Norwood or Sydenham
never did a lot for their characters, while Kensington,
Chelsea, Fulham, Hammersmith, Chiswick and Wimbledon may
be counted among the low-lying suburbs which yet enjoyed
considerable success. Certainly possession of a hill helped
make a district a desirable development, but by itself it
was not enough. The previous standing of the hill was also
critical. At Hampstead, curiously enough, the pre-Victorian
activities on the hill were anything but middle-class.
Hampstead began to emerge from the agricultural village
stage in the seventeenth century, as a retreat for wealthy
Londoners and a suitable perch for the country houses of
a few discerning notables, such as Sir Henry Vane. It
blossomed at the end of the century with the commercial
exploitation of its mineral waters, which created the small
business precincts of Well Walk and Flask Walk and gave it
a brief career as a smart and fashionable spa patronised
by the aristocracy and high society. It acquired the
equipment of a high-class resort, with pleasure gardens,
assembly rooms, pump room, an ample supply of inns, and
above all suitable accommodation for visitors. Speculative developments in Church Row, Elm Row and New End
provided early eighteenth-century town housing of considerable distinction - of three- and four-storeys and mainly
arranged in groups of three or four houses or in longer

88

rows - which was chiefly used for letting to visitors or
to summer residents. The attractions of the waters had
faded by the 1730s, but the upper-class habit persisted
of wealthy City men sending their families up to Hampstead
for the summer. (3) Memories of its role as a fashionable
resort and hill-station refuge from insalubrious, smelly
summers on the city plains lingered long, and may still
have been influencing estate agents' purple prose as late
as 1908. 'Hampstead', ran the plug for North End Place
in that year,

> '... one of the most beautiful and most healthful
> suburbs of the great metropolis, with its wide-
> spreading breezy heath and smooth velvet turf, the
> great bulk of which, so far as human probability
> goes, must for ever remain unbuilt upon, has been
> well described as a watering place in all respects
> but one, the exception being that there is no sea
> there. All the other attributes and accessories,
> however, are present: its donkeys and bath chairs,
> its fashionable esplanade, its sand and sandpits,
> its chalybeate spring, its old church and new, its
> chapel of ease, its flagstaff, its fishing ponds,
> and its tribes of rosy children with their attendant
> nursemaids.' (4)

The highest reaches of Hampstead, indeed, in the hamlet
setting of North End and in the mansions and large villas
scattered round the heath uplands, retained in 1908 and
later 'their claim upon those cultured and well-to-do
circles which desire select secluded residence entirely
without the great city's murk and fret and fever, and yet
all the same within easy reach of the fashionable West
End and the more prosaic City'. (5) The nursemaids
pushing prams, however, were from middle-class nurseries
lower down the hill, and if the buckets and spades of their
children had no real sea in view they nevertheless
represented the delights of the sea of middle-class housing
which by this time lapped round the uplands of the élite.
By the end of the nineteenth century the upper-class visitors
and the aristocratic and patrician residents had departed;
their grand country houses and splendid garden-parks which
had once lined Haverstock Hill and West End Lane were for
the most part demolished, turned into building estates or,
in the case of Kidderpore Hall, taken over by Westfield

College of the University of London. The glory that had
passed, however, was a condition of the present; for the
ambition to imitate and emulate the life of the élite, to
absorb some of the dash and glamour of the old Belsize
House, to live in the orbit of Rosslyn House, to feel
proximity to the leisured gentry of Church Row or Hampstead
Grove, was a powerful motive for the middle-class drive to
reach up towards the old town on the hill. The obliteration
or transformation of the object of emulation was necessarily
proportional to the success of the drive to turn open country
into desirable residences not for the few, but for the
thousand.

The beginning of the embourgeoisement of Hampstead can
be dated almost precisely to the moment in 1819 when Colonel
Henry Samuel Eyre, owner and chief developer of St John's
Wood, first planned some public turnpike roads to run through
the northern part of his estate connecting it to Hampstead,
West End Lane and Kilburn; and to the moment in 1820 when
his surveyor, Peter Potter, gave evidence to the House of
Commons Committee on the Marylebone and Hampstead Road Bill,
the sole - but equally abortive - survivor of these first
proposals. Eyre's idea was to open up the rest of his
estate to development and to create building frontages
partly at the expense of the travelling public, rather than
solely by estate roads built by himself, and to justify
this turnpike method by proposing that his access road
should seem to lead somewhere. In this case it was to lead,
through the present Swiss Cottage, to the cart-track known
as Belsize Lane and thus across to Haverstock Hill. Eyre
imagined that his road improvement would be welcomed by all
the property owners concerned - by Sir Thomas Maryon Wilson,
the lord of the manor of Hampstead, whose farmland bordered
Belsize Lane, and by the owners of the handful of secluded
houses towards the Hampstead end of the lane - as an obvious
convenience and carrier of development values. But, just
in case, he also placed his road on the side of public
morality. 'It is a private way', his surveyor Potter agreed
in answer to a question, 'but if I may make an observation
I should say it was too private for as I went along the lane
I saw two women as naked as they were born washing in the
pond at the end of the lane... There is no respectable part
where their (the Belsize Lane householders') families can
walk out without meeting with nuisances; and the nuisances
are so common that no respectable female can walk in the
lane'. (6) The cause of seemliness and of banishing bare

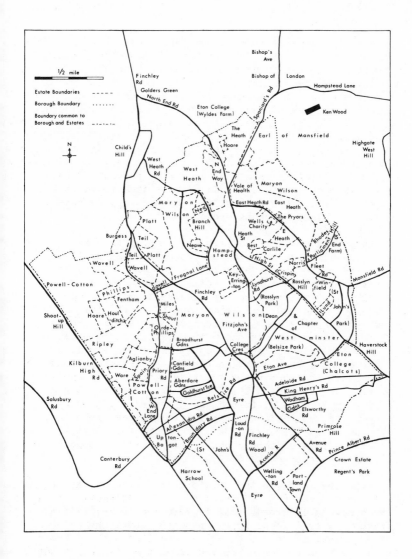

Fig 7 Building estates in Hampstead, c 1840-80
       (base map c 1960).

bottoms by exposing them to the public gaze left Sir Thomas
Maryon Wilson and the Belsize Lane houseowners entirely
unmoved, and they successfully countered morality by
deploying conservationist arguments. Resistance was on
the double ground of damage to the farm and damage to
amenities. Such a road would be very detrimental to his
farm, Sir Thomas claimed, 'as exposing it to the depredatory
practices of dishonest people, both as to cattle ... and
as to fences, and also as facilitating great and serious
annoyances, trespasses and injuries thereon which are likely
to be committed by idle and disorderly persons of both
sexes whom such intended road might induce to go to that
quarter'. (7) More generally he argued that Hampstead
would be ruined by being opened up:

> 'Hampstead is a very eligible situation from its
> nearness to the Metropolis. It has enough publicity
> at present. It is desirable, in order to meet the
> taste and choice of the residents there for privacy,
> not to put in practice any measure to make it more
> public. The gentlemen there who fill official
> situations, or are in professions, or are merchants
> of the first rank in the Metropolis, wish to preserve
> about their dwellings the quiet and privacy which
> the country should secure for their refreshment and
> necessary retirement from active duties and pursuits
> daily prosecuted in the Metropolis. This quiet and
> privacy will be disturbed and diminished if, by a
> new road, as designed, the idle, or pleasurable (not
> to say the vicious) members of any portion of the
> Metropolis are to be drawn to Hampstead for objects
> of pleasure or crime.' (8)

These arguments, with the aid of a few political friends,
were enough to fend off the threat of middle-class morality
and a new public road, both in 1820 and in several later
attempts when Colonel Eyre turned to other schemes which
were variations on the Finchley Road line. The schemes
produced such colourful opponents as the leading valuer
of brewery properties, John Thompson, who stoutly defended
the privacy of Frognal Priory, the extraordinary house he
had created, with its squirrel-mixture of Gothic, Norman,
Tudor, Dutch whipped up into baronial fantasy. His house,
he deposed, had been carefully sited for its extensive views

'the estate of Col. Eyre in the vale or flat southward
of Mr Thompson's house is wholly or nearly so
overlooked from it or the pleasure ground. Mr
Thompson's view would be interrupted, certainly
stripped of much of its beauty, by any road carried
through Col. Eyre's lands especially if buildings
be made on the sides of it. The value of Mr
Thompson's property would consequentially be
affected by such a measure as a public turnpike
road ... which would lead to the erection of houses
and buildings of every description so that manu-
factories and other offensive works may be established
and carried on.' (9)

A privileged few thus strenuously resisted the threatened
intrusion of new roads on their peace and privacy,
Thompson being joined by the great merchants of Belsize
Lane and Frognal, and by the grandees of West End, General
Orde and Lady Headfort of West End House. But the defence
of open country and natural beauty, however spirited, did
not long prevail over Colonel Eyre, his friends and their
money; in 1826 an Act was obtained authorising the construction of the Finchley Road to connect St John's Wood with
Finchley, via Golders Green and the ancient Ballards Lane.
A curious feature of the episode was the appearance of the
Maryon Wilsons,father and son, as staunch conservationists
and champions of the open country against profit-making
despoilers, since the son, also Thomas, was to spend the
rest of his life being reviled, quite wrongly, as an arch-
fiend and despoiler of the worst money-grubbing sort plotting
the rape of Hampstead Heath and its conversion into
building estates. (10)
   Finchley Road was built between 1826 and 1830, constructed
southwards from Finchley into London in obedience to a
prudential clause inserted by the suspicious Maryon Wilson
who was not going to allow Colonel Eyre merely to make the
first section of the road at the St John's Wood end, with
its critical estate importance, and then quietly abandon
the rest of the scheme. Nevertheless, although physically
its junction with the Great North Road at Finchley made it
an arterial road, throughout the nineteenth century the
chief function of Finchley Road was that of a principal
estate road forming building frontages and giving access
to building land on either side. As Maryon Wilson had
predicted, the great volume of through coach, carriage,

waggon and cart traffic from the north anxious for a direct
route to the West End, which the Eyre faction had visualised
was largely fictitious. Little through traffic developed,
and the Finchley Turnpike was in constant financial
difficulties from its low toll income until it was taken
over by the Metropolitan Road Commissioners from 1850. (11)
The misfortune of being built on the eve of railway
development no doubt contributed to disappointing toll
receipts; and in the twentieth century no one can deny that
Finchley Road has been saturated and overkilled by motors
as an arterial route. In the short run, however, it was
an immediate success as an estate developer's road; Eyre's
building advanced steadily along the converging axes of
Finchley Road and Avenue Road in the 1830s, reached Swiss
Cottage in 1838 rendering the adjacent land ripe for
development, and continued towards the northern boundary
of the estate along Belsize Road in the 1850s and 1860s.
It was the means of introducing good-class speculative
housing development into Hampstead, and of tying it firmly
to a pedigree which was rooted in the Portman estate and
the aristocratic quarters of Portman Square and Bryanston
Square, and which descended through Dorset Square to St
John's Wood.

Every consideration of economics and geography should
have made Finchley Road the vehicle for channelling middle-
class development speedily northwards towards Golders
Green. Land law prevented this and, for more than a
generation, from 1830 until the late 1870s, all building
stopped abruptly at the frontier of the Eyre estate. This
was because Thomas Maryon Wilson, the younger, who inherited
the family estate and title in 1821, held it under the
provisions of his father's will as a life-tenant, with no
powers to grant more than 21-year leases, and naturally no
powers to sell any land. His persistent efforts to remove
these disabilities were as persistently frustrated by those
who professed to believe that he had designs on the Heath,
with the result that the entire Maryon Wilson estate in
Hampstead was effectively sterilised from building development during his lifetime. (12) This was sad for Sir Thomas
but probably fortunate for Hampstead, since it meant there
was no opportunity on his long stretch of Finchley Road
for the straggling ribbon-development which was what the
prevailing level of demand for housing at that distance
from the centre would have supported. Even if this hypo-
thetical development had been a high-class ribbon of large

94

villas for merchant princes, which is unlikely, it would
still in all probability have created serious problems of
layout and ownership that would have hampered, distorted
and downgraded the subsequent higher-density development
and infilling which was bound to follow. The development
which was disallowed on the Maryon Wilson estate accrued
to the other building estates in Hampstead - insofar as it
was not chased out of the district altogether - and in turn
permitted them to enjoy a more compact, more uniform and
more single-class development than might otherwise have
been the case. In this way sterilisation of one part, in
fact a very large part since it was 416 acres, acted as a
stimulus to middle-class fertility in other parts, and was
a contributory factor in the success of the Chalcots,
Belsize and Kilburn Priory estates.

It was on the Chalcots estate, 200 acres in the south-east
of the parish owned by Eton College and running from
Primrose Hill to Haverstock Hill, that the Finchley Road
signal was first sighted; not too surprisingly since the
John Shaw whom the college appointed as their architect-
surveyor for the estate was the son of John Shaw who was
the architectural consultant for the St John's Wood
development. The direct ties of Chalcots were with Camden
Town, vigorously being built in the 1820s but not settled
in its social character and reputation; the only conceivable
line of residential advance to Chalcots was by Hampstead
Road, and this was the route used by all traffic to the
old town. But the influence of the Camden Town neighbours
on residential atmosphere and property values was unreliable
and ambivalent, though it was many years before this adjacent
quarter was definitely taken over by skilled workers and
canal-side trades. As a precaution, therefore, Shaw proposed
that Eton's development should open with a variant of the
Finchley Road ploy, a lateral thoroughfare driven through
to join Finchley Road itself thus tapping its supplies of
wealth, elegance, and distinction. In 1826 the college
obtained an Act conferring powers to grant 99-year building
leases, and in 1829 John Shaw issued a prospectus of the
Chalcots estate:

'... which is too well known to render necessary
any description of its eligibility in all respects,
for Villas and respectable Residences, combining
the advantages of Town and Country. It is proposed,
in the first instance, to offer to the Public that

'part of the Estate adjoining the Hampstead Road
at Haverstock Hill, containing about 15 acres, in
lots of not less than half an acre, for the erection
of single or double detached Villas. Two roads,
with proper drainage, will be immediately formed
by the College; and are intended hereafter (should
the Buildings go on) to be continued and connected
with other Roads, particularly with the new Turnpike
Road from Marylebone to Finchley, now in progress;
but if not so continued, the Roads at present
proposed will afford very desirable Frontages for
Buildings, having the advantage of adjoining the
main Hampstead Road, and being at the same time
secluded from its publicity.' (13)

This launch contained the basic ingredients for success,
in specifying the type of development aimed at and in
providing an outline machinery for attaining it, in the
proposed general covenants in the 99-year building leases
stipulating 'the erection of substantial and respectable
private houses and offices', and in the stipulation that
plans and elevations of every house 'shewing the thickness
of the walls and scantlings of the main timbers, with a
general specification of the nature and character of the
building' were to be submitted for approval by Eton's
surveyor. (14) Success, however, was not instantaneous,
partly because the machinery of covenants was imperfect,
even more because the estate administration to back it up
was inefficient and lackadaisical, but most of all because
as luck would have it proposals for the London & Birmingham
Railway, running clean through the Chalcots estate on the
approach to Camden Town, began to be talked about almost
as soon as Shaw's prospectus was issued. Not until the
railway upset was over, the line safely tucked into the
Primrose Hill tunnel, and fashionable sightseers watched
the astonishing spectacle of the first trains emerging
from it in 1838, did developers, builders, and home-seekers
recover from this first railway fright and decide that
after all the college land would make good building ground.
Hence while the Chalcots estate went very slowly indeed in
its first decade, and was in no little danger of misfiring
through inability to find any builders willing to take more
than one or two lots apiece, from the 1840s, especially
after the general revival in the London building trade from
about 1844 - the first since the building boom of the 1820s

collapsed in 1825 - it went ahead rapidly and confidently
towards its comfortable middle-class goal. (15) It went
ahead literally along the new lateral artery which Shaw
had proposed as the essential link with St John's Wood
and its class.

Lacking the turnpike impulse and finance of Colonel
Eyre's Finchley Road, Eton's new road at first moved with
the snail's pace of a private road dependant on private
finance. Started with a flourish in 1830, and named
Adelaide Road after the queen who was then also new, the
college tired of the labours of road-making after the first
couple of hundred feet, and gave up any idea of investing
in the development of its own estate. Thereafter the progress
of the new road depended on the appearance of builders
ready to construct a bit more in order to create more
frontages for themselves and, not surprisingly, by 1844
only a third of the intended length had actually material-
ised. (16) Then in 1844 the first true developer appeared
on Chalcots, with the resources and vision to operate on
a grand scale on large blocks of building land. This was
Samuel Cuming, a carpenter from Devon who had already made
his way in the London building business, who negotiated
a large take from the college of nearly 40 acres at a
ground rent of £35 an acre. He proceeded to make the rest
of the new road, and by 1850 he achieved the long-desired
junction with Colonel Eyre's Avenue Road at Swiss Cottage,
and Adelaide Road was at last completed. (17)

Since it was twenty years in the making it is doubtful
whether Adelaide Road ever did perform the grand character-
forming functions for which it had been originally intended。
For by the time Cuming's men reached Avenue Road in 1850,
behind them stretched a mile of new road whose residential
character was already settled, for good or ill, and it was
too late to think in terms of a break-through to a promised
land, via a corridor which would funnel some part of the
charms, attractions, reputation and property values of St
John's Wood out into the land of Chalcots awaiting social
irrigation. The early residents in Adelaide Road, to be
sure, were anxious that their road should lead somewhere,
and became distinctly restive at the prospect of being
left indefinitely in an elongated cul-de-sac with attendant
dangers of neglect, casual accumulation of insanitary
rubbish tips suspected of encouraging cholera, and perhaps
growing risks to persons and property in the lengthening
dark defile. (18) Hence both college and developers had

97

a strong incentive to make the road into a thoroughfare
giving through-communication in order to provide consumer
satisfaction and amenity, and thus preserve property values
and enhance the attraction of the riparian lands. Nevertheless, the roots of the residential character of Adelaide
Road were firmly planted house by house as Cuming advanced
towards Swiss Cottage, building there and in the parallel
Fellows Road in step with his road-making. Those roots
were unpretentious but solid middle-class. The Adelaide
Road houses were fairly uniform in design, with basement
and three storeys, usually providing seven bedrooms but
sometimes nine, on minimum frontages of about 30ft though
a substantial minority spread to 50ft, allowing ample
rather than impressive principal ground-floor rooms, with
scarcely any front gardens but a good 100ft and more at
the back. They were built in pairs, without being true
semi-detached, in plain stock-brick in plain style rendered
faintly classical by pillared porches and little flights
of steps leading to them, these being essential marks of
middle-class status indicating domestic servants beneath.
The appearance was of a street of town housing, dreariness
and monotony being avoided by the occasional tree and by
arrangement in short runs interrupted by provision for cross
streets giving access to the back land on either side.
Such a neighbourhood bore practically no resemblance to
the leafy semi-detached villadom of St John's Wood any more
than did its comfortable middling middle-class professional
and commercial residents seek to emulate the smart or risqué
side of the St John's Wood reputation. It would be misleading
to suggest that Samuel Cuming's brand of development was
home-grown, since it was highly conventional and familiar.
Indeed its appeal to that element of the middle class which
sought conventional respectability and which was no part of
the world of smart fashion and high society, came from
precisely that quality of familiarity, which showed that
Cuming and his customers were unimpressed by the social
influences of the Eyre estate with which the link-road
was desired, and were interested only in the convenience
of physical communication. Such a quality, moreover, set
the course for the development of the bulk of the Chalcots
estate into a residential district for the unfashionable
and unpretentious middle classes. (19)

  Other Hampstead estates likewise depended on an initial
strategic road for the foundation of their character,
though until Fitzjohn's Avenue was laid out in the late

1870s there were no more roads on the scale of either
Finchley Road or Adelaide Road. The small Kilburn Priory
estate on the south-western edge of the parish, inherited
by Colonel Arthur Upton from Fulk Greville Howard in 1846,
was adequately served by the short Priory Road which Upton
built in 1850. This bisected the estate, and formed a
direct link between Kilburn High Road and ancient West End
Lane avoiding the pocket of low-grade tenements and workshops which Greville Howard had unintentionally helped to
create. Upton found a builder-developer in the Cuming
mould, George Duncan who had previously been active on the
Eyre estate. Duncan's seems to have been the decisive
influence, for although the estate already had a small
upper-class quarter in Greville Road and Greville Place
of detached villas, some with their own stabling, Upton's
ambitions for the 15 acres leased to Duncan were limited
to semi-detacheds 'every house to be of not less than the
third rate... and to be of value of £400 at least, and the
plot to be at least 25 feet frontage and not less than 75
feet in depth'. (20) Duncan built rather better than this
and, in the 1850s, Priory Road, Priory Terrace and part of
Abbey Road became a new district every bit as respectable
as anything by Cuming. The houses were on 33ft frontages,
very much the same size as in Adelaide Road, but a shade
more stylish and dashing with more liberal use of stucco
and ornamented eaves; the building cost was a good deal
more than the £400 minimum, and the selling price nearly
double. (21) Moreover Duncan played a useful part in
ensuring that the desired class of residents was attracted,
by taking care that an estate church, St Mary's, was provided
for the district at an early stage in the development;
this was a great improvement on Eton's performance, for
the Chalcots estate did not get its first church, St Saviour's,
until nearly thirty years after building had been started. (22)

The Belsize estate of the Dean and Chapter of Westminster,
surviving remnant of the medieval abbey's ecclesiastical
manor of Hampstead, was far from small when it came to
building ripeness, and indeed with 240 acres was larger
than all save Maryon Wilson. But the especially ecclesiastical post-Reformation habit, or indulgence, of letting
their lands under leases for three lives had led the dean
and chapter into a tenurial tangle with five different
principal leaseholders, eight separate sub-estates, and
eight different leases for lives each with its own set of
three named lives. (23) As a result there was never any

unified landlord control over this great tract of choice
land, stretching from Swiss Cottage to Parliament Hill,
and never any question of a master plan for the orderly
development of what became the heartland of nineteenth-
century middle-class Hampstead and the capital of
twentieth-century bed-sitterdom. To be fair, the administration of the capitular estates showed little sign of
possessing the necessary vigour and initiative for taking
charge of large-scale development in any case, so that
the awkward tenurial situation was no particular handicap;
the administration much preferred things just to happen
to the estate, confining itself to protecting the dean
and chapter's pecuniary and other interests. It did not
follow, however, that the development of Belsize just
happened, without design or direction. The directing
function descended to the leaseholders or lifeholders,
acting as quasi-owners of their sub-estates, five of whom
doubled as both owners and developers, while one converted
himself from a dairy farmer into a builder and developer.
Each of these could necessarily only make plans and schemes
within the context of one particular sub-estate, an area
of perhaps 30 acres. The end product was a mosaic of
building estates and street layouts echoing the patchwork
of earlier fields and country villa-parks, held together
more by the happy chance that the ancient public road up
Haverstock Hill provided a spinal column for most of the
Belsize estate than by anything else. Nevertheless the
internal arrangements of each sub-estate were conceived
and controlled with care, and their execution was generally
pleasing. Only one definitely failed to make the grade,
the property alongside Fleet Road. Here the natural disadvantage of being low-lying was compounded by proximity
to the working-class districts of Kentish Town and Gospel
Oak, and a couple of blows in the 1870s and 1880s proved
fatal to its chances of attracting people of means: first
a smallpox hospital came to rest on the doorstep, scaring
the middle classes; then the horse trams arrived, setting
up their depot and stables in Fleet Road. Hence this
district was developed with artisans' dwellings, of a
mildly superior sort, and came to house railway workers,
tram workers, small shopkeepers and the like. It was the
only part of the Belsize estate on this social level: the
rest was all successfully covered with middle-class housing,
though of varying size, appeal and standing.
    The very first development on the Belsize property was

a short stretch of gentlemen's ribbon-development in the
1820s when Haverstock Hill between England's Lane and
Belsize Grove was planted with villas and lodges for rich
merchants and retired East India Company men; a swathe of
individualised gentility which set a tone rather than a
pattern, and which survived until ripe for more intensive
redevelopment after 1918. For this particular pattern of
large houses - Gilling Lodge, Devonshire House, Haverstock
Grange - set in their own grounds, equipped with stables
and coach houses and inhabited by carriage-folk, was not
followed elsewhere. Rather, the aim was to strive to
replicate its social tone and to manufacture gentlemen's
houses by the hundred, at much higher densities and with
communal not individual horse-and-carriage trimmings;
such move to production in bulk inevitably carried the
ensuing neighbourhoods a notch or two below the patrician
and upper-middle-class-levels. It was not far below in
central Belsize over the site of the old Park, or in the
highest reaches close to the old town, but it declined
perceptibly to the east of Haverstock Hill. The ingredients
of the operation were much the same on all the sub-estates
which were launched as building ventures at various times
between 1850 and 1880 in response to the pull of the market
and the dropping of lives in the lifeholds: a developer
to produce schemes and to help procure initial finance, a
good name for the building estate for promotional use, a
good road to start it off, a handy church (if necessary
specially provided), and the good fortune to attract a
builder able to work on a large scale and not in penny
packets.

Charles Palmer, the solicitor who had acquired the head
lease of the Belsize Park section of the estate, achieved
all this. He turned himself into a developer, obtained a
building agreement for the whole property from the dean and
chapter, produced a comprehensive plan for the development
of the estate, drove through Belsize Park as his first road
to open up the land, promoted the building of St Peter's
church in the square laid out close to the site of the old
house, made use of the obvious and attractive name of
Belsize Park to publicise his estate, and luckily found in
Daniel Tidey a first-rate builder able to undertake most
of the risks and work of all the house-building. (24)
Henry Davidson, a City merchant who had purchased Rosslyn
House and its sub-estate in the 1820s, was not so successful.
He too turned himself into a developer in 1853 by taking

the estate on a building agreement, had a ready-made label
for his development as the Rosslyn Park estate and a suitable
first road which he named Lyndhurst Road, while he felt no
need to provide a special estate church since the area was
quite close to Hampstead parish church, and later on closer
still to the new St Stephen's, Rosslyn Hill. But he was
never able to stumble upon any builder in a large way of
business who was willing to tackle the major part of the
estate as a single enterprise; largely, according to his
own account, because the intrusion of a railway tunnel
running through the centre of his estate, a hundred or more
feet below ground, had made builders nervous about the
safety of foundations. (25) Be that as it may, building
went on slowly on the Rosslyn Park estate, in small lots;
though it maintained a high character. It was only some
years after Davidson had sold out and departed from the
district that his successor found a single builder,
William Willett, who completed the development in the
1880s and early 1890s in one operation. (26) Less successful
still, and less fortunate, was William Lund who began to
turn his 45 acre residential estate of Haverstock Lodge
into a building speculation from 1851. He invented an
appealing name for his scheme, the St John's Park estate;
advertised its closeness to 'the Hampstead Road Station
of the Blackwall & Fenchurch St Railway' in reference to
the newly-opened East & West India Docks & Birmingham
Junction Railway, later the North London Railway; laid out
two good roads through the estate, Upper Park and Parkhill
Roads, and quickly found in Richard Batterbury a builder
keen to take many plots and to push ahead ambitiously with
large, soundly-built pairs of villas. All went well for
a time, and St John's Park was in a fair way to establishing
itself as a highly desirable district, until the smallpox
hospital came to the Fleet Road end of the estate in the
epidemic of 1869 and inflicted a blow from which the
reputation and value of that section never recovered, and
causing a band of open territory to be preserved, until
after 1914, to separate the infected district from the
posh end of the estate. (27)

Nevertheless all three estates achieved some measure of
success in the upper end of the middle-class bracket.
The last of the Belsize sub-estates to be developed settled
unimaginatively for the solid middle of the spectrum.
This district, adjoining the Heath and Parliament Hill
Fields, had great potential as an area with immense natural

102

attractions and the advantage of Hampstead Heath railway
station at a true, not an estate agent's, three-minute
walk. Its possibilities had, certainly, been somewhat
marred by the neighbouring development of South Hill Park
from 1871, with its routine suburban cramped houses grouped
in fours rather than twos and mainly packed on to frontages
so narrow, at 22ft, that middle-class classification had
to be maintained more by height than by width. All the
same, when the adjoining Belsize property of South End Farm
was also developed unimaginatively it was because of the
passivity of the dean and chapter more than the spoiling
effects produced by Thomas Rhodes in South Hill Park.
From want of energy and any concept of the development of
their Hampstead properties as a whole the dean and chapter
simply allowed Joseph Pickett, until then the dairy farmer
of South End Farm as a yearly tenant, to propose himself
as estate developer and builder. Pickett was then left
very much to his own devices, and his ideas of building,
though reasonably substantial as to construction, were
limited and unimaginative when it came to layout and design.
In the Parliament Hill and Nassington Road, which he was
largely responsible for building in the 1880s, he worked
on rather more generous 30ft frontages to supply more spacious,
nine-bedroom houses than Rhodes had done; but even so they
attracted the middling ranks of doctors, nonconformist
ministers, civil engineers, minor civil servants, printers,
wine merchants, retired officers, solicitors' clerks, railway
clerks, and of course droves of widows, rather than the more
prosperous carriage-trade elements. (28)
   Attention to the needs of horses was one of the key tests
of the quality of a district. On the Chalcots estate in the
days of Cuming only scanty provision of mews was made, on
a scale of perhaps one stable to every twenty houses, and
after 1870 there was a regular estate policy against building
mews on the grounds that they created islands of poverty
and dirt. There was never any intention of providing any
stabling at all on the South End Farm estate, indicating
a realistic appraisal of the status of the prospective
residents, although Rhodes did erect a small mews block at
the entrance to South Hill Park for the more affluent
occupants of the centre of his lozenge. St John's Park,
by contrast, was at first planned with an extensive range
of mews and housing for stable servants at the lower,
Fleet Road, end of the estate, on a scale which would have
allowed practically a stable to each house. With the coming

of the smallpox hospital these plans were abandoned, but
the only effect was to confirm that the residents higher
up were respectable, even artistic, rather than wealthy. (29)
Similarly on the Belsize Park estate the original plans
envisaged lavish provision of mews and servants' quarters
in their own separate precincts, again at the level of a
stable to each house, and again these plans were abandoned
as building went along, though not as a result of an
external shock but out of realisation that even quite
wealthy middle-class families were dropping out of the
carriage-owning world by the 1850s and 1860s. The prestige
of displaying a private carriage was beginning to be out-
weighed by the difficulty and expense of horse-keeping
and carriage-driving in London; convenient access to horse-
bus routes and jobmasters for occasional carriage hire
settled the issue. All the same Daniel Tidey set aside
space for a considerable number of mews on Belsize Park
and the adjoining estate, even if these were in different
places from the original plan, and by 1880 when all was
covered with houses there was an average of one stable
to every four houses. Some were no doubt tenanted by
private householders on the estate, but it seems that the
great majority were let to commercial concerns: livery
stables, looking after privately-owned horses; cab owners;
or jobmasters providing horses or carriages for hire.
Belsize Park of the late nineteenth century was very
comfortably off, rather smart, but on the whole not
carriage-owning. (30) Families with private carriages
were catered for on the Rosslyn Park estate, which as well
as a small mews block provided several large detached
houses on sites with ample room for stables and coach
houses; but above all they were catered for on the Maryon
Wilson estate when that was released for building development from the late 1870s onwards. (31)

After the death of Sir Thomas Maryon Wilson in 1869 the
family estate at last became available as building land
when a standard collusive action between Sir Thomas's
brother and heir, Sir John, and his son, Spencer, broke
the restrictive provision in the old will and imported a
power to grant 99-year building leases. When some stiff
bickering between father and son had died down it was
mainly through such leases that the lands were developed,
although in a few instances tracts of building land were
sold outright to raise part of the capital for estate
road-making. The Maryon Wilson estate in Hampstead was

very large for a building property, and it was large outside Hampstead with urban property in Woolwich and landed estates in Essex and Sussex; thus it was furnished with an estate administration reasonably well equipped to take on the tasks of organising building development. In effect the estate, unlike its institutional neighbours, came to act as its own developer in matters of planning, construction of key roads, and dealings with major builders. The result, however, was that the Maryon Wilson agent proceeded to follow the model quite fortuitously presented by the Belsize estate, in the sense that the huge area of development land available, some 400 acres, was divided into sub-estates which were treated separately. The creation of smaller units was necessary to ease the task of management, to mark out areas for rather different classes of housing and keep them separate, to provide spatial limitations on the danger of causing a glut by putting too much building land on the market at the same time, and to set the framework for a rolling programme of road finance which would not overstrain the Maryon Wilson's resources. As the Maryon Wilson agent put it: '... if roads and sewers are to be made over a series of building estates in Hampstead it will ruin any man even with a stronger back than Mr Spencer Wilson's'. (32) The original intention was to have five such separate building estates, with the idea that they would be developed more or less in sequence. One of these, however, long known as East Park in anticipation of its eventual development as a district of wealthy villas on the eastern edge of the Heath, was snatched away for public enjoyment when it was acquired by the Metropolitan Board of Works in 1886-9 as the key part of the Hampstead Heath Extension; Sir Spencer Maryon Wilson was compensated for this disappointment at the rate of £1,800 an acre, a very full building value without any of the trouble of working to realise it. The remaining four areas, although becoming a little blurred at the edges and difficult to conform to the concept of sequential development, by and large ful- filled the planner's intentions.

The showpiece was to be a superior and wealthy residential district of the highest quality, occupying the attractive slopes of Conduit Fields and created by driving a major new road from Swiss Cottage to the old town of Hampstead. This was Fitzjohn's Avenue, started in 1875, named after the Maryon Wilson's country seat in Essex, built on the grand scale as 'a kind of boulevard planted with trees', resplendent with fashionable and stately houses, and

following a line which the despised Colonel Eyre had
proposed over fifty years before for one of his road
schemes. (33) The tract over Finchley Road and westwards
to the boundary with Colonel Cotton's estate near West
End Lane was regarded as the 'land in the worst part of
the estate, namely the Kilburn end' because of its less
attractive situation, and this hundred acres and more was
set aside for much less expensive, much more crowded, much
more middling middle-class housing: the region of Priory
Road, Canfield and Broadhurst Gardens in the late 1870s,
Compayne, Greencroft and Fairhazel Gardens in the late
1880s, and Aberdare Gardens and Goldhurst Terrace in the
1890s. (34) A third area, alongside Finchley Road, had
once been presented with almost a mile of building frontages by the turnpike alone, but this valuable gift to the
estate, albeit one thrust on Sir Thomas Maryon Wilson
against his wishes, had become tarnished over the years.
By the end of the 1870s no less than three railways,
emerging from their tunnels, swept across the estate between
Finchley Road and West Hampstead: from north to south in
chronological order the Hampstead Junction, the Midland,
and the Metropolitan (later joined by the Great Central).
Apart from abstracting much land this complex of lines
effectively sterilised the intervening slices or made them
into sites for coal yards, rubbish tips, contractors yards,
municipal works depots, and eventually for Hampstead's first
electricity power station. This bundle of influences was
not promising for the residential prospects of the areas
still left in the hands of the estate, and inevitably
development of a mixed character was permitted. Parades
of shops with apartments over were built in the sections
of Finchley Road nearest to unseemly activities, and the
illusion that these were not there at all was fostered by
continuing the line of shops over the railway tracks on
iron stilts. Intermixed with the shops came large blocks
of apartments and flats in the 1880s and 1890s, respectable
but still viewed as ungodly by conservatives, and decidedly
not acceptable as family homes; their height, maybe, helped
to obscure the eyesores which lay behind many of them,
particularly on the western side of the road. The final
area of the estate, however, returned to the social distinction of Fitzjohn's Avenue, and eventually surpassed at least
its wealth. This area lay roughly between Frognal Lane,
Telegraph Hill and the West Heath, and was reserved for
last place in the sequence of operations, though some

building on its road fronting the West Heath did begin
in the 1880s, and its spinal estate road, Redington Road,
was laid out a few years earlier. The main activity in
this district, however, came considerably later, in the
1890s and 1900s, and crowned what was virtually the final
phase in the building of Hampstead with a new style of
luxury development with large detached houses which dispensed with the obligatory mid-Victorian kitchen basement,
but which still accommodated their nine or ten bedrooms
within not more than three storeys, and which stood in
large gardens of perhaps 75 x 200ft. An earlier generation
going to live in a house in, say, Belsize Avenue, with
much the same number and size of rooms, not merely had many
more stairs to climb, but also had a garden barely one-
quarter the size.

The Redington Road style was not entirely new, and in
some respects it shows the influence of the garden city
idea for the rich. It was certainly very different from
the Fitzjohn's Avenue style, where despite a handful of
architect-designed houses - some pleasing and well-mannered
by Norman Shaw, others heavy in hand - the greater part of
the district was the work of speculative builders, Herbert
and Edward Kelly, who built large, tall, houses with every
convenience and embellishment to suit their wealthy market
but no new ideas. But it was anticipated in Hampstead by
the work of William Willett, who emerged as the second
creator of the fortunes of the Eton College estate in the
late nineteenth century. Head of a father-and-son building
firm, which he made into one of the largest enterprises
in the country, and famed for his persistent campaigning
for daylight saving, William Willett came into Hampstead
building, from Kensington, by way of the Belsize estates
and his father's work in Belsize Avenue and on Rosslyn Park,
where in Lyndhurst Gardens and Wedderburn Road in the
1880s William first developed his ideas for large detached
houses with lower profiles and more display of pitched
roofs than had been acceptable to previous tastes. His
main work came when he moved on to the Eton estate as well
and took agreements for their undeveloped lands in 1881
and 1890, becoming responsible for most of Eton Avenue,
as well as for Elsworthy Road and Wadham Gardens. It was
with Wadham Gardens in particular, built on a cricket
ground, that Willett was able to use the curves of an
irregular road pattern to set off to greatest effect his
detached houses, with their gables and tiled porches of

vaguely Dutch influence, their bay windows and tile-hung
gable-ends, and their neat privet hedges and small front
gardens which replaced the area steps leading to the
banished basement kitchens. The contrast with the treatment
of a curving street half a century earlier - for example
Buckland Crescent with Tidey's semi-classical regular flow
of stucco fronts - with its strictly urban manner, is
complete. It was for this that Willett earned the reputation
of introducing 'garden city lines' to Hampstead. (35)

Wadham Gardens was completed soon after 1900, the Redington
Road district was well over half-built by 1914 though building
there was still going on in the 1920s; with these the building
of middle-class Hampstead was practically complete. It
ranged unbroken from Primrose Hill to the West Heath, flanked
by areas of considerably lower social status in Fleet Road
to the east and West Hampstead and Kilburn to the west.
It could cater for the wealthiest members of the upper
middle class in Avenue Road, Belsize Avenue, Lyndhurst Road,
Fitzjohn's Avenue, Wadham Gardens or Redington Road; for
the well-to-do family man in business or the professions
in Adelaide Road, Fellows Road, Belsize Park Gardens, Lawn
Road, Priory Road, Boundary Road or Aberdare Gardens; and
for the family in tighter circumstances, or the clerical
lower end of the middle class, in such roads as Parliament
Hill, South Hill Park Road, Ainger Road, or Belsize Road.
Moreover by 1914 within each grade a whole range of houses
was available, of different sizes, dates, styles and prices:
from 5-bedroom to 12-bedroom, from 1820 to 1914 dates, from
late Regency classical all the way through Italianate stucco,
domesticated mock Grecian, garbled and garreted Gothic,
speculative builders' nondescript, Queen Anne revival, back
to neo-Georgian, at prices from £750 to £3,000 or £4,000.

This result, this large expanse of broadly middle-class
development, and the wide range of choice of houses within
it, was in only a few instances brought about by the
decisions and acts of the men who had the disposition of
the land, the landowners. It was in a broad sense determined
it is true, within the general framework of topographical
and social forces which indicated possible directions for
particular classes of development, by the idiosyncracies
and accidents of the landowners' legal and tenurial arrangements carried over from pre-building days. But at the
detailed brick-and-stucco level the character of the place,
and its different neighbourhoods, was determined by the
builders themselves, or more strictly, by the developers -

those large builders, for the most part, who took large
leases of building land and organised its disposition,
saw to the laying out of the lesser residential roads,
the making of sewers and the provision of water supply,
and who generally arranged sub-leases with smaller builders
for individual houses or small groups of houses. With a
few exceptions, as when the Maryon Wilson estate sold off
some freehold sites either to raise money or as a favour to
prominent purchasers, the entire area was developed under
the leasehold system of 99-year building leases; though it
is true that in all of these, with a few exceptions in
early leases granted in the 1820s, the ground landlords
inserted restrictive covenants which were binding on the
builder and on succeeding lessees. (36) These covenants
were designed first to create, and subsequently to protect,
the tone of a district. They commonly stipulated the
number and value of the houses to be built, and in order
to prevent aberrant and jarring intruders into the peace
and quiet of an area, thus spoiling its attractions and
its property values, it was usually expressly provided that
no factories or workshops should be built, but dwelling
houses only, and further that these should never be used
for any trade or business. Shops and public houses were
permissible, indeed absolutely necessary, exceptions to
the complete non-commercial purity of residential estates;
but their location was carefully considered and controlled
by the terms of building agreements. Enforcement could
be rigid, as when the Ecclesiastical Commissioners firmly
refused to permit a parade of shops on Haverstock Hill in
the 1890s, on the grounds of preserving residential
amenities. They could also be fickle, for after an admittedly
frugal allowance of three public houses had been permitted
in separate quarters of Belsize - Belsize Lane, England's
Lane, and Haverstock Hill - chiefly in recognition of the
thirst of stablemen, the Ecclesiastical Commissioners
announced in 1895 that teetotalism must prevail, and refused
to contemplate a licensed grocer opening shop in England's
Lane. (37) Religion might be a stern master in other ways
too, for the Dean and Chapter of Westminster regarded it as
their duty to insert covenants to prevent any buildings
on their estate 'being used for ecclesiastical, collegiate
or other purposes of the Church of Rome', although their
willingness to use building control to secure exclusively
Anglican colonisation did not extend much further than
this. (38) Other covenants of a routine character sought

to ensure that individual houseowners and occupiers should
keep their property in proper repair over the whole 99-year
term of the lease so that when it expired a house, in as
sound order as when it was built, should be surrendered
to the ground landlord. It is, however, slightly surprising
to find such landlord supervision carried to the length of
requiring that lessees 'shall paint, color and whitewash
at the end of every seventh year, inside work, and outside
at the end of every fourth year'; a provision both for
prudent maintenance of an individual house, and for ensuring
that an entire street should at all times look well cared
for, bright, and attractive. (39)

All this amounted to a formidable armoury of instruments
of planning and building control, and might seem to place
responsibility for determining the social character of
residential districts firmly in the hands of the ground
landlords. Nevertheless the crucial building covenants,
those governing the number of houses to be erected on a
given take and their type and value, were almost universally
inoperative in the middle-class districts of Hampstead,
even though the reverse tended to be true in what became
the lower-class quarters. The most obvious evidence is
that the developers habitually fulfilled their targets of
the number of houses they were bound to erect, when anything from one-quarter to one-half of their building land
remained untouched. The other aspect of this situation
was that the total ground rent due to the ground landlord
was habitually 'secured' or 'satisfied' by the sum of
individual ground rents charged on individual houses when
a similar proportion of ground still remained uncovered.
Different financial arrangements were then made for the
'surplus' houses which remained to be built, and they were
charged with only nominal ground rents of a peppercorn or
one shilling a year payable to the ground landlord,
although a separate 'improved ground rent' of an ordinary
commercial cash value would usually be created, payable
to the developer himself. This happened on the northern
section of the Eyre estate, on Kilburn Priory estate, on
both Cuming's and Willett's contributions to the Chalcots
estate, at Belsize Park, St John's Park, Rosslyn Park and,
Parliament Hill and, although no direct evidence is
available, it very probably happened on the Maryon Wilson
building estates as well. Its significance is to show
that the provisions imposed by ground landlords were
minimum conditions, and so much below the practical

possibilities of the districts concerned that the effective
decisions on the style of development were clearly being
made by the developers themselves.

Confirmation comes from the second main leg of building
controls, the regulation of the value of the houses to be
erected, where there is a similar lack of relationship
between the stipulations of leases and agreements and the
actual handiwork of the builders. It was common form for
building agreements to contain a clause, such as that in
the 1853 Rosslyn Park agreement, requiring that 'each
detached house shall be of the cost value of at least £600,
and semi-detached houses £1,000 the pair, exclusive of walls
and fences; in the event of houses being built in terraces
or rows, the cost value not to be less than £400 for each
house'. (40) Any connection between this agreement and
the houses of Lyndhurst Road, Eldon Grove, Thurlow Road,
or Lyndhurst Terrace which were built under it, is extremely
tenuous. The option to build terrace housing shows that
the ground landlords had no definite ideas about the future
of the area; more important, the very large and substantial
family houses, costing more like £3,000 than £1,000 the pair,
were plainly the idea of the developer and not the ground
landlord. (41) The highest cost value which the dean and
chapter ever required was £1,000 for detached houses and
£800 for each semi-detached house, in the Belsize Avenue
agreement of 1868; but the grand houses which the elder
Willett built there, semi-detached, all sold for at least
£2,400 and some for over £3,000, suggesting that he must
have been providing not far short of three times his
contracted values. (42) The experience on other Hampstead
building estates was similar, though without such extreme
divergence between stipulated and actual values; equally,
there appears to be no instance in which a ground landlord
had to take a builder to task for putting up inferior
houses, though one did get into difficulties for erecting
stabling on a site reserved for residential use. (43)
The conclusion is inescapable that, in the middle-class
end of the building business, it was the developer who
generally decided what kind, size and price of house to
build, in the light of his assessment of the potentialities
of the district; and that his assessment of its future
quality was likely to be higher, or more optimistic, than
that of his ground landlord, whose minimum aspirations
formed the basis of the fundamental building covenants.
The covenants, in other words, formed a floor or safety

net which could have been called into action to arrest
too calamitous a fall from social grace should things go
wrong and expectations prove too sanguine.

Landowners proposed, developers disposed. In the short
run the developers of Hampstead pitched their operations
about right, in the sense that houses built for a particular section of the middle-class market generally succeeded
in attracting that kind of middle-class occupant. There
were, naturally, some years of over-building when new
houses were difficult to let and stood empty for months
or even a year or two; there were some very localised set-
backs, as when the proximity of the smallpox hospital
caused some intended family houses to be occupied instead
as tenements; and as early as 1884 the excessive size of
one of the houses in Belsize Park Gardens made it unlettable
and it was demolished to be replaced by a large block of
flats. (44) But by and large the new houses filled up
with the kind of people who had been expected, presumably
because facilities, room space, appearance, locality and
price were about right for the tastes and pockets of the
different groups at the appropriate time. But although
the initial success rate was high and few of the 'wrong'
people got into a neighbourhood to start with, success
was inherently impermanent because Hampstead had shifting
social frontiers as well as moving building ones. It was
not that the middle class surrendered possession of any
of its territory or suffered lower-class invasions, but
rather that the type of middle-class use of housing and
of neighbourhoods changed. It was no doubt quite normal
that professional men should be allowed to use their
private houses for their callings, but when such as music
teachers, singing teachers or dancing masters were added
to the somewhat superior surgeons, doctors and dentists,
even this discreet business use could begin to influence
the residential quality of neighbouring houses. It was
altogether more serious when the largest family houses
of Belsize Park and Rosslyn Park became decreasingly
desirable to the largest middle-class families from the
1880s and 1890s, because they were too large or had too
many stairs or did not have modern equipment like bathrooms, and became difficult to let any longer as family
houses. At that point the ground landlords were forced
to relax their covenants requiring exclusively residential
use, and permission was increasingly freely given for
some of these large houses to be used as small schools -

kindergartens or schools for young ladies; boys, even authenticated sons of gentlefolk, were banned as too noisy - as boarding-houses, or as guest-houses. (45) The process accelerated in the first decade of the twentieth century, with applications to convert the once grand houses in Belsize Avenue into boarding-houses; the path was already prepared for the almost wholesale conversion of the older Victorian houses into flats and bed-sitting rooms in the interwar years. (46)

The advertisement columns of the local paper reflect this drift from private single-family occupation to commercialised accommodation. Already by 1895 a typical week would see two full columns in the <u>Hampstead</u> <u>and</u> <u>Highgate Express</u> devoted to advertisements of furnished and unfurnished apartments, and board residence. It is true that a proportion of these related to working-class districts, where taking in lodgers had always been part of the household economy; but many of them concerned indisputably middle-class roads - South Hill Park, Parliament Hill, Adelaide, King Henry's and Belsize Park Gardens, and Broadhurst Gardens, to name a few. By 1910 the business had expanded, these advertisements were classified into their three main categories, and together they took up 4 -5 columns each week, and covered a greater range of middle-class addresses especially in Belsize Park. (47) The impression could easily be formed that the Hampstead of substantial middle-class families had become the Hampstead of middle-class bachelors and spinsters, of servantless and childless families, and of middle-class widows living on their rents. That was a fate which, in 1914, still lay in the future. It was already foreshadowed by the signs of widows in Broadhurst Gardens providing hot baths for their gentleman lodgers, proving that the framework of housing supplied by the developers over the previous century, however successful in its day, could not make Victoria's reign last for ever.

Chapter 4

Royal Leamington Spa
T. H. Lloyd

'To say the truth, unless I could have a fine English
country-house, I do not know a spot where I would rather
reside than in this new village of midmost Old England.' (1)
Leamington in 1857, the year in which Nathaniel Hawthorne
wrote these words, was something more than a village for
at the last census its population had numbered 15,274.
But if Hawthorne did less than justice to the size of the
town, in every other respect his description of it is
resonant with superlatives. The Jephson Gardens was the
most pleasant public garden which he had ever been in, the
shops were the most brilliant he had seen outside the
capital, while the 'almost palatial ranges of edifices
and separate residences, look quite equal to any in London'.
   Although this was not Hawthorne's first visit to Leamington
one is bound to question whether the enthusiasm represented
his considered opinion or whether it reflected more his
profound relief at having escaped from a sojourn in Manchester
of which he had grown weary. The change of scene struck
him forcibly and he wrote in his notebook that 'there could
not possibly be a greater contrast than between Leamington
and Manchester; the latter built only for dirty uses, and
scarcely intended as a habitation for man; the former so
cleanly, so set out with shade-trees, so regular in its
streets, so neatly paved, its houses so prettily contrived,
and nicely stuccoed, that it does not look like a portion
of the work-a-day world. "Genteel" is the word for it;
a town where people of moderate income may live an idle
and handsome life, whether for a few weeks or a term of
years'. (3) Hawthorne's dissatisfaction with Manchester
was caused in no small measure by his lodgings, 'a specimen
of the poorer middle-class dwellings, as built now-a-days',
for which he paid £5 a week. This figure reflects,
admittedly, the temporary demand for accommodation created

by some of the million and more visitors to the great
Exhibition of the Art Treasures of the United Kingdom
held in the city in 1857. In Leamington Hawthorne and
his family lodged at 10 Lansdowne Circus, which he
described as a 'nice little circle of pretty, moderate-
sized houses, all on precisely the same plan, so that on
coming out of any one door, and taking a turn, one can
hardly tell which house is his own'. (4) The house
contained a scullery, kitchen, hall, small sitting-room,
modest dining-room and drawing-room, three bedrooms,
dressing-room and three attic rooms. Hawthorne does not
record the terms on which he took the house, but soon
after it had been built, some twenty years previously,
it had been let for £40 a year.

Leamington was crowded with houses of this size and price
range, all providing accommodation for visitors. There
was a danger that after a while the uniformity, of function
if not of style, might have a depressing effect and eclipse
any favourable impression which had first been created.
Looking back upon his stay in the town Hawthorne wrote:

'...it may fairly be called beautiful, and, at some
points, magnificent; but by and by you become doubt-
fully suspicious of a some-what unreal finery: it is
pretentious, though not glaringly so; it has been
built with malice aforethought, as a place of gentility
and enjoyment. Moreover, splendid as the houses
look, and comfortable as they often are, there is a
nameless something about them, betokening that they
have not grown out of human hearts, but are the
creations of a skilfully applied human intellect:
no man has reared any one of them, whether stately
or humble, to be a life-long residence, wherein to
bring up his children, who are to inherit it as a
home. They are nicely contrived lodging-houses,
one and all, - the best as well as the shabbiest
of them, - and therefore inevitably lack some nameless property that a home should have. This was
the case with our own little snuggery in Lansdowne
Circus, as with all the rest; it had not grown out
of anybody's individual need, but was built to let
or sell, and was therefore like a ready-made garment,
- a tolerable fit, but only tolerable'. (5)

Hawthorne was by no means the first to observe that the

charms of Leamington lessened with the duration of one's stay. In 1840 A.B. Granville had commented that 'Leamington, in fact, is one of the most monotonous of watering-places. Families of the first ton, who have resided there for two or three successive seasons have complained of its dullness. Private and exclusive circles in the evening are indeed formed among people who have been long acquainted with each other, but hardly ever is introduction into them allowed to a stranger'. (6) Granville's criticism was occasioned, no doubt, by the fact that he expected to find all the appurtenances of a flourishing spa, and in this he was disappointed. Already Leamington was hardly less staid than the mid-nineteenth-century town visited by Hawthorne. This was due only partially to the fact that in 1840 the town was in the depths of an economic depression, for it had begun to assume this character at the very time when speculators were investing most recklessly in its future as a spa. The failure of Leamington as a resort left the town with a surfeit of houses, which had been built to accommodate visitors who failed to arrive in the expected numbers. These houses were slowly filled by a resident middle class, very different in manners and outlook from the traditional spa society.

Leamington's misfortune lay in the fact that its main period of growth, beginning in 1825 and ending in 1837, came just as the inland spa was about to decline as a social institution. The future lay with the seaside resort. Well before 1830 the hazardous nature of investment in the town was all too apparent. W.G. and H.T. Elliston who had opened assembly rooms in 1822, at a cost said to have been between £20,000 and £30,000, became bankrupt in 1827. The bankruptcy in the same year of W.L. Lubbock, lessee of the older assembly rooms, brought to an end the traditional type of spa assembly. Henceforth both establishments operated on a much more restricted basis. Investments in circulating libraries, pleasure gardens, theatrical entertainments and other enterprises appropriate to a resort were equally dangerous. As early as 1831 the editor of the Leamington Courier (7) commented that 'perhaps in the general round of speculative business, there is not one branch more subject to vexatious disappointment or less certain of securing to its projectors a fair remuneration for trouble and anxiety, than that of catering for the public amusement... Were the public to consider the risks thus encountered, and the ruinous consequences which

116

occasionally fall on those, whose aim, next to a fair reward for their labours, is to gratify them, and to afford both rational and intellectual amusement, we should not have so often to record the failure of efforts made with those laudable intentions'. The provision of accommodation attracted speculators long after doubt had been cast upon the wisdom of investing in enterprises catering for the other needs of the visitor. Their optimism was not based upon any firm economic foundation. In 1840 Granville noted that 'the hotel-keepers, as well as the proprietors of houses, make but a sorry business of their respective concerns, and the speculators in both, I trow, are burning their fingers. The old town has hardly had time to grow older, when a new one starts into existence. Who is to inhabit all these flimsy semi-palaces, it is not easy to conjecture'. (8) This refrain might have been repeated several times before the century had run its course.

The great increase in the number of houses available for renting by visitors may have been partly responsible for the decline in the importance of hotels. Earlier in the nineteenth century, when there were complaints of a shortage of accommodation, hotels were an attractive form of investment. Although the Royal was entirely rebuilt on a grand scale in 1827, and several lesser hotels were built in later years, hotel building became a relatively minor form of speculation. The existing establishments did not, of course, go out of business and Granville claimed that the town 'now boasts of a dozen of the most superb hotels in England'. Some of the smaller hotels were both dearer and more fashionable than the very large Royal and Regent, probably because they were managed according to the old custom of providing for all the needs of a family in private rooms. The latter both operated the modern system, then termed <u>table d'hôte</u>, of providing all services, other than sleeping, in public rooms. The all-in cost at the Royal was about 6 guineas per week, of which one-third went in gratuities. With the decline of the spa the hotels seem to have fallen upon hard times. The Clarendon, assigned by Granville to the fashionable group, was described in 1855 by Nathaniel Hawthorne as 'by far the most splendid hotel I have seen in England'. Yet the Hawthorne family were its sole occupants and on examining the visitors' book he found that no more than 350 or so people had stayed there throughout the previous two years. He estimated that a popular American hotel would have had as many visitors in one week as this place

117

in five years. Hawthorne stayed but a day or two in the Clarendon and then took a furnished house. His description of the move possibly provides a clue to the decline of the hotel in mid-nineteenth-century Leamington: 'This English custom of lodgings has its advantages, but is rather uncomfortable for strangers, who, on first settling themselves down, find, that they must undertake all the responsibilities of house-keeping at an instant's warning, and cannot even get a cup of tea till they have made arrangements with the grocer. Soon, however, there comes a sense of being home, and by our exclusive selves, which never could be attained at hotels or boarding houses'. (9)

House building was undoubtedly the main form of investment in Leamington for much of the nineteenth century. It was essentially speculative, and one of the main aims of this chapter is to demonstrate the precariousness of this form of investment in a situation which was dependent on the patronage of a leisured class. Even in a town like Leamington, however, not all the houses were occupied by the middle class. It would be difficult, if not impossible, to assign each individual dwelling to a precise social category, but a rough guideline is provided by an estimate made in 1846 in connection with a proposal to establish a new waterworks company. It was calculated that there were 462 first-class houses, capable of paying a water rent of £2 per annum; 492 second-class houses, rent £1; 980 third-class, rent 10s; and 818 fourth-class, rent 5s. The first- and second-class houses, which may safely be identified as residences of the middle class, together make up more than one-third of the total, a very substantial proportion. When one takes into consideration the great difference between the average cost of middle-class houses and that of working-class houses in Leamington in this period one is forced to conclude that the prosperity of the building industry was closely geared to the middle-class market. Whenever demand in this quarter slackened, much of the capacity of the industry was made redundant. In this, of course, it was little different from other sectors of the economy of the town. Since there was virtually no industry the livelihoods of most people depended upon the prosperity, or merely upon the whims, of the leisured class.

Before examining in greater detail the economics of house building it is necessary to describe very briefly the main stages in the growth of the town. Leamington at the

beginning of the nineteenth century was a mere village
entirely on the south bank of the River Leam; a community
of 72 families occupying 67 houses, with a further 3 houses
unoccupied; 315 souls in all. Although descriptions of
the mineral waters had been in print since the sixteenth
century no attempt was made to exploit them commercially
until the late eighteenth. The first bathing establishment
was opened in 1786 and a second in 1791. Apart from a new
inn built in 1793 these did not lead to any secondary
development. In the early years of the spa there were
complaints that shortage of accommodation combined with
the hostility of local landowners to act as a brake upon
progress. The earliest surviving estimate of the number
of visitors dates from 1809, when it was claimed that there
were not less than 1,500 'exclusive of servants and
children'. (10) If this is an accurate statement of the
number staying in the village it indicates a very promising
future for the spa. The first investments in urban development had already been made, but as yet actual growth
had been small.

The urban growth of Leamington really began about the
year 1806 with the opening of two new bathing establishments.
The following year an acre of land in the village was sold
for 700 guineas and this seems to have been the signal for
some of the principal landowners to make land available
for building. The first phase of the expansion ground to
a halt amidst a flurry of bankruptcies at the beginning of
1815. However the period of real activity had been of
much briefer duration. In 1811, when over most of the
country the building industry was in a depressed state,
Leamington was in the middle of a building boom. The
census showed that the number of occupied houses had
already increased to 125, while a further 50 were in the
course of construction and 13 were unoccupied. This burst
of activity was apparently sufficient to satisfy demand,
for the Rate Book of 1814 accounted for only 170-180 premises
of all types, (11) suggesting that during the intervening
three years there had been little or no new building. At
this time the so-called 'new town', on the north bank of
the River Leam, contained an assembly rooms, the Bedford
hotel and twenty-two or twenty-three houses on the west
side of lower Union Parade, about a dozen houses in upper
Union Parade and two dozen in Cross Street. Since a
similar number of premises had been built on the land
made available on the other side of the village the centre

of gravity remained firmly on the south side of the river.
About 1818 a new wave of investment began, but although
more houses were built during this second period of
expansion, the boom was equally short-lived. By 1821 it
had been brought to an end, probably by the difficulty
experienced in letting new houses. The census of that
year recorded 399 occupied houses, 23 in the course of
construction and no less than 59 unoccupied. During the
next few years there was little new building, for the
Rate Book (12) of May 1825 accounted for roughly 520
premises of all types. One important result of this
activity was that it brought the two halves of the town
into balance, so that there were now some 270 buildings
in the new part against 250 in the old, and a rateable
value of £3,520 in each half.

The recession of the early 1820s was probably more
apparent than real, for plans were already being made
for the town's main phase of expansion, which had begun
by the spring of 1825, when new streets were being laid
down in both the new and old towns and a building boom
was already gathering momentum. The boom lasted without
interruption until 1837 when it was brought abruptly to
a halt by the failure of the Leamington Bank, caused
partially by the deteriorating economic climate of the
country as a whole. The bank failure was one of the most
important events in the history of Leamington and its
consequences were felt in the property market for at least
twenty years. The decay of the spa as a fashionable
institution in the 1840s added to the economic depression,
which the advent of the railway relieved only slightly.

The growth of the town during the 1820s and 1830s can be
seen from the census reports, although they disguise the
fact that most activity was concentrated into the years
1825 to 1837. The population of the town, which had grown
from 315 in 1801 to 2,183 in 1821, increased to 6,209 in
1831 and to 12,864 in 1841. The total stock of housing
increased from 481 in 1821 to 2,607 in 1841, the net
additions in each decade being 712 and 1,414. Great as
were the achievements of the developers during this
period their hopes and ambitions were even more grandiose.
Contemporary maps show that plans were on foot to develop
parts of the parish which, in the event, were not to fall
to the builder for decades. Many streets existed only on
paper while others, although staked out on the ground, were
equally unreal. In social terms the setback of 1837 may

have been a blessing in disguise, for ten years later the railway came to the centre of Leamington, ploughing a track through these grassy streets. Although a number of houses and public buildings were demolished to make way for it, the toll would have been far greater if building had been continuous during the intervening years.

The depressed state of the property market in 1841 is shown by the fact that at the time of the census there were no fewer than 250 unoccupied houses, 10 per cent of the completed stock. This surplus held back new building for many years to come. During the 1840s the net increase in the stock of housing was only 358, well below the rate of population growth. In the following decade the net increase was 370, equal to the current rate of population growth, which had meanwhile fallen by half. Even more eloquent of the depression in the building industry is the fact that these decades were two out of the only three in the nineteenth century when the net increase in total housing stock was less than the net increase in the number of occupied houses. The balance was made up from stock of empty houses.

The revival of the fortunes of the building industry began during the late 1850s and the full extent of the recovery is shown in the report of the 1871 census. During the previous decade the total stock of housing had grown by 898, an increase of 27 per cent. This investment was encouraged, no doubt, by a higher rate of population growth, which amounted to 20 per cent in the same period. Building continued at a steady pace into the 1870s and by the end of that decade there had been a further addition of 705 houses, an increase of 17 per cent, compared with a population growth of only 10 per cent. An indication that Leamington was over-built is provided by the number of empty houses, which increased from 154 in 1861 to 221 in 1871, and to 313 in 1881. The number of partially built houses in the same years was 21, 49 and 62. The danger was apparent as early as 1873, if not before, when a commentator remarked 'noticing in my rambles in and about the town, the very great number of first and second class houses there are "to be let", one cannot but infer for a moment that Leamington is going down'. Whether or not that inference was correct there was clearly justification for his further observation that 'Leamington would seem to be overbuilt with private town-houses, and if such is the case, and as a large and new building estate is just formed on which

121

Table 3

Population and Houses, 1801-1901

	POPULATION		HOUSES		
	Numbers	Intercensal increase	Occupied	Building	Empty
1801	315	–	67	–	3
1811	543	228	125	50	13
1821	2,183	1,640	399	23	59
1831	6,209	4,026	1,003	51	139
1841	12,864	6,655	2,308	49	250
1851	15,724	2,860	2,736	44	185
1861	17,402	1,678	3,160	21	154
1871	20,910	3,508	3,963	49	221
1881	22,979	2,069	4,563	62	313
1891	23,124	145	4,809	12	464
1901	22,889	235	5,062	11	445

Total	Intercensal increase (all houses)	Intercensal increase (occupied houses)	Population per inhabited house
70	–	–	4.70
188	118	58	4.34
481	293	274	5.47
1,193	712	604	6.19
2,607	1,414	1,305	5.57
2,965	358	428	5.75
3,335	370	424	5.51
4,233	898	803	5.27
4,938	705	603	5.04
5,285	347	246	4.81
5,518	233	253	4.52

more villas will, I hear, be forthwith erected, more of
the town-houses will soon be tenantless, unless something
is done very fresh and reviving to bring more tenants
into them'. (13)

During the 1880s population growth came to a halt entirely,
but the building industry, as ever, seems to have been
somewhat slow in responding to the lessening in demand.
Although the number of people in 1891 was virtually identical
with that in 1881 the net stock of housing had increased
by 7 per cent, bringing the number of unoccupied houses
to 464, nearly 9 per cent of the total. In the final decade
of the century, with population actually declining, the
building industry ground to a virtual halt and the net
increase in the housing stock was only 4 per cent. By
now the industry was probably responding only to a real
demand for new houses and the increase was slightly less
than the increase in the total of occupied houses. The
days of speculative building were long past.

Although the over-building which characterised Leamington
over much of the nineteenth century resulted in financial
losses to many individual speculators, it may have yielded
some real social benefits. It is possible that part of the
remarkable drop in the average number of persons per
inhabited house, which occurred during the second half of
the century, was attributable to the housing surplus.
However it is unlikely that the benefits were spread equally
throughout the community. They probably did not reach
below the lower-middle and artisan classes. Not until after
World War I did the local authority embark on a housing
programme and the widespread poverty in the town in the
late nineteenth century must have prevented the lowest
classes from improving their housing conditions by their
own efforts. Although the buildings of nineteenth century
Leamington must have appeared to the casual observer as
overwhelmingly middle-class, they disguised some appalling
slums. The human misery generated in these rookeries was
real enough, but their influence upon the social geography
of the town was limited. A few areas were solidly lower-
class, with clearly distinguishable boundaries; elsewhere
there were small lower-class enclaves in predominantly
middle-class areas; there was, however, no suggestion of
an east end and a west end, and most parts of the town
were capable of supplying the middle class with a respectable
address. This resulted partly from the comparatively small
size of the town and partly from historical circumstances.

Until about 1820 the sheer puniness of Leamington would
have made nonsense of any claim by one part of the town
to be more fashionable than another. The place was not
yet established as a residential centre and much of the
increase in the permanent population was made up of
businessmen and tradesmen. These found it convenient to
settle in and around the old village, which remained the
busier and more populous part of the town. The developers
of the new town undoubtedly sought to create a fashionable
suburb, but they found very few takers. In the second
period of expansion around 1818 no attempt was made to
preserve the social character of the estate and most of
the remaining land was covered with lower-class houses.
One of the most noisome slums in the town grew up at the
bottom of the gardens on the east side of upper Union
Parade.

In the early 1820s the future of the new town may have
looked bleak. Union Parade was being surrounded by
inferior buildings, while the attraction of the old town
had recently increased with the opening of a new assembly
rooms and yet another bathing establishment. These developments probably drew speculators into the estate of
Thomas Read, who in 1818 had laid down new streets on the
further side of the Grand Union Canal which traversed the
parish several hundred yards south of the village. He
disposed of the land on building leases, which contained
covenants that each house must cost between £800 and £1,000.
Building in this area probably post-dated the 1818 boom
and coincided with the social decline of the new town.
A map (14) of 1820 shows very little evidence of building,
but by 1825 some fifty or more houses had been erected.
In the event the speculators burned their fingers, for
this part of the town was not destined to remain fashionable.
In 1830 one of their number, James Bissett, (15) wrote
about a house which he owned in Ranelagh Terrace, 'it has
been built upwards of seven years, at the cost of above
a thousand pounds; and has never been inhabited, altho in
a pleasant part of the town...' A house in Brunswick
Street which he had formerly let for £50 now yielded only
25 guineas. On another occasion Bissett wrote 'my spirits
have not yet failed me, tho I am sometimes apprehensive
I shall sustain a great loss if compelled to sell any of
my houses...'

Bissett himself realised the cause of his misfortunes,
which lay in the fact that 'the Bias of the Town has

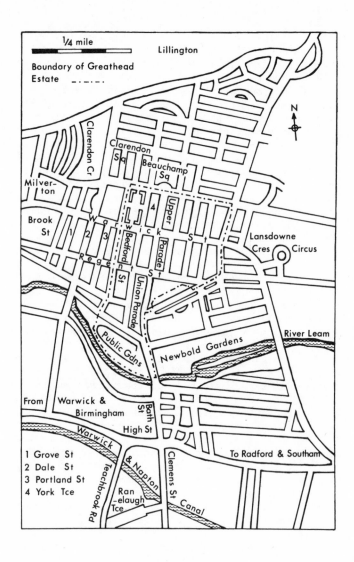

Fig 8   Royal Leamington Spa, c 1850.

recently varied from the South to the North...' In the
third phase of expansion the speculators had returned to
the new town, leap-frogging the inferior streets on either
side of the Parade and sinking their money in land owned
by the Willes family. Initially Edward Willes jr offered
a choice of two developments. The cheaper land was in
Quarry Fields, which lay immediately to the west of the
Greathead estate beside the River Leam, and this began
very quickly to be built up with moderately priced middle-
class housing. The land to the north of the new town was
more expensive, and was also burdened by covenants designed
to ensure that only very superior houses were built.
Despite this the land was quickly taken up by speculators
and Willes began to plan an even more grandiose development, extending down the entire eastern sides of the new
and old towns.

During the 1830s, even before the failure of the
Leamington Bank, a vast amount of land was released on to
the market and there was a substantial fall in prices.
This had a profound and permanent effect on the pattern
of middle-class housing. The plenitude of land offered
great choice of location in which to build, while its
comparative cheapness meant that detached villas with
large gardens became the predominant style. The movement
towards extensive, low density building was encouraged
by an anomaly in the rating provisions of the Local
Improvement Act. The fact that householders in streets
which lacked either street-lighting or flagged pavements,
paid only two-third rates led the middle class to build
in the more distant areas, which lacked these amenities.
In 1848 an editorial in the Leamington Courier commented
that 'The general complaint made by strangers frequenting
Leamington, is its straggling and unfinished appearance,
and it is actually the fact that individuals intending
to build have frequently selected detached and remote
pieces of land to escape the expenses attendant upon paving
and lighting'. (16) The correction of this rating anomaly
in the Public Health Act, which was implemented in 1852,
tended to aggravate the problem of extensive building, so
that during the next building boom many large villas were
erected just outside the boundaries of the local board of
health, in the neighbouring parishes of Milverton and
Lillington. Here they enjoyed the prestige of a Leamington
address, while paying much lower rates. This meant that
late nineteenth-century Leamington extended over an area

127

which was large in relation to its population. Most of
the town was the preserve of the middle class and much of
the working class was crowded into comparatively small
central areas. It is important to note that this
occupation by the working class was an original feature of
the town's history. It had not resulted, as in many large
cities, from a middle-class migration to the suburbs with
the vacated houses being taken over by the working class.

The occupation of houses sets the seal upon a long chain
of events. Therefore before describing the middle class
of Leamington and its living-accommodation it is appropriate
to analyse the various links in the chain, beginning
with a general comment on the sources of the capital which
went into the building of the town. The pre-urban landowners appear in the history of Leamington largely as the
recipients of a sudden and, no doubt, unexpected increase
in the value of their property. Bertie Greathead put a
small part of his profits into the companies operating
the assembly rooms and the pump room in the new town,
while Matthew Wise, to his cost, left purchase money on
mortgage with builders. Apart from this the main function
of the landowners was to make sites available for building.
This meant that all the capital had to be brought in from
outside, for Leamington was beginning from virtually nothing.
Although it would be a mistake to discount the amount of
capital invested in the town, it would be equally unwise
to exaggerate it, particularly during the first and second
periods of expansion. This seemingly obvious point has
to be made in order to prevent unnecessary speculation
about possible sources of capital. It has, for instance,
been suggested that surplus money from the Duke of Bedford's
estates went into the building of Leamington, although,
as far as the present writer is aware, there is no concrete
evidence that this was so. (17)

Both inspiration and much of the capital for the initial
growth of Leamington came from near at hand, from a group
of businessmen in the county town of Warwick, which lay
only 3 miles away. Into eighteenth-century Warwick flowed
a substantial amount of agricultural wealth, mobilised by
the early development of banking, and augmented in the
1790s by the profits of the cotton-spinning and weaving
and worsted-spinning factories which were set up in the
town. In 1810 machine-made lace was added to the range
of industries, which altogether provided employment for
about 800 people. (18) There can be little, if any, doubt

9. Leamington: part of terrace, east side of Beauchamp Square, 1820s, by P. F. Robinson (*T. H. Lloyd*)

10. Leamington: house occupied by Nathaniel Hawthorne, Lansdowne Circus, 1830s (*T. H. Lloyd*)

11 & 12. Nottingham: 12 Cavendish Crescent North (street and back views) (*J. R. Young*)

that it was to provide an outlet for surplus money that a
number of businessmen and bankers, mostly independents in
religion and politics, persuaded Bertie Greathead to
develop his land. They formed a consortium, known as the
Union Society, which is shown in Greathead's account (19)
as the purchaser of the entire western side of lower
Union Parade for the sum of £4,090. The precise legal
status of the society is uncertain, but it probably
comprised individuals who had agreed to provide a guaranteed market for a certain amount of land, without which
it may not have been worthwhile for Greathead to take his
land out of agricultural tenancy. The leading members of
the same group, together with Greathead, provided the
capital for the assembly rooms and the pump room.

The financial interest of Warwick businessmen in the
development of Leamington grew stronger rather than weaker,
for the continued growth of the spa was essential to
Warwick's prosperity. It provided alternative employment
for both capital and labour as Warwick's textile industries
disappeared in the face of competition from Lancashire.
In 1837 the report of the Royal Commission on Municipal
Boundaries recorded that Warwick 'is thriving, and distinguished by an appearance of respectability and neatness.
Trade seems to be increasing rapidly, which may be accounted
for in a great measure by its proximity to and connexion
with Leamington, where most of the Warwick Tradespeople
have shops, and where the chief speculators from this town
invest their capital'. (20) The economic catastrophe which
overtook Leamington in 1837 was felt even more severely
in the neighbouring town. By 1841 no fewer than 334 houses
out of a total of 2,336 were unoccupied in Warwick, while
throughout the 1840s the extent of pauperism in Warwick
was greater even than in Leamington.

In the first period of urban expansion, the old town
seems to have attracted a wider circle of investors than
the new town, which was dominated by the tightly-knit
Warwick group. Some of the early building in the old
town was financed, directly or indirectly, by Coventry
money, the profits of the silk industry. The cosmopolitan
individuals who were drawn to try their fortunes in a new
spa also found the old town the more attractive part.
The already mentioned James Bissett, painter and medallist,
brought himself and his museum from Birmingham in 1813,
together with sufficient capital to build half a dozen
houses. It is true that not all the newcomers had money

of their own, but the circle from which they borrowed was probably wide. Later this difference between the two parts of the town disappeared, so great was the need for capital.

Consideration of the methods by which capital was mobilised must first draw a distinction between direct investment and loan capital. If the assumption is correct that the new town was established to provide a safe investment for the profits of Warwick businessmen it is likely that many of them put their own money into its development. Loan capital, of course, was not absent even in the early days and some buildings were mortgaged as soon as they were built. Nevertheless, it is probably safe to conclude that as the town grew direct investment by those who had a proprietary interest in its development became relatively less important and loan capital a proportionately greater source of finance. The unsecured loan was a rarity and most loans were advanced against a mortgage on land or buildings. The examination of loan finance becomes, therefore, an investigation of the mortgage market.

Today most mortgages are provided by building societies, but in the early nineteenth century the situation was otherwise. In Leamington some of the earliest houses in the new town were built through the agency of a building society which was an offshoot of the Union Society. However, this was not a long term source of finance, for it was a terminating society, which came to an end when the shares were fully paid up in 1811. There is no evidence of a permanent building society until 1848, when the Leamington Building and Investment Society was formed, with the declared object of assisting the industrious classes to buy their own homes.

Since landowners, with the exception of Matthew Wise (p 128), were unwilling to leave purchase money in the hands of the buyers, the only possible sources of mortgages were banks and private mortgagors. In the eighteenth century two country banks had been founded in Warwick, one of which, despite changes in the partnership, remained private until its failure in 1887. By the beginning of the nineteenth century the other bank was the property of John Tomes and John Russell. Tomes and Russell invested their own money in the development of the new town and undoubtedly advised their clients to do the same. To what extent, if any, they made use of the bank's money for this purpose is unknown. In the early

1830s the bank granted overdraft facilities to William Buddle & Son, builders, and when they exceeded their limit of £1,000 took a mortgage on houses for a short period. The circumstances make it quite clear that it was not the usual practice of the bank to advance money on mortgage. Clearly a bank could not afford to have a large proportion of its assets tied up in securities which were not readily negotiable.

In June 1834 Tomes and Russell introduced joint-stock banking to the district when they launched the Warwick and Leamington Banking Company, handing over their own business in return for shares in the new company. In May 1835 a second joint-stock company was formed, the Leamington Bank, and in September a third, the Leamington Priors and Warwickshire Banking Company. By now Leamington was clearly overbanked, even for a town which aimed at providing homes for a wealthy middle class. Given the fierce competition which existed between the banks it was essential that they observe sound banking principles if they were to survive. The directors' minute book (21) of the Leamington Priors and Warwickshire shows that this company took great care not to get its money tied up in property speculation and this may well be true of the Warwick and Leamington. The same cannot be said about the Leamington Bank. Some of the directors were themselves prominent speculators and were afterwards accused of lending themselves money from the bank. They also advanced money to builders and others on mortgage of property. By the end of 1836 the Leamington Bank was having difficulties in meeting its obligations to its London correspondent, the London and Westminster Bank, and was asked to reduce its overdraft. (22) It was unable to do this and by June 1837 the overdraft had increased to £50,554. Shortly afterwards news of the bank's troubles became common knowledge in Leamington and steps had to be taken to wind up its affairs. This was a long and complicated process, for much of the bank's assets were tied up in property and could not be realised quickly. On 2 December 1837 the bank owed £35,593 to the London and Westminster and £11,921 plus interest to individual creditors. More than twelve months later these figures had been reduced only to £27,105 and £8,010.

The failure of the Leamington Bank resulted directly or indirectly in the bankruptcy of nearly all the builders in Leamington and many other persons as well. Even those

whose debt to the bank was less than their own real assets
became bankrupt, since in the crisis of confidence they
found it difficult to sell property or to obtain credit
elsewhere to fulfil their obligations. Various suits were
initiated in chancery, as a result of which in August 1839
an enforced auction sale was held of property owned by
debtors of the bank. (23) This consisted largely of middle-
class houses owned by speculators. At a conservative
estimate the value of the property was at least £200,000.
This was by no means all the property which changed hands
as a result of the smash, for wherever possible debtors
had tried to settle with the bank before this stage was
reached.

The bank's claims against the auctioned properties were
exceeded by those of other parties, who held mortgages
totalling at least £130,000. The vast majority of the
mortgagors were private persons, drawn from all over the
country, but mostly from the counties of Warwickshire and
Worcestershire. This, undoubtedly, was the main source
of finance for the building of Leamington. It is a common-
place of economic history that from the end of the seventeent
century the East India Company, the Bank of England and
the National Debt put an end to the monopoly previously
enjoyed by land of being the only completely safe form
of investment. It is too often forgotten that while these
institutions were very convenient for the retired London
merchant they were less useful to persons of moderate
means in the provinces. For most of these, properties,
or a mortgage on property, remained the easiest form of
investment until the growth of the stock exchange in the
railway era. Leamington provided the gentry and tradesmen
of the neighbouring towns and countryside with an ideal
investment. If they were disinclined to speculate themselves, then a mortgage on the speculations of others
appeared to provide absolute security for their investment
and a guaranteed return of 5 per cent per annum. In the
early 1830s Thomas Woods Weston of Barford, a retired
partner in one of the Warwick banks, advanced £14,000 to
William Buddle & Son on mortgage on houses. (24) They
undertook not to sell the properties without his consent,
since he wished to leave his money there for a long period.
Weston and others like him undoubtedly financed a very
large part of the building in Leamington.

Turning next from the general question of finance to the
actual stages of building, we find that by the late eight-

eenth century, ownership of land in the parish was highly
concentrated. The anciently-enclosed land north of the
river was divided between the Earl of Aylesford, Bertie
Greathead of Guy's Cliffe and Edward Willes of Newbold
Comyn, the last being the only one of the three who
resided in the parish. South of the river the only
estates of consequence after the enclosure award of 1768
were those of Willes, 194 acres; Aylesford, 21 acres;
Matthew Wise, who lived in the village, 473 acres; and
the yeomen families of Lawrence and Lyndon, with 76 and
68 acres respectively. The Lyndon estate was bought by
the Earl of Warwick for £1,800 in 1789, but two years
later he gave it to Thomas Read, wool-stapler of Kidder-
minster, in exchange for land in Warwick. The Lawrence
estate was bought for £3,200 in 1800 by Francis Robbins,
a local gentleman. In this situation, which was neither
one of monopoly nor one in which ownership was so divided
that no single person could seriously influence the market,
it behoved each landowner to watch his neighbours carefully.

In 1808 preparations began to be made for the development
of the Read, Robbins and Greathead estates. There is no
evidence of any co-operation between them and it is more
than probable that they were in competition. The method
of development was different on all three estates. The
first two, which lay adjacent to one another on the south
of the village, were not ideally suited to the requirements
of the town planner, since the enclosure award had left
them with inconvenient boundaries. Each had only a short
northern boundary fronting the High Street, but stretched
southwards for a considerable distance. Moreover both
were bisected by the canal, which in the case of the
Robbins estate cut off most of the land from the village.
A better prospect for the developer was the Greathead
estate, a farm of some 75 acres lying on the virgin north
bank of the river hard by the bridge into the village.
However, although described by contemporaries as the new
town, and often hailed by historians as an example of early
town planning, the development of the estate deserves only
a very small accolade, for little real planning went into
it. The grid pattern of streets was probably laid down
at the outset, but for the first ten years or so building
was confined to the two principal thoroughfares, Union
Parade and Regent Street, and most of the land in the
other streets remained unsold.

Francis Robbins shelved the problem of developing his

133

estate by putting it up for auction in lots. The only
piece which had immediate building potential was the
Bancroft, a close of 2 acres lying between High Street
and the canal. This was bought for £1,303 and straight
away began to be developed with good quality housing.
The potential value of the land to the south of the canal
decreased in proportion to its distance from the village
and this was reflected in the prices realised: James Crump
of Coventry gave £847 for 4 acres and Edward Treadgold,
a local builder, gave £488 for 2 acres; Matthew Wise
bought 42 acres of the most distant land for £4,561 17s.
In the short term this was not a good buy, for ten years
later it was valued at only £3,650, including buildings
and timber. The remaining Robbins land was bought by
Thomas Read, who had already begun to develop his own
estate in association with John Webb, a Birmingham builder.
They solved the problem of the awkward boundaries by laying
a single street, Clemens Street, as far as the canal,
pushing beyond that point in the second phase of expansion.
The Reads did not dispose of their freehold interest,
probably because they could not, or would not, redeem
mortgages of £2,000 and £1,500, which they had already
charged upon the estate as a whole. Instead they granted
99 year building leases. The choicest site, 909 sq yd
on the corner of High Street was leased in 1809 for a
ground rent of £8 19s 2d. Two years later the adjoining
site of 621 sq yd commanded a ground rent of £33 13s.
What premiums, if any, were charged for the leases is not
known.

Bertie Greathead left the development of his estate
entirely in the hands of the Warwick banker, John Tomes,
and Richard Sanders, a timber merchant turned architect.
Their chief consideration appears to have been to obtain
the maximum immediate return and they disposed of the
freehold interest, probably with only rudimentary building
covenants, if any. Until 1814, land was sold at a standard
price of 5s per square yard, except for some 3 acres sold
to Tomes and Sanders at a rate of 1s 5d per square yard,
clearly in consideration of services, and a piece of low-
lying land sold to the pump-room company at 2s per square
yard. In the summer of 1814 land in lower Frost Street
(later Bedford Street) sold at 4s and 3s 3d and, although
this may merely reflect the fact that all the best sites
had now been sold, the price of land in this street subsequently fell to 2s 9d. During the periods of slump and

recovery, prices in other streets averaged between 3s 5d and 4s per square yard, but by 1822 at latest had increased to 5s. They did not fall again below this figure, except for a large block of about 18 acres north of Warwick Street, which was sold in 1824 to Richard Tomes for £11,000. Between 1808 and 1826, the time taken to dispose of the entire Greathead estate, sales produced a gross income of £37,827 0s 10d. (25) Against this sum must be set a total of £2,013 13s 3d laid out in development costs and a final payment of £1,000 to John Tomes, probably for services rendered. Greathead therefore received a net price of almost £500 an acre, contrasted with the £26 an acre paid for the Lyndon estate in 1789 and the £42 an acre for the Lawrence estate in 1800.

Except for the layout of the streets there is, as already mentioned, no evidence of any plan for the coherent development of the Greathead estate. Absence, or at least abandonment, of an overall design may well account for the social deterioration of the new town in the second period of expansion after 1818. The situation was different on the Willes estate where, in contrast to Bertie Greathead, the owners exercised a degree of personal supervision over the development. The Willes family employed pro-fessional architects to produce designs, beginning with local men and, as their ambitions grew, moving on to men of greater eminence and ability. That these designs largely came to nothing was the result of adverse economic circumstances.

It was about the time that the second period of expansion was beginning, that Edward Willes sr decided to develop the 23 acre Quarry Fields lying immediately to the west of Greathead's land. In November 1817 he commissioned Henry Hakewill of Warwick to draw up a design for the area. (26) Willes was offered a plan for detached villas ranged around four sides of a square, each in its own plot of just over 900 sq yd. The central square, presumably intended as a pleasure ground, measured 350 yd x 480 yd and was bisected by a road 65ft wide joining up with Cross Street at its eastern end. Besides being totally unimaginative, the plan was extremely prodigal of land since it accommodated only about forty-five villas. An alternative plan was prepared by Samuel Beazley of Carlton Chambers, St James's, London, the architect of the new assembly rooms in Bath Street. (27) This was almost as extravagant of land as the earlier design,

allowing for seventy-three detached villas ranged in three
concentric circles separated by very wide avenues. Neither
of these plans was adopted and in 1821 T.C. Bannister
produced a more conventional design, (28) the main feature
of which was a modest central square, measuring 72yd x 66yd,
probably intended to contain a church. About the same date,
or slightly later, Bannister drew up an alternative plan
showing the area divided into a simple grid pattern of
streets with a church just outside Quarry Fields on the
opposite side of the bridleway coming from Milverton parish.
(29) This, more or less, was the plan finally adopted.

Edward Willes died in December 1820 and was succeeded
by a son of the same name, who played a major part in
launching the town upon its third period of growth. The
younger Willes appreciated the need for co-operating with
Greathead's agents, who still held 18 acres or so at the
top of the Parade. Co-operation took the form not only
of integrating their street plans but also of improving
access to this part of the town from Warwick via Milverton
parish and of providing a church, both measures being
intended to encourage the middle class to settle here.
Willes donated the land and some of the materials for the
new chapel, which opened in 1825, but most of the cost was
borne by the vicar of Leamington, who became proprietor
of the building. Like Greathead, Willes decided to dispose
of the freehold interest and in 1821 sold a site of just
over one acre behind the Regent Hotel for the record price
of £3,000. His main sales drive began in 1824 when most
of Quarry Fields was quickly taken up by four local
speculators, each buying large blocks of several acres.
The price, 3s 4d per square yard, works out at about £800
an acre if no allowance is made for land going into streets.
While selling Quarry Fields, Willes was planning the
development of a further 100 acres or so along the north
side of the new town. This was intended to be a prestige
development and to supervise it Willes engaged the services
of Peter Frederick Robinson, a former pupil of Henry
Holland. In May 1823 Robinson submitted a design in which
the central feature was a large circus approached by an
extension of Union Parade through the Greathead land. (30)
The first sales promotion was probably based on this plan,
for one piece of land was sold and Robinson designed and
built for Willes a Gothick cottage, Binswood Cottage, (31)
possibly intended as a sample or speculation. Then, however, the entire ground plan was altered to a more formal

grid of wide avenues with mews streets behind (32); the
circus was replaced by Beauchamp Square, said to be based
on Grosvenor Square, London, while a little to the west
lay the somewhat smaller Clarendon Square. Besides laying
out the estate Robinson drew terraced façades for all the
buildings, (33) which purchasers were required to accept
under covenant. Before the end of 1825 Willes had disposed
of most of the land in the Beauchamp Square estate at a
price of 6s per square yard, about £1,450 an acre. The
land which remained, together with that remaining in
Quarry Fields, was sold in 1828 at lower prices. The
buyers were probably selected carefully to avoid upsetting
the market. In all, slightly less than 50 acres of building
land were sold in Quarry Fields and around Beauchamp Square
for £50,975. The inclusion of land going into streets and
squares reduces the overall return to rather more than
£400 per acre.

Encouraged by success Willes planned to develop all his
land on the east side of the town, a total of 369 acres
north and south of the river. Since this meant abandoning
their own mansion and park, the family retired to Berkshire.
In October 1826 Robinson drew a series of plans for the
development of the entire estate, the emphasis being on
terraced housing, although each plan incorporated a number
of villas in large gardens. (34) Robinson submitted a
number of alternative designs, but each of them shows
very clearly his limitations as an urban planner, for he
seems to have been incapable of breaking away from the
concept of the grid. In 1827 Willes commissioned John
Nash and James Morgan to make a design and it was on the
basis of their work that he laid out the estate. (35)
The plan, with its sweeping curves and large areas of
parkland, shows unmistakeable traces of Nash's work in
Regent's Park, London. By the middle of 1827 the principal
roads in the estate had been staked out and a new bridge
across the river was being built by the firm of Sowter
& Dale of London. Thereafter, however, the project hung
fire. The explanation is not difficult to find; so much
money had already been invested in land and the capacity
of the building industry was so deeply committed that
there can have been very little to spare for a project
as ambitious as that which Willes was now trying to launch.
By the 1830s it was apparent that the estate could not be
exploited as a whole and Willes must have consented to
its piecemeal development. He appointed as his resident

agent John George Jackson, a pupil of Robinson, who obtained commissions for his own work in various parts of the estate. Large plots were acquired by builders and speculators, who were allowed to develop them more or less as they pleased. Although there was no standard price the usual rate was about 3s per square yard, half that charged in Beauchamp Square, where, incidentally, most of the speculators were still holding on to their purchases. In the north-east of the estate a few streets of artisan houses were built, but most of the development consisted of low density, middle-class housing - the villas for which Leamington is famous. Only a comparatively small amount of land had been sold by 1837 and with the financial crisis of that year sales dried up. Within a few years, however, the bolder investors were beginning to look for bargains and between 1841 and 1844 Edward Greaves, a Warwick builder, laid out £3,183 on various sites totalling nearly 13 acres. In order to encourage middle-class residents Willes promoted the building of a church and donated the site for the episcopal chapel of St Mary, which opened in 1839. Within a few months of being appointed, the incumbent sought to divide the parish and quickly won over the bishop to his side. The parish authorities protested strongly that the new church had been built in the midst of open fields and did not serve an existing congregation, nor could it do so until that area was developed. Despite the opposition the parish was divided in 1840. The population of the new parish numbered about 2,500, few of whom lived near the church, and even this figure could be achieved only by careful manipulation of boundaries.

Willes' decision to give up the idea of developing his estate along the lines indicated by Nash and instead to sell the land off cheaply was probably influenced by the threat of imminent competition from the Wise family. Despite the fact that they owned many gardens, closes and orchards in the village and hard-by, the Wises had released little land for building during the first and second periods of expansion. By the mid-1820s these were ripe for development and it would have been foolish not to capitalise them. The sites were disposed of on building leases, at ground rents ranging from 4d to 2s per square yard. It is unlikely that premiums were charged, but the rents provided a good income and building covenants established a large reversionary value. Shortly afterwards Matthew Wise began to build a new mansion in the south of

the parish and by the early 1830s he was ready to abandon
his old house and gardens. These were included in a
planned development covering about 99 acres immediately
west of the old village. At the same time Wise began to
sell land to the south east of the village. In 1834 a
firm of local builders, James Hill & William Peace,
contracted to buy the old Wise mansion and 45 acres of
land for £23,000. Edward Clarke, another builder, gave
them £8,000 for about 25 acres. Hill and Peace accepted
covenants binding them to build residences costing at
least £800 if villas, or £1,000 if built in terraces. By
the time of their bankruptcy in 1838 they had built Eastnor
Terrace, a row of thirteen fine houses soon to be demolished
to make way for the railway. Clarke became bankrupt about
the same time and, apart from Eastnor Terrace, a mere handful of houses had been built. Only in the late 1850s did
building recommence in this area, perhaps encouraged by the
proximity of the railway station.

Wise was the only landowner willing to leave part of the
purchase price on mortgage of the property. In the case
of Hill and Peace it was agreed in 1833 that they should
pay £5,000 cash within twelve months and keep the remaining
£18,000 on mortgage. Interest was to be 3 per cent for
the first 3 years, 4 per cent for the next 3 years and
5 per cent thereafter. Subsequently it was agreed that
£6,000 should be paid off after 10 acres had been built
over and sold, and another £6,000 after a further 10 acres
had been sold. The £5,000 cash was raised from a third
party by means of a mortgage. In January 1837 the land
was further pledged to the Leamington Bank for £15,000
owed by Hill and Peace. By now it was mortgaged for far
more than its value.

After 1837 no more grand designs were set on foot by
the pre-urban landowners. They continued to sell land
whenever the opportunity arose, but they were now in
direct competition with speculators who had acquired
large stocks of this commodity. The majority of those
who had bought land directly from the landowners may be
classed as speculators, although they can be separated
according to the nature of their speculation. Some were
builders, for whom buying of land was but the first stage
of a speculation in house construction. Among these
some bought only sufficient to engage their limited
resources, venturing upon no more than two or three houses
at a time. A few bought much larger amounts in anticipation
of future needs, although they were willing to resell at

139

a profit or if they needed to raise cash. Except in the case of the sales made by the Wise family the acquisitions of builders were out-weighed by those of the non-builders. The latter can also be separated into two groups. The small purchasers usually bought sites for between one and four houses, presumably with the intention of commissioning houses, in a few cases for their own occupation, but mostly for letting. The other group was composed of those buying large amounts of land in anticipation of a future increase in value. They hoped to make a profit by reselling as growing demand forced up the price. Speculation of this nature was a very risky business as long as large reserves of land remained in the hands of the landowners, for while this situation lasted it was the latter who regulated the price. This is demonstrated very clearly by the sales made by Willes in the 1820s, which attracted all types of speculator. All the Quarry Fields land went to local speculators. Stephen Peasnale, a Leamington glazier in partnership with Theophilus Taylor, a Warwick builder, paid £3,022 for 26,686sq yd. Benjamin Smart paid £2,825 for 16,955sq yd. Smart was a Quaker; his father had held Rock Mills, Milverton, since at least the 1770s and had converted them to cotton spinning in the 1790s. He had already invested heavily in the old town of Leamington, where he had opened the Imperial Fount Baths in 1818. In the 1820s he gave up the mills, although whether as cause or consequence of his further speculation in Leamington is not known. The third buyer was Daniel Winter Burbury, solicitor, a member of an old-established Warwick family. In 1825 he paid £1,420 for 8,523sq yd and in 1828 gave £1,600 for 14,884sq yd which, almost certainly, was the whole of the land which had remained unsold in Quarry Fields. Burbury played a prominent part in the affairs of the Leamington Bank when it came to be founded. This land was sold subject to covenants which enforced the making of sewers and forbade premises to be used for offensive trades, but beyond this little effort was made to regulate building. This, and the fact that the price was sufficiently low to enable the speculators to resell at a profit, resulted in early development. Virtually the whole area was covered with middle-class houses of varying degrees of opulence, but built to a typical urban or suburban density. Two exceptions are worthy of mention, because of the contrast they make both with one another and with the other houses. The whole of the site between Grove

Street and Dale Street, 10,911sq yd originally acquired
by Benjamin Smart and D.W. Burbury, came into the possession
of Henry Jephson, the most prominent physician in the town.
On this site he built his own residence, Beech Lawn, which
became something of a legend in Leamington. Less than a
hundred yards west of Beech Lawn, on the land acquired
cheaply by Burbury, grew up Brook Street, one of the most
notorious slums in the town. Here several hundred people
were packed into an area considerably smaller than
Jephson's 2 acre garden.

This timely development of Quarry Fields meant that the
first speculators were able to realise a profit upon their
investment before the collapse of the market. The situation
was very different on the neighbouring Beauchamp Square
estate, where most of the speculators suffered heavy losses
as a direct consequence of sluggish demand. Robinson had
planned for at least 300 first-class residences, but by
1829 there were only five houses on the estate. The delay
is probably to be explained by the presence of cheaper
land just to the south, the high cost of building in accord
with the covenants and the likelihood that there were a
very limited number of firms capable of working to that
standard. In 1829 the firm of William Buddle & Son began
to build in the vicinity of Clarendon Square. Other builders
started to follow suit, perhaps encouraged by the easing
of the covenants over some of the land. Whatever hopes
this may have raised in the hearts of the speculators,
they were dashed a year or two later when a glut of cheap
land came on to the market in other parts of the town.
Unless they were willing to sell at cost price, or even
at a loss, most were unable to dispose of their holdings.
Building was reduced to a mere trickle, which dried up
even further after 1837. The number of first-class houses
on the estate increased from 72 in 1837 to 108 in 1851,
although by the latter date there were also a score of
working-class cottages here. The biggest disaster in the
estate was Beauchamp Square itself, which had been designed
to have terraces of fifteen houses around three sides.
No houses were ever built on the western side, but three
were built in the north terrace by Robinson himself and
two in the east terrace by Burbury and Morris.

The most prominent local speculator in the Beauchamp
Square estate was again D.W. Burbury, who invested heavily
in his own right and in partnership with John Morris,
a Warwick builder. Morris also bought 4 sites for himself,

while other local builders bought a total of 10. No more
than a dozen or so sites went to other local people,
including five to Henry Baly, a Warwick druggist. Birmingham was represented by J.W. Phipson, who bought 31 sites
for £4,249; W. Phipson, with 41 sites for £5,704 and a
further 18 sites for £1,800 after the price was reduced;
and J.V. Barber, with 38 sites for £5,274 and later 20
sites for £410. The remaining speculators were mostly
Londoners, probably introduced by P.F. Robinson.
Robinson himself gave £3,645 for 26 sites, but failed to
complete arrangements to buy more when the price was
reduced. The chief London investors were Isaac and
William Darby, builders, who gave £2,923 for 21 sites,
and the Thesiger family. Charles Thesiger, former chief
customs collector of Jamaica, gave £4,253 for 32 sites;
his barrister son, Frederick, £1,392 for 10 sites; and
Miss Caroline Thesiger £278 for 2 sites. John George
Jackson bought a site for one house, while the remaining
Londoners, many of whom failed to complete their contracts,
were gentlemen and tradesmen.

On the basis of existing evidence only one speculator
seems to have escaped unscathed from the Beauchamp Square
adventure. This was J.V. Barber, who was encouraged to
make a further large investment in the land sold by Willes
during the 1830s. One example must suffice to illustrate
the losses made by the others, and by some of those who
speculated at one remove. D.W. Burbury and John Morris
in partnership paid £2,096 for 6,989sq yd which made up
all the fifteen sites on the eastern side of Beauchamp
Square. At the south end they erected two houses, which
they furnished and let. On these they raised a mortgage
of £2,000 at 5 per cent. Burbury died in 1840 but, because
of the complexity of his will, the heirs continued in
partnership with Morris until 1846, when the partnership
was dissolved by order in chancery. Despite the fact
that since Burbury's death Morris had been receiving the
rents of the houses to service the mortgage and repairs,
the property was charged with £1,000 arrears of interest,
as well as the principal sum of the mortgage. After
building the two houses Burbury and Morris had managed to
sell very little land, clearly because they were unwilling
to lower their price. In the early 1830s one J.H. Craber
contracted to pay them £5,523 10s for 5,814sq yd. This
deal was never completed, but in July 1833 Burbury and
Morris conveyed 638sq yd for £606 2s to John Prosser, in

completion of an arrangement made between Craber and Prosser.
In December 1834 Prosser sold the plot to Edward Clarke,
builder, for the price at which he had bought it. Clarke
became bankrupt in 1837 and in his assignment the site
was valued at only £150. It remained in assignment until
it was sold for £150 in 1854. It changed hands in 1862
for £250, and only then was a house built on it. The
only other site which Burbury and Morris managed to dispose
of was 522sq yd sold to the Buddles for £495 18s in 1836.
After the latter's bankruptcy in 1839 the site went to
John Lampray who had granted them a mortgage on it. When
Lampray himself became bankrupt in 1845 it was sold for a
mere £150.

The collapse of land prices in the early 1830s makes it
impossible to determine whether, in the normal course of
events, the speculator in land fulfilled a useful economic
function or whether he was merely an intruder causing an
unnecessary increase in price. The former possibility
cannot be ruled out, for one of the leading firms of
builders, William Buddle & Son, apparently chose to acquire
their sites exclusively through the speculators. This
firm, the only one whose activities can be reconstructed
tolerably well, specialised in opulent middle-class
housing and thus provides a useful case history.

In 1829 the Buddles made an agreement to buy from J.V.
Barber a large piece of land on the west side of Clarendon
Square. In 1825 Barber had given £1,809 12s for this land,
designed for 13 houses, and alleged to measure 6,032sq yd
at 6s per square yard, although it actually contained
7,830 sq yd. The Buddles agreed to lease the land for 99
years at a ground rent of £382, with an option to acquire
the freehold at the end of 3 or 7 years for £3,650; the
price was reckoned to be 9s $3\frac{3}{4}$d per square yard plus $2\frac{3}{4}$d
in every £10. In the event they bought the freeholds in
5 parcels before the end of 3 years. On this land they
built 11 houses as a speculation, 6 of which they sold.
While building in Clarendon Square the Buddles were
negotiating with the Thesigers for the adjacent sites, on
which they built Clarendon Crescent. In 1830 they paid
Charles Thesiger £1,406 for 3,397sq yd which he had bought
for £724 in 1825 and later years, the present price being
8s and 9s per square yard, although they were allowed two
years to pay, free of interest. By July 1831 Frederick
Thesiger was willing to sell 4,640sq yd at 6s, the price
he had paid six years before. On this land the Buddles

143

prepared sites for 10 houses and sold the leases for £300 each and annual ground rents at £5. They then built the houses by contract with each purchaser. After speculating in a few more houses on adjacent sites the Buddles removed the centre of their operations to Binswood Avenue, in the same estate. Here they built between 15 and 20 houses, all on land acquired from J.V. Barber. In 1837 they still owned at least 8 of these houses.

The Buddles also had dealings with Barber outside the Beauchamp Square estate, buying some of the land which he acquired in the area laid out by Nash and Morgan. On this they built four houses at the south-east end of Lansdowne Crescent and, just opposite, Victoria House and Lansdowne House, two enormous piles, the one classical and the other Gothic. They also bought Robbins Baths and the adjoining properties of Woburn House and Bedford House in Bath Street, all of which they pulled down in the mid-1830s. After selling some of the land to the improvement commission for street widening they built Victoria Terrace, a development much praised by Granville when he visited the town.

In 1837 William Buddle & Son owned at least 22 houses and various other properties with a total rateable value in excess of £1,400. (36) Many of these houses were held by tenants on leases of 3 and 7 years. This case was far from unique, for all the builders in the town owned houses and the leading builders owned more houses than any other speculators. John Toone, for example, owned at least 11 houses with a total rateable value of £934, as well as Toone's Buildings, a block of 44 tenements rated at £6 10s each. James Hill owned properties rated at £1,300 and William Peace owned properties rated at £1,900, including at least 11 of the 18 houses in Lansdowne Circus, all of which he had undoubtedly built. Ownership of these properties did nothing to stave off bankruptcy, for all were mortgaged nearly to the hilt. It was easy enough for builders to obtain mortgages, but after paying interest of 5 per cent there was not a great deal left for repairs, management costs and landlord's profits. For example, in 1834 the Buddles valued their 5 houses in Clarendon Square at £10,700. The total rents amounted to £605, but interest accounted for £535, leaving an average of only £14 per house for all other charges and profit. It is true, however, that in the case of unfurnished tenancies the occupier was usually required to keep the interior in good repair and decoration.

144

13. Sheffield: Endcliffe Hall, the home of Sir John Brown, completed in 1863 (*J. N. Tarn*)

14. Sheffield: a villa in the Gothic style, Broom Hall estate, built after the middle of the nineteenth century (*J. N. Tarn*)

15. Sheffield: Oakholm, a neo-classical house of the period before 1851 (*J. N. Tarn*)

16. Sheffield: Broomhall Place, built about 1830 (*J. N. Tarn*)

In view of the apparently small net profit which a builder made by renting a mortgaged property, it might be suggested that he would resort to this course of action only if he were unable to sell a house built as a speculation. This proposal is contradicted by the fact that the Buddles arranged to lease houses for a period of years, even before they were completed. The explanation seems to be that a mortgage for the full market value, or something near it, was as useful to a builder as an actual sale, since it allowed him to realise the profit on his building operations, which was his major concern. As long as the rent paid the interest on the mortgage and left a little over as a fund for insurance, future repairs and the like, the builder was probably quite satisfied. He may also, of course, have been anticipating a future increase in value.

There is, unfortunately, no means of ascertaining what proportion of houses were put up as a building speculation, either in the hope of a sale or in the certainty that they would have to be mortgaged by the builder, and what proportion were built under contract from a customer. Many contractors were themselves speculators, since building houses for renting to visitors was regarded as a good investment. In the 1850s rented property was expected to yield 6½-7 per cent on capital and there was probably a similar expectation in the 1830s when both property values and rents had been at a higher level. Although it is impossible to obtain any precise information about building costs there are a few pointers to the general level of prices. Building covenants suggest that in the first half of the century a good house was expected to cost at least £800-£1,000, although many undoubtedly cost two, three or more times as much as this. After mid-century the general level of expectancy was probably lower. Covenants attached to land sold by the executors of J.V. Barber in 1857 stipulated minimum building costs of £400, £500 and £700 per house. The nearest villa on adjacent land, built in the 1830s, had been offered for sale in 1855 for £950. These figures are put into perspective by the prospect held out to artisans in 1848 by the building society that, over a period of ten years, they might become the owner of a house valued at £60. During the 1840s there was undoubtedly a real fall in house values, although no prices can be quoted for the sale of the same house over a number of years.

During the first half of the nineteenth century the owner-occupier was a rarity, except in the case of persons who

had a vested interest in the town. As late as 1834 it was
regarded as a great advance when visitors began to rent
unfurnished houses. The Warwick Advertiser (37) commented
'Many furnished houses have been taken, and it is within
our own knowledge that several highly respectable persons
have engaged large and moderate-sized unfurnished houses.
The latter is a presage of the prosperity of Leamington -
for although the inhabitants are ever forward in their
exertions to please visitors, they are, of course, anxious
to secure a large, respectable, and wealthy resident
population'. Granville in 1840 observed that despite
the many empty houses the rent of a whole furnished house
was 'very dear'. A considerable saving might be effected,
however, by taking unfurnished property. In July 1832
a Captain Somerville took a 3 year lease of a furnished
house from the Buddles at £245 a year, with liberty to
sub-let whenever he wished. Before the lease expired
he renewed it on an unfurnished basis at £110 a year.
Furniture was easily acquired, for there were frequent
auction sales of new and second-hand pieces. Furnished
accommodation remained plentiful for those who intended
to stay for only a few weeks or months. Prices may,
however, have fallen. In 1851 an advertiser asked for
a well-furnished house in the best part of the town for
a period of four to six months. It was required to have
six good bedrooms and three good reception rooms, but he
was not prepared to pay more than £120 a year.
    It may be asked why visitors who intended to stay in the
town for several seasons, or as permanent residents, did
not further reduce their costs by buying a house rather
than renting unfurnished property. The answer appears
to be that in the first half of the century house buying
in Leamington was essentially a matter of speculation.
It was not regarded, as in the present inflationary age,
as a form of personal saving. Most of the leisured people
who came to live in Leamington were persons of independent
means, whose assets were securely invested in stocks which
paid dividends wherever the recipients chose to live.
Their income enabled them to pay rents which began at about
£40 for modest houses and ranged from £80 to £160 for the
best. They would not have made any substantial saving by
withdrawing their capital to buy a house, which was initially
expensive and which also saddled them with the bother of
management or selling if they decided to leave the town.
Moreover the capital of many of the newcomers was tied up

146

in annuities and other non-negotiable stocks and was
therefore not available for house buying.

It remains to be asked who were these newcomers to
Leamington and what sort of accommodation could they
command? These questions are best answered by looking
closely at two locations and examining the houses against
the background of the 1851 census. The first area to be
considered is Clarendon Square, on the Beauchamp Square
estate. This was one of the most fashionable parts of
the town. With the exception of three or four smaller
houses on the south side of the square prices in the
early 1830s ranged from about £1,500 to £3,000 or more.
The second area is Portland Street in the Quarry Fields
estate, a distinctly less fashionable address. The most
expensive houses in this street probably commanded at
least £1,500 in the early 1830s.

There were 43 houses around Clarendon Square, one of
which was occupied by Leamington College as a boarding
house for pupils. None of the remaining houses were
unoccupied, but in two instances the family was absent
on census night, leaving servants in charge. Among the
40 families in residence 16 were headed by spinsters or
widows, 14 of whom recorded their occupation as annuitant,
fundholder, landowner or railway shareholder. One entered
no occupation, while the last gave 'daughter of an Earl'.
Among the 24 male householders 4 were absent, while the
occupations of the remainder were army or navy 4, church
4, funds 5, land 4, magistrate 1, retired merchant 1 and
the familiar figure of James Hill, builder employing 4 men.
The average size of the families in residence was only 3.2,
but the households were swollen by the addition of resident
servants. Most families had a least 1 male servant, the
average being 1.1 per household, and all had female servants,
average 3.4. No doubt most families also enjoyed the
services of non-resident grooms, gardeners, daily women and
the like. On census night the population of the square was
completed by the presence of 5 governesses, 1 male
companion, 10 visitors and the wife and 2 children of a
coachman.

The average size of each household in Clarendon Square
was small in proportion to the accommodation provided,
for most of the houses were very large. The east side
of the square was made up of a terrace of 14 houses,
begun at the south end before 1829 and completed in 1838
or 1839. Only the first house has a façade which was

147

built more or less to the original design of P.F. Robinson.
The later houses, although still classical in style, were
distinctly inferior, both in design and execution. No 42
was occupied by the largest household in the square. The
master of the house was absent, but present were his wife,
Lady Louisa Ramsay, their 5 daughters, aged 9 months to
6 years, 9 female general servants and 3 male general
servants. The accommodation consisted of a basement
containing cellars, larder, kitchen, scullery, housekeeper's
room, and servants' hall; ground floor - hall, dining-room
28ft x 18ft, breakfast-room 19ft x 18ft, butler's pantry,
water-closet; first floor - front and rear drawing-rooms
29ft x 19ft and 28ft x 18ft, connected by folding doors;
second floor - two principal bedrooms with dressing-rooms,
closet and water-closet; third floor - 4 bedrooms and
closet; 4 attic rooms. In 1839 this house had commanded
a rent of £160. No 35 in this same terrace, almost
identical in size and layout, was occupied by a widow with
2 grown-up daughters, who were served by a housekeeper,
cook, lady's maid, housemaid, kitchenmaid and 2 footmen.
The house, together with stabling for 7 horses and double
coach house with servants' quarters above, all of which
were lacking in No 42, was sold in 1851 for £1,750. The
current rent was £120, although a previous tenant, Edward
Bolton King, one-time Member of Parliament for Warwick,
had paid £150.

This pattern of living was duplicated in terraced housing
in various parts of the town. No 32 Lansdowne Place was
identical in the number, lay out and dimensions of rooms
to 42 Clarendon Square. No 20 York Terrace, at one time
the property of Sir Edward Mostyn, was similar, but on a
larger scale. In the basement were 2 large kitchens,
servants' hall, waiting-room, housekeeper's room, larder,
beer, wine and coal cellars. On the ground floor was an
entrance hall 50ft long with a double stone staircase,
dining-room 33ft x 20ft, morning-room 27ft x 19ft and a
large pantry. On the first floor were two drawing-rooms
33ft x 31ft and 22ft x 20ft connected by folding doors.
Above were 6 large best bedrooms with 3 dressing-rooms,
bedrooms for the lady's maid and housekeeper and 6
chambers for servants. Outside there was stabling for
16 horses, coach houses and chambers for grooms.

Although Portland Street can only be described as
middle-class it belonged to a lower stratum than Clarendon
Square. It was, moreover, even more dominated by women.

Out of 31 households no fewer than 20 were headed by
spinsters or widows. Six of these described themselves
as lodging-house keepers, 3 gave no occupation, while the
remainder said that they were annuitants or had some other
form of independent income. However, it is beyond dispute
that many of the latter supplemented their income by taking
in lodgers. They might well be described as gentlefolk
in reduced circumstances. Their lodgers were visitors to
the town, people of much the same social rank as their
hosts, people who travelled not with a retinue of servants,
but at most a lady's maid. The occupations recorded for
male householders were coal merchant, general practitioner,
upholsterer, baker, retired surveyor of taxes, retired
dealer in fancy goods, gardener, magistrate, dentist and
house proprietor; in one case the occupation was not
entered. Many of the female householders lived alone,
except for servants, and because of this the average size
of family was only slightly in excess of 2 persons. But
servants were also far fewer than in Clarendon Square.
Only 4 households had a male servant, and while only the
gardener had no servants at all, 19 households had only
1 female servant, the remainder having 2 or 3. The fact
that the census was held early in the season, on the night
of 30-31 March may help to explain the comparatively small
total of lodgers and visitors, 36 in all.

The largest houses in Portland Street were four detached
villas built in the early 1830s. One of these, Portland
Villa, was bought, probably in an unfinished state, by
William Buddle & Son for £1,300. When completed it consisted
of a basement with the usual offices, dining-room, double
drawing-room with folding doors, butler's pantry and water-
closet on the ground floor, 3 bedrooms and 3 attics. In
the 1830s it was rented by J.M. Cottle, surgeon, for £80.
The occupant in 1851 was a bachelor, Charles Milward,
magistrate, who lived alone with 1 male and 1 female servant.
Next to these villas was a pair of semi-detached houses,
one of which was taken about 1839 by George Brown, dentist,
for £35 a year. It contained a basement with kitchen and
usual offices; dining-room and breakfast room, connecting
by folding doors, on the ground floor; drawing-room and
bedroom on the first floor; 2 bedrooms, dressing-room and
water-closet on the second floor and single attic above.
Brown still lived here in 1851 with his wife, unmarried
daughter and 1 female servant. The rest of the houses
on the west side of Portland Street were in a single terrace,

149

although not on as grand a scale as those in Clarendon
Square. No 69 was probably typical. It contained a
basement with 3 cellars, 2 kitchens, larder, and housekeeper's room; drawing-room, dining-room, breakfast-room,
2 sitting-rooms on the ground floor and first floor; and
9 bedrooms and dressing-rooms above. The inhabitants
in 1851 were Elizabeth Kinsey, lodging-house keeper, her
sister, 1 female servant and 5 visitors, including a
maidservant. Mrs Kinsey, paying a rent of £55, was still
the tenant when the house was put up for sale by auction
in 1855.

When villa building became the vogue during the 1830s,
a few speculators were tempted to run up accommodation
far more extravagant than anything so far described. The
Buddles erected Victoria House, still standing as solid
and four-square as a Norman keep, but with the addition
of a classical portico. In the 1839 auction it was
described as having 36 good bedrooms, but many of these
were secondary bedrooms and servants' rooms. The reception
rooms were larger and more numerous than usual, but the
only extra accommodation was a library. More exotic was
Furze House in Holly Walk. Besides having exceptionally
large reception rooms and a library it had a music saloon,
a picture gallery with a glass lantern in a leaded dome
and a bathroom with a marble bath. At an auction in 1851
this house failed to attract a buyer, but its 2 acre garden
was divided into lots and sold off for building. Most
villas, however, provided accommodation which was comparable
in scale with that of the first-class terrace residences
already described. The layout was much the same, although
there may have been a tendency to save the cost of making
a basement by putting the domestic quarters at ground level.

The basic accommodation of a middle-class home in
Leamington in the nineteenth century consisted of dining-
room, breakfast- and one or two drawing-rooms. If there
were two drawing-rooms they could almost always be made
into one by opening folding doors. Presumably this was
intended for large gatherings. Two or three principal
bedrooms were essential, but only the best houses had
dressing-rooms attached to them. The number of secondary
bedrooms, servants' rooms and domestic offices varied
according to the size of the establishment, but on the
whole the accommodation seems to have been very generous.

Most of the amenities which made life comfortable, except
for electricity, had been introduced by the middle of the

century. Lighting by gas was universal, since a company
for the manufacture and sale of gas had been established
as early as 1818, one of the first in the provinces.
Cooking by gas had not yet been perfected, but, when it
was, Leamington was probably one of the first towns to
benefit, since it was the home of Flavels, one of the
leading pioneers in this field. The firm had already
patented a coal-fired cooking range which won great
acclaim. At least one property, 24 Lansdowne Place, let
for £150 in 1851, had a central-heating system operating
with hot water. The water-closet was already universal,
most of the better houses having at least two. Bathrooms
were mentioned comparatively infrequently, but were
clearly becoming established by the 1850s, some of them
having showers as well as bathtubs.

Although this study has deliberately concentrated on
the economic aspects of house building in Leamington it
would be unfair to conclude without saying something,
however briefly, about the aesthetics of the subject.
Unfortunately, although it is possible to draw up a
tolerably complete list of architects who practised in
Leamington in the first half of the nineteenth century,
very few houses can be attributed with any degree of
certainty to particular individuals. Moreover the architects
themselves are very shadowy figures.

In the first phase of the development of the new town
most of the houses were built under the supervision of
Richard Sanders, the Warwick timber merchant turned
architect, who was himself a prominent speculator. His
work induced nothing but scorn in Mary Berry, a guest of
Greathead in 1810, who recorded that 'the houses now
building are in rows, like any street in London, and are
in the very worst possible taste'. (38) Miss Berry's
opinion of Sanders' work may have been shared by his fellow
speculators for, when they built the Royal Pump Room, the
architect, C.S. Smith of London, was appointed by public
competition. Clearly, however, Sanders cannot shoulder
sole responsibility for the mediocrity of the architecture
of Leamington in the first and second periods of the town's
expansion. The fault lies in the fact that there was no
development sufficiently large or integrated to justify
the commissioning of any of the best architects of the day.

This fault was corrected only when Edward Willes brought
in P.F. Robinson to plan the development of his estate.
This step undoubtedly gave a tremendous fillip to the

architecture of Leamington, although it would probably
be a mistake to attribute all of the fine buildings of the
late 1820s and early 1830s to Robinson himself. Robinson
evidently saw the grand terrace as being best suited to
the needs of Leamington, and Waterloo Place and York
Terrace are very much in his vein, although whether they
actually came from his drawing-board cannot be established.
Unfortunately his grandest plan, that for Beauchamp Square,
did not come to fruition. The three houses which he built
on the north side of the square have long since been
demolished, but the two rather less palatial houses which
still remain on the east side show what might have been
achieved.

Leamington has very few terraces which can vie with
those of London and of other spa towns. This is to be
explained by a combination of the late date at which
developers began to concern themselves with architectural
detail and the switch, a few years later, to villa building.
The economic circumstances which influenced the latter
development have already been discussed in detail. In
place of the elegance imparted by the uniformity of the
grand urban terrace Leamington acquired variety. From
their earliest days the villas, in their wide, tree-lined
streets, were built in a wide variety of sizes, shapes
and styles. Who is to say that the town was any poorer
for that?

Chapter 5

The Park Estate, Nottingham
K. C. Edwards

In the years preceding the Victorian era and continuously
through the forties and fifties of the last century, the
effects of the Industrial Revolution, including the widespread use of coal for steam power, the growth of the
factory system in industry and the developments in transport,
focussed attention on the towns, both large and small.
The census of 1851 marked a change in that for the first
time in a population of 16 million, over half (54 per cent)
were urban; and an ever increasing number lived in towns
of 50,000 or more. (1) By 1881 there were fifty towns
which exceeded this figure. As Professor Asa Briggs has
affirmed, the future welfare of the nation lay in the
large cities. (2)
   This great experiment in modern urbanisation affected
society in various ways, not only in economic terms.
In science and technology, in the arts, in religion and
in political thought it gave rise to achievements which
evoked new and often acute problems. Besides these
general manifestations of change there were local conditions
making the towns different in detail from one another,
environmental controls playing a leading part in establishing
their individuality. The large town, according to Briggs's
monumental study, 'was a characteristic Victorian achievement, impressive in scale but limited in vision, creating
new opportunities but also providing massive problems'. (3)
Nottingham like its neighbours, Derby and Leicester, shared
in the changes mentioned above, but for a time it suffered
a major disadvantage for, unlike its neighbours and indeed
most other of our leading cities, though it grew in
population, it was not permitted to expand territorially.
Thus it became a sordidly overcrowded town. Not until
twenty years after the Nottingham Enclosure Act (1845)
was it freed from this grave handicap.

In the pre-industrial phase Nottingham was an outstand-
ingly attractive place, a truly garden city, about which
travellers from home and abroad were consistent in their
chorus of praise. In 1720 its population was about
10,000, living in 2,000 dwellings, covering an area of
some 1,000 acres. This was forty years after William
Cavendish, the first Duke of Newcastle, had built his
mansion (1679) on the site of the castle which lay in
ruins on its sandstone eminence. Beyond, to the west,
the duke planted an extra-parochial area with trees which
became known as the Duke of Newcastle's Park. (4) By
1841 Nottingham's population had risen to 53,000 huddled
together in the identical area, but the building of
hundreds of back-to-backs in the form of courts and alleys,
the squares or courts often closed at both ends and
entered by a narrow tunnel, numbers of dark grim streets,
and even underground dwellings where the local sandstone
was easy to excavate, were among the ways by which the
additional people were accommodated. To take but one
example of the effects of serious overcrowding in an
uncleansed and unscavenged town - the danger to public
health - there were outbreaks of cholera in 1832, 1845,
1853 and 1865. In the first instance there were 1,100
recorded cases of which 289 proved fatal. (5) Soon after
it Thomas Hawkesley was appointed engineer to the newly
founded Trent Bridge Water Works Company; almost immediately he effected improvements to the town's water supply
and in a few years inaugurated a piped supply to 8,000
houses (35,000 inhabitants), to brewhouses, dye-works and
factory steam engines. Hawkesley, who afterwards moved
to London, was perhaps the world's greatest water engineer.
With the extension of water supply came sewage removal
and increased sanitation, and with the slow abandonment
of the widespread slums - though some lasted till the
present century - the lot of the poor in Nottingham
gradually improved as mid-century was passed. (6)
    The chief reason for the transformation from a spacious
to an excessively overcrowded town in a period before
modern civic institutions were given legal basis, was
the unwillingness of the burgesses or freemen to sell or
commute their common lands for purposes of building. Not
once but many times efforts were made to dislodge them,
but their resistance to enclosure and to loss of their
rights and privileges, largely grazing rights, lasted
until 1845. (7) It is generally agreed that this power

of the burgesses was disastrous for the development of the town, for the period of their stranglehold included the years of industrial change, especially the growth of the factory system for which there was so little room in the crowded town. The population inevitably spilled over into surrounding villages such as Arnold, Basford, Beeston, Carlton and Sneinton, which much later became part of the city or city-region. Even so the town was girt by lands owned by aristocratic families who would not part with an acre. In the east the parish of Colwick was owned by the Musters and, to the west, Wollaton was the property of Lord Middleton, descendant of the Willoughby coal-owners. The Duke of Newcastle, who owned the Castle and its grounds, occupied a like position but without the monopolistic control adopted by the others. Leicester and Derby suffered no such disadvantage and were already developing other industries, unlike Nottingham whose fortunes depended on lace and hosiery. At the same time, however, coal mining to the north-west of the town proved indirectly a compensating factor and led to the later enrichment of the entire district. The congestion in Nottingham is well shown by a comparison of the map by Badden and Peat (1744) or that by J.F. Straw (1969 for 1800, through historical research), with Staveley and Wood's plan of Nottingham (1831) indicating the density of building. There were 1,400 acres of unenclosed land around Nottingham and, until the Enclosure Act of 1845, the town was compressed within an area only slightly larger than it had been in medieval times.

As early as the 1820s the Duke of Newcastle considered the development of The Park. A hundred years before, his forbear had rid the area of deer and had taken in cattle for grazing, while at the southern margin the fish ponds were converted to a reservoir for the old water-works company but were later allowed to become silted and nearly dry sometime before 1831. They were converted into cultivable plots known as Fishponds Gardens. On the north-west periphery of the Park a barracks for militia quartered in the town had been built in 1794 and, though it was demolished in 1855, its existence is recalled by Barrack Lane, a thoroughfare leading off Derby Road. (8) In 1828 Lenton Road was constructed, leading from the town to Lenton, and passing north of Fishponds Gardens.

In 1831 the Reform Bill rioters pillaged and burned the Castle. The house was not inhabited by the Newcastle family and was without articles of any great worth, but the fire was so severe that only the walls were left standing. (9) The mansion was never used again as a ducal residence but the fifth duke in 1851 decided to convert his Park, still extra-parochial, as a private estate for the villas of Nottingham's well-to-do citizens. Although it was many years before the scheme was completed, this was an illuminating experiment and, despite its relative isolation owing to conditions of residency, was an example of successful district planning so near to the town centre and many of the factories and warehouses that Nottingham was at last to be envied. The creation of The Park was one of the first steps by which the town began to return to its earlier spaciousness. Moreover, in the absence of aristocracy and local gentry, the social élite was composed mainly of manufacturers in lace and, to a lesser extent, hosiery, with lawyers, doctors and, later, local government officials. The factory owners at least were wealthy and their resources enabled them to form an urban aristocracy, their local connections ensuring a measure of social philanthropy.

In Leicester the early nineteenth-century development of New Walk, a tree-lined residential stretch closed to vehicular traffic, came into being as a result of the enclosure of the South Field. Development here also included the building of high-standard villas along London Road, but the town reserved much of the land for future uses - open spaces, schools, cattle market, fire station and university. (10) Even earlier were the Georgian houses of Friar Gate in Derby, but these were small in number and lined an important thoroughfare. (11) In Nottingham The Park became more fully developed, another area of large villas for the prosperous citizens was founded at Mapperley Park, a suburb well to the north of the town centre. Mapperley Park, lying between the Mansfield Road and Mapperley Road with its continuation along Woodborough Road, was a larger area than The Park. It was partially wooded, was outside the town, and was enclosed by Act of Parliament in 1792. Much of it was allocated to Ichabod Wright, a member of a local banker's family, who established new plantations in parts, but left other areas free for building. Prosperous citizens built themselves villas there at about the same time that many were drawn to The Park. Thus Mapperley Road, Magdala Road (1880), and other new thoroughfares such as

Lucknow Avenue and Drive, Cyprus Drive and Mapperley Hall
Drive were lined with spacious residences. Development
also took place along one side of Forest Road, overlooking
the great recreation ground (the Forest) and the cemetery,
to the west of St Andrew's church. Another extension of
this form of development took place at Alexandra Park,
linking Mapperley with both sides of Woodborough Road, at
the end of the century. Members of the Hine family,
relatives of Thomas C. Hine who did so much for The Park,
owned the land and they opened it out for building on a
speculative basis. This large and fashionable area
supported three churches: St John's (Carrington, 1842),
St Andrew's (1870) and St Jude's (Mapperley, 1877); and
formed part of the northward spread of the city. There
were thus two outside localities in which were concentrated
those inhabitants who formed a notable section of
Nottingham's new urban aristocracy, while others were
distributed in the town.

The Park was an area of 155 acres, in the form of a
broad valley, leading from Derby Road at an altitude of
250ft down to Castle Boulevard (opened in 1884) which was
only 85ft above sea-level. The valley however was not
symmetrical, the slope on the east side adjoining the
castle and curving round to the Ropewalk and Derby Road
being much steeper than the western side. Houses built
high up on this east side have extensive views overlooking
the Vale of Trent and beyond. From Derby Road to Castle
Boulevard is about half a mile and the breadth at the
lower end of the valley rather less. The underlying rock,
as in the case of the Castle and the town, is Bunter sandstone (pebble beds), the physical properties of which make
it an admirable material for building. It is a coarse-
grained rock, highly porous, giving rise to a prevailingly
dry land surface and infrequent streams. Although readily
excavated, it is a highly stable material. (12)

A prominent local architect, Thomas C. Hine, was given
the task of laying out The Park as a residential estate.
He was the brother of Jonathan Hine who, with his partner
A.J. Mundella, were owners of the first hosiery factory
in Nottingham to be steam driven (1851). (13) Except for
the configuration which determined the position of the
roads on the eastern side, a geometrical plan was adopted
(Fig. 9). This was based on two tree-lined circuses,
Lincoln Circus the more northerly, and Newcastle Circus
the larger and more southerly, which were linked by a

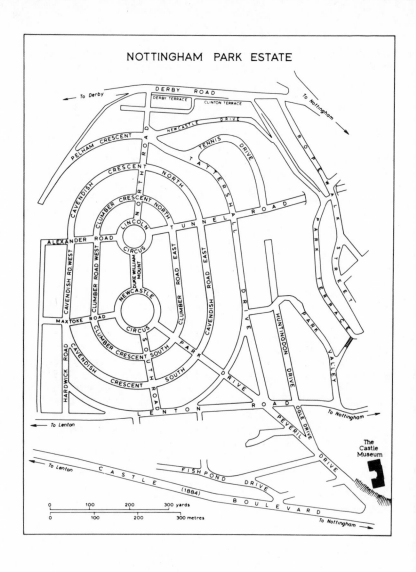

Fig 9   The Park Estate, Nottingham, c 1970.

central axis or avenue, consisting of North Road, Duke
William Mount and South Road running from Derby Road to
Lenton Road. North and South Roads were not strictly
in alignment with the compass points. Around the circuses
ran a series of crescents, these in turn being flanked
by more or less parallel drives. One road, Alexander
Road, which was continued from Lincoln Circus by Tunnel
Road, led from west to east and terminated in a pedestrian
tunnel under the Ropewalk, emerging on Derby Road on the
townward side of the hill now named Canning Circus. The
tunnel was closed in 1962. (14) Similarly Maxtoke Road
led to Newcastle Circus from the west, but from here a
road once called Station Drive (now Park Drive and Peveril
Drive), led directly south-eastward to Lenton Road. It
was to continue to Castle Boulevard as soon as that was
constructed. Within this framework the plots of land,
available leasehold, were of varying size and shape.
The smallest were along Derby Road where the houses were
of terrace type, while the average within The Park proper
were distinctly larger, some being a quarter of an acre
or more and available for greater and more elaborate
villas.

The first house in Hine's geometric plan was built in
1854 and in the years which followed almost 600 were
completed so that, by 1887, the scheme was virtually
brought to a close. (15) Hine himself, together with
his assistant, C.J. Evans, was responsible for designing
many of the earlier houses, especially some of the
larger ones on which he consulted the intending owners.
Before 1850, however, Georgian stuccoed villas with
uninterrupted views over the Trent Valley had been built
along the Ropewalk followed, a little later, by others
slightly lower on the steep slope. The first houses in
Park Valley came in 1853. This first phase of development
is well seen on a map by John Bromley of Derby (1853)
entitled 'An Extra-Parochial Estate comprising Nottingham
Park, the Castle and Precincts etc. etc., the property of
His Grace the Duke of Newcastle'. (16) On the scale of
4 chains to the inch it shows the barracks before they
were demolished and the houses built before the imposition
of Hine's geometrical layout (Fig. 10). These were the
houses in Derby and Clinton Terraces (Derby Road), along
the Ropewalk, in Newcastle Terrace (later Drive), Park
Terrace and Park Valley and a few in Western Terrace.
There were others on the south side of Lenton Road and

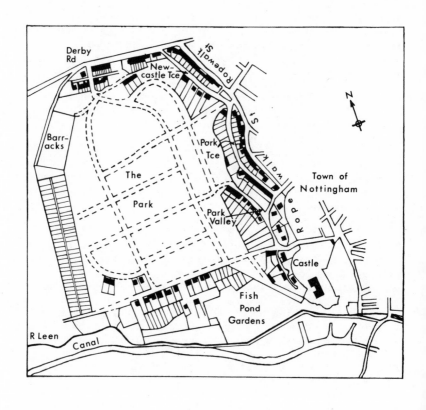

Fig 10   The Park, Nottingham (after J. Bromley, 1853).

four aligned on the curve of what was to become Cavendish Crescent South. Fishponds Gardens are also included in some detail. Thus the eastern parts, the northern extension confronting Derby Road and the beginning of development in the south, were the first to be realised.

Little has been built in the area, except for the present period, since the 1880s and quite a number of vacant plots remain as well as other unfilled land. One of the earliest recreational sites was a bowling green of 1807 near Fishponds Gardens patronised by tradesmen and other local inhabitants, but this has been moved to a site on the western side while another, laid out in 1957, is near the centre of The Park. Next to it are tennis courts, where the annual Nottingham Tournament is held, and more recently a squash court has been added. These recreative facilities now draw their members from outside The Park as well as within; but the subscriptions are nevertheless high.

Being essentially a private speculation, the early history of The Park is somewhat obscure. The project was supported however by W.E. Gladstone, a staunch believer in liberalism and local democracy. In the 1860s he visited Nottingham, understood the conditions, and praised the work of Hine – one of the larger houses, still surviving, was called Gladstone House. Gladstone was one of the trustees of the Duke of Newcastle when he leased Nottingham Castle to the corporation in 1875; Hine restored it so that it was opened three years later as the first municipal museum and art gallery. (17) Locally, the estate was encouraged by William Felkin, author of History of Machine-Wrought Hosiery and Lace Manufacturers (1867), who was a JP and mayor of Nottingham in 1851 and 1852. Felkin was much more than this. He was an agent for the sale of hosiery and lace goods, and for years he collected information about workers' conditions in the local trades, contributed articles to the press, and submitted evidence to House of Commons enquiries and government commissions dealing with social questions. (18) He lived in The Park at Derby House.

Though a few of the houses were of stone, most were of red brick, for this was the period when local brickyards began to be extensively used, their new material coming from the Keuper marls which spread around the eastern portions of the town. They were typically Victorian in style with Gothic and even Tudor detail, and three or four storeys in height. Except for the larger ones they were sited close to each other along the frontage but had

ample garden space at either front or back. Many had
cellars, owing to the ease of excavating the sandstone,
and often the tradesmen's entrance was at the back, a
floor-level below that of the front door. Many also
had shelters for carriages and stables or mews, often
quite elaborately designed. Stained-glass windows in
porches and passages were a typical Victorian detail.
(Fig. 11.)

The Park remained a purely residential area. There was
not a shop, public house, bank or post-office, and the
situation is the same today. Neither was there, nor is
there today, a single commercial advertisement, only the
tree-lined roads. There were no schools. The Boys High
School, an ancient foundation moved from the old town
to its present site in 1867, was not far away and, in
1875, a Girls High School was started nearby under the
auspices of the Girls' Public Day School Trust. Later,
at Clinton Terrace on the Derby Road, there was a private
school for girls which was described in 1892 as 'giving
a thoroughly good education for young gentlewomen in a
system which combines all the educational advantages
of a modern high class school with the comforts and
refining influence of a superior home'. (19) Perhaps
surprisingly there was no church. In the hope of making
The Park an independent parish a church was proposed at
Newcastle Circus but, because the large majority of the
residents, many of whom were non-conformists, opposed
the project, it was never built. This is not to say
that the householders were godless, but there were
political issues involved and in any case many people
favoured other forms of worship than that offered by
the Church of England. Moreover the residents were near
existing churches: St Peter's, a medieval parish in which
the area remained even after the demolition of St James's
in 1934; St Nicholas, an ancient foundation; St James's
(1809); St Matthew's (1853); Holy Trinity, Lenton (1842);
Pugin's Roman Catholic Cathedral (1842); the Baptist
Chapel in East Circus Street (1859) and the Congregational
Chapel, Derby Road (1882), were all within little more
than half a mile, and easily reached by horse-drawn
carriage or by walking.

Though the plots in The Park continued to be taken up
until the late 1880s, it was the houses built in the
sixties and seventies which established the tradition of
a new élite in Nottingham. A measure of wealth and with

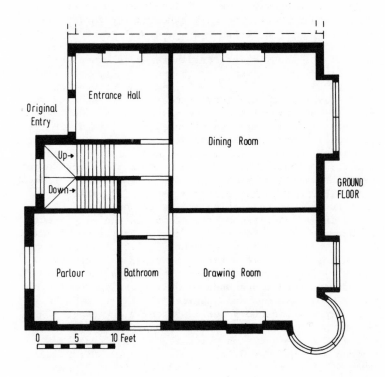

Original
Entry

Entrance Hall

Up→
Down→

Dining Room

GROUND
FLOOR

Parlour

Bathroom

Drawing Room

0   5   10 Feet

Fig 11   12 Cavendish Crescent North, 1885-90 (drawn by
J.R. Young, Department of Geography, University
of Nottingham).

it civilised living ensured social recognition and whatever other personal achievements were to be found in
business, the professions, local government or religious
leadership; such people lived in close touch with one
another and within half a mile of the scene of activities
promoted by a growing town. Their location was ideal,
for in many respects The Park repeated the garden-like
city of a previous century in which Low Pavement, Castle
Gate and Houndsgate sheltered the leading inhabitants.
In contrast, the similar residential development at
Mapperley Park Road was 2 miles away. These were the
years of unprecedented economic development when industry
became diversified and many branches of engineering were
added to the expansion of lace and hosiery. The tobacco
business of John Player was founded in 1877 and, in the
same year, Jesse Boot began his career as a pharmaceutical
chemist which led to the establishment of Boot's Cash
Chemists in 1883. Later in the same decade Frank Bowden
began the making of Raleigh cycles in the street of that
name. Thus Nottingham became a centre for varied industries,
the town grew in population and, with the advent of newcomers including persons from abroad (especially France
and Germany, some from the latter country being of Jewish
faith), there were many who came to live in The Park and
in the course of time entered the urban aristocracy.
Many were first-generation business owners who, among
others, embraced the causes of Nottingham's poor in the
aims of philanthropy and justice.

   In Wright's Directory for 1853 nearly 200 names of
persons in The Park are included, among them representatives of those callings which illustrated broadly the
emergence of the new élite. (20) There was Sir Samuel
Johnson, the town clerk, born and bred in Nottingham,
who was a believer in local autonomy and enjoyed an
enviable reputation for integrity; and Edward Goldschmidt,
JP, who was born in Germany, came to Nottingham in 1851,
successfully followed a career in manufacturing silk and
stationery and was mayor four times. Both lived in
Pelham Crescent. Muncaster Howard, a barrister who was
clerk to the Nottingham Board of Guardians, lived in
Newcastle Drive. The Misses Sarah and Hannah Guildford
of Lenton Avenue earned respect and admiration for their
support for the education of women in the locality.
Marriott Ogle Tarbotton, who served the town extremely
well for many years, resided in South Road. In 1860 as

Borough Surveyor, Tarbotton reported the need for a modern
bridge over the Trent but this was delayed until 1870-1.
In the meantime he was engaged on the problems of health
in the growing town, and prepared reports on improved
housing, sewage and drainage long before they were
implemented. After 1877, when Nottingham was at last
enlarged by borough extension, Tarbotton was put in charge
of the gas and water undertaking as well as the sewage
works, while his work as borough engineer and surveyor
fell to his assistant, Arthur Brown, who was also involved
with social and religious problems until the end of the
century. (21) There was also William George Ward, JP,
twice mayor, who in his later years lived in Newcastle
Drive. An astute businessman, he entered the lace trade
and was financially successful. He was chairman of the
School of Art Committee and devoted time and money to
assist in negotiating the lease of the Castle and its
Grounds from the trustees of the Duke of Newcastle to the
corporation. In this Ward was ultimately successful,
his firm giving a large donation. (22) There were a
large number of other influential business folk. Thus in
Lenton Road alone were Robert Hutchinson, a miller;
Henry Lewis, a timber merchant; J.P. Cox, a lace dresser;
Matthew Walker, a bone and linseed crusher; Samuel Parr,
an aerated-water manufacturer; Joseph Wilson, a toy and
fancy goods dealer. (23)

Later, an analysis of members of the borough council
shows the same predominance, as far as aldermen and
senior councillors were concerned, of The Park residents.
For the year 1889-90 the council consisted of 16 aldermen
and 48 councillors. Of the 16 aldermen, 6 lived in The
Park, 4 in the Mapperley district and 6 elsewhere; of the
6 members who lived in The Park, 4 were JPs and 3 had been
mayor. (24) Of the much larger number of councillors
coming from many different districts, though in general
they were of humbler stature, some distinguished ones
were domiciled in The Park. In more recent times Sir
Jesse Boot, the first Lord Trent, the city's greatest
benefactor, lived in the house called St Helier - named
after the Jersey township, near which he later resided.
This house was among the first to be demolished and
rebuilt as self-contained flats. Claremont House in
North Road, once the home of J. Birkin, one of the fore-
most lace-manufacturers, suffered the same fate and
became twelve flats. Clumber Court, the mansion owned

by Sir E. Jardine, lace-maker and engineer, was divided
after his death into four lavish flats in 1950, but was
demolished in the sixties. Mrs Kaplowitch, another
leading lace-manufacturer, well-known in the city and
district, lived in Peveril Towers until she died recently,
while Alderman Sir William Crane, Chairman of the
Corporation Housing Committee, lived in The Park until
he died some years ago.

A comparatively recent description of The Park has been
given by Cecil Roberts in the first book of his autobiography. He was a Nottingham-born novelist of high
repute and recalls the scene and his own boyhood experience
in the early part of the present century:

'From the retaining walls of the Castle one looks
down over the splendid amphitheatre known as The
Park. It is a residential area, enclosed, laid
out by the Duke of Newcastle about 1850. It was
forest land until the middle of last century.
Italian, Regency and Victorian villas are spaced
out over the steep slopes. The concentric planning
in terraces, drives, crescents, circuses, all wooded,
shows the Nash influence. England has no lovelier
residential quarter, secluded, sylvan, yet built
into the heart of the city... In the days of my
youth, this was an exclusive area inhabited by
millionaire industrial tycoons and others. If,
in a shop, you gave a Park address, the bow was a
little lower. In later years, I had a friend,
a rich and gifted eccentric, who had a lease of
one of these ducal houses, fifteen rooms, hall and
garden, for eighty pounds a year. Often his guest,
in a dwelling crammed with art treasures, I looked
down on St. Helier's, built by Jesse Boot, and
across to a high rampart of villas known as The
Ropewalk, where perched the house of 'Festus'
Bailey, the poet, who died there, forgotten, in 1902.
Those late Victorian magnates, many of whom
lived in the stately Park houses, were very much
of a pattern. From humble beginnings they rose
to wealth. They got themselves baronetcies, and
established commercial dynasties, their careers
touched romance. Jesse (for instance) was on the
way up. Thence a peerage, Debrett: residence,
The Park.' (25)

166

Today many of the houses are a hundred years old, more
or less and, although The Park survives as a residential
estate, there have been changes in its organisation and
in those who are domiciled within it. These changes,
brought about by conditions both within The Park and in
the large city in which it is situated, date chiefly from
World War II and particularly to the last twenty years.
As early as 1938 the Newcastle interests in the estate were
acquired by the Nuffield Trust and passed thence to the
University of Oxford, the present owners. Since 1953
residents have been able to convert their property from
leasehold to freehold and over three-quarters of them
have done so. Because many of the houses are too large
for modern families and maintaining domestic staff has
become too expensive, their adaptation to flats, largely
for professional people, has been a logical outcome.
More than a quarter of the older houses have been so treated.
    From the start the roads and sewage have been privately
organised and maintained. The roads, with a total length
of 6½ miles, are in as good a condition as any in the town,
and the sewage system is inspected every three years so
that any irregularities are made known. Sewage falls
into the nearest corporation main of low elevation, which
is in Castle Boulevard. Water, gas and electricity are
obtained from local supplies. There is however a problem
of street illumination in some parts of the estate, for
the lamp-posts are outmoded and do not work since the area
was converted to North Sea gas a year or two ago.
    The Park remains very much as it was and is believed to
be the only surviving private residential estate in the
country, those at Bristol, Bath and Manchester now being
defunct. Privacy is maintained by closing the gates at
all main entrances one day in the year, though there is
no gate leading into it from Castle Boulevard in the south.
Thus, in practice, though the gates are no longer manned
by members of staff working for the manager who lives in
the estate, The Park is formally closed from 8am until 4pm
on a day in December shortly before Christmas. Whether
tenure is freehold or leasehold, roads and sewers are
maintained by the estate, as formalised under the Nottingham
Borough Extension Act of 1877. For the maintenance of
these an annual rent charge of 15 per cent of the general
rates is allowed by the city to The Park ratepayers.
    Among minor conditions householders may not build
additionally unless the cost of labour and materials exceeds

£2,000; they may not keep pigs, fowls, doves or pigeons; they may not expose the drying of clothes or other articles within the sight of neighbours; neither may they utilise their property for functions other than residential. Though over a hundred years old The Park reflects almost ideal planning conditions, although clearly the latter were imposed and did not arise democratically from consensus of opinion. These conditions, which still benefit the inhabitants and the municipality, anticipated modern planning regulations. The estate began as a model of town planning and today it survives as such, the only exception being part of the northern fringe, Derby Road (Derby Terrace, Clinton Terrace) and to some extent the Ropewalk which, adjoining the General Hospital, is traditionally the home of the medical profession and increasingly of the legal profession. In keeping with the Town and Country Planning Act of 1947, the two terraces are likely to become more and more used as offices.

The coming of flats, though these are not inexpensive to run, has markedly changed the personnel living in The Park, as has the disappearance of the old family mansions. Some of the influential citizens remain but as time passes these become fewer. The motor-car carries many of the residents to places of work beyond the city though the latter still claims its share. The staff of Nottingham University, which has grown enormously since it received independent status in 1948, find The Park a convenient residential area. (26) Today twelve professors live within the estate (in pre-war days there were three), to say nothing of other members of the senior staff, and some lecturers from other higher educational institutions.

The location of The Park between two main roads leading into the heart of the town - Derby Road to the north and Castle Boulevard to the south - meant that it was close to bus and tram routes, although public transport has never been allowed in The Park itself, thus reducing pollution. Once again, with the gradual cessation of smoke from factory chimneys in the surrounding area, the estate is now free from another form of pollution, though it lies to the south-west of most of Nottingham's industrial sites and thus has been generally upwind of their smoke.

In 1972 the houses in The Park consisted of the following:

Old houses	288
New houses (built since 1953)	125
Maisonettes (built or converted since 1953)	119
Bungalows (built since 1953)	19
Mews (converted to houses)	6
Flats (about 250 houses)	707

It is estimated that some 3,250 people live in The Park,
the number tending to increase. In a town whose population
has been made secure since the end of World War I by the
corporation's efforts to clear slum areas and to build
council estates, and which at the same time enjoys full
employment, the difference between the inhabitants of
The Park and other districts has lessened. Although many
families of the urban aristocracy have left, greater
general wealth is bringing a new generation in, utilising
the new forms of housing which supersede the old. The
private estate was once described by the late Professor
A.C. Wood as 'a transition from disciplined Georgian to
variegated villadom', to which we should now add a phrase
to take account of the increasing number of flat-dwellers.

Chapter 6

Sheffield

John Nelson Tarn

Samuel and Nathaniel Buck's 'The East Prospect of Sheffield
in the County of York', (1) engraved about 1740, shows a
small country town dominated by its parish church - a
wealthy late medieval fabric, cruciform in plan, with a
fine tower and crocketed spire. The artist must have sat
roughly where are now the great bastions of the modern
Park Hill flats, while at the foot of the hill the River
Sheaf flows through almost open country to join the Don
just out of the picture. The Don itself is on the northern
edge of the town, with a few houses around the two bridges
which cross it, then open country. The Earl of Shrewsbury's
hospital (1673) dominates the foreground, the elegant
classical chapel of St Paul stands in suburban calm near
the southern extremity of the town - its site is now the
Peace Gardens next to the Town Hall - elsewhere the scale
is entirely domestic: a dense huddle of houses sweeps
around the east-facing bank of the Sheaf, past the site
of the castle and round to the north of the town. But
west of the parish church there is little sign of building.
The Manchester road disappears through open country over
the dome of Hallamshire while Broom Hall can be seen in
the middle distance, a country house at the heart of a
large estate which will soon become the first suburban
middle-class development. Some lesser houses are randomly
scattered high up the valley but there are not many of them.
The town is surprisingly small and insignificant, an overgrown medieval market town, quaint, but old-fashioned and
with very few classical public buildings. What is particularly noticeable, however, from this topographical view
of the town, is its setting: the domed hills are much more
clearly marked than now, so too are the deep valleys of
the Sheaf and the Don. The only feature which the Bucks
share with us is the long steady line of moors at Ring-

inglow in the distance. It was this pronounced topography which was to influence the character of the nineteenth-century town more than any single factor after the growth of the steel industry. When the great days of affluence came, with the successful commercial manufacture and marketing of steel, the newly rich envisaged a way of life and style of living which was a fitting response to this great natural challenge. The western suburbs of Sheffield remain, then, unique in urban history.

The Sheffield of the Bucks was nevertheless already an industrial town. Its prosperity in medieval times had been closely related to its geographical position, at the confluence of two rivers. These rivers, or their numerous tributaries, had already in the sixteenth century provided water power to propel the grinding wheels for the rapidly developing cutlery industry which had developed largely through the influence of that great local family, the Shrewsburys. (2) Iron had been smelted with the aid of local timber in and around Sheffield since the twelfth century, now in the sixteenth it became an important local industry, with smelting and forging carried on in the well-wooded valleys near the abundant fast-flowing rivers and streams. Only in the second industrial age did the centre of the heavy steel industry shift downstream, ultimately to settle in the Don Valley, first near the newly built canal, and then beside the new railway. Even then, the cutlery trade remained a remarkably small-scale industry, with the works of the 'little masters' dotted about the town in a way which today seems amazingly inconsequential.

Perhaps its essentially commercial character made Sheffield what it was by mid-eighteenth century. It was not a particularly rich town and was said to be very parochial in its outlook, partly no doubt since it was so isolated geographically. Ralph Gosling's plan of the town made in 1736 - about the time of the Bucks's view and before the major industrial upheavals - shows a pattern of tight streets, narrow alleys and general lack of amenity. Then came the rapid national sequence of industrial changes which heralded the new age: steam engines replaced the wasteful use of water power; crucible steel began to replace iron. In Sheffield, specifically, the process of silver plating copper was discovered and the local resources of coal were exploited, which, in the pre-railway age, helped the economic growth of the town as a centre of smelting and forging considerably. This growing industrial significance of the area was to break down the traditional isolation and bring Sheffield more fully into the national picture. Although some of the squalor and dirt associated with successful heavy industry was to come in later years, and despite the fact that the town was neither rich nor physically attractive at the outset of this period of expansion, the evolution of the steel industry did not bring in its wake the usual housing problems, public health crises or general domestic squalor and deprivation that affected so many northern industrial towns. Ugly as industrial Sheffield may have been, the ugliness was less extensive. Sheffield remained more healthy than most comparable towns; it avoided the iniquities of cellar dwellings, for example, and of mile upon mile of back-to-back housing probably because the major growth period in the steel industry came later than the period of expansion of Leeds, Manchester or Liverpool. (3) Steel was to carry Sheffield on a continuing but never steady wave of prosperity well into the twentieth century. The borough became a city only in 1893 and its Town Hall was not completed until 1897. It was during the mid- and late nineteenth, rather than the eighteenth century, that consolidation of the commercial enterprises took place, and this therefore pinpoints the major period of suburban growth.

But before that period the luxury trade of Sheffield Plate had already given the town its first taste of prosperity and even an international reputation. The silver plating of copper which began in the 1750s and finally gave way to electro-plating in the 1840s, although it was carried on in Sheffield, was not a local speciality. But Sheffield Plate was indirectly responsible for the first sign of gracious domestic building that the town had seen. Paradise Square, north-west of the parish church, was built because of the enterprise of Sheffield's most famous eighteenth-century banking firm, the Broadbents. The first five houses - tentative in the extreme - on what was to become the north side of the square were completed in 1736, and the bolder decision to proceed with the other three sides followed in 1771. So the town possessed its first and only truly classical square, elegant but persistently domestic in scale and uncomfortably sited so that it looks as though it were sliding downhill. Nevertheless a real effort had been made to create a domestic environment similar to that considered desirable in other towns:

172

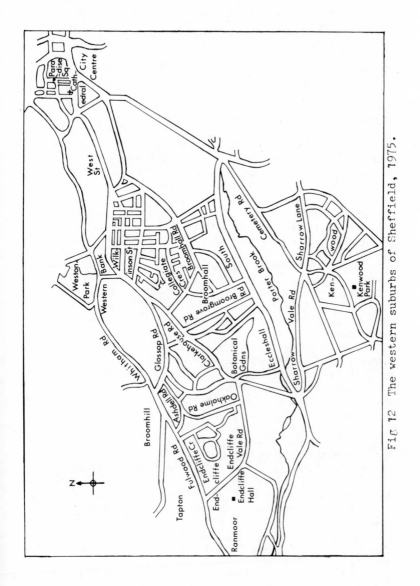

Fig 12 The western suburbs of Sheffield, 1975.

Sheffield was becoming self-conscious. Other interesting
domestic developments followed during the early nineteenth
century, as the town continued to expand, but none had
quite the same degree of gentle classical consistency and
the trend was now for a picturesque setting and more formal
individual building, which successfully prevented the
building of urban squares. The finest pieces of domestic
building were, first, Broomhall Terrace on the edge of
the Broom Hall estate, built about 1830 and, second, The
Mount at Broomhill, built about the same time. Other new
developments were still rather mean and small in scale,
alterations to streets in the town itself were not yet
undertaken with any real conviction that Sheffield was
growing into a great town. Civic buildings were constructed
later than elsewhere and even William Fairbank's layout
between Porter Street and the Porter Brook south of the
town, late in the eighteenth century, for Vincent Eyre,
Steward to the Duke of Norfolk, was already planned as a
mixture of housing and factories, in the way which was
to become so common in the next century. The housing was
in itself attractive, but like so much housing inextricably
mixed up with other developments at this period, it was
doomed to eventual decline.

The modern scale of the town, as we know it, emerged
only in the nineteenth century with the steadily increasing
industrial momentum. If the greatest effect of the
development within the steel industry was not to be
experienced in the town as a whole until the sixties and
seventies, nevertheless the old attitude of insularity
gave way to a feeling of expansiveness and genteel
affluence much earlier than this. Shortly after 1800,
suburban expansion up West Street began, marking a
definite turning of the tide in the attitude to upper-
and middle-class housing.

A number of factors helped to end the era of insularity.
Road communications were improved with a whole series of
turnpikes after the road to Chesterfield was built in 1756.
There were regular stage coaches from Sheffield to London
and several other large towns after 1760. Then in 1819
the Sheffield canal was constructed, parallel to the Don,
opening up commercial outlets to the east and boosting
the local coal trade. The railway from Rotherham arrived
in 1838, making it easier and cheaper to bring in raw
materials and take out steel products. The commercial
heart of the town was then drawn downstream to the east,
and the western hinterland, climbing towards Derbyshire,

174

was marked out permanently for residential purposes. How fortunate for this beautiful area that the influence of charcoal and water power were permanently replaced by those of coal and the railway. On the whole it was the long south-facing slopes on either side of the road to Fulwood, falling away to the Porter Brook, and the south-facing slopes at Sharrow that attracted the best developments; the bleaker, higher and north-facing slopes rising to Eccleshall and Crookes were, and still are, noticeably less attractively developed and obviously were less sought after by most people with some choice and money to spend. (4) The nineteenth-century housing developments also showed the first signs in Sheffield of a separation of the classes which was common to all industrial communities. The workers followed the industries, increasingly downtown to Attercliffe and beyond until Sheffield and Rotherham were almost joined together. The curious nature and small scale of the cutlery industry to some extent counterbalanced the pull of the great steel works so there were a number of other industrial areas, some indeed to the west of the town centre. As far west as St George's church there was a distinct belt of mixed industrial and housing development. Many of the little works have still survived and some of the related housing can still be distinguished although much less of it than the industrial buildings. Nevertheless the distinction was made and gradually the character of suburban Sheffield emerged. From Broomhall Place westwards was marked out as the preserve of the masters rather than the men. (5)

There are basically three distinguishable physical patterns of development in the westward expansion. First, the linear patterns of streets which lie parallel to Glossop Road with a neat overlay of connecting roads creating what might be termed a vestigial classical grid. With them can be linked, stylistically, the groups of neat villas which line at intervals the existing roads out of town and share the same rather restrained classical style, sometimes reminiscent of the eighteenth-century Paradise Square but more usually noticeably severe in appearance with Regency and neo-classical detailing which is consciously architectural. Secondly there were the planned estates, with their curved roads and studied designs for villas, at Sharrow and Broomhall. They are picturesque and more purposefully romantic in their effect and clearly suburban in intention. Thirdly there were

the great mansions, some of them older houses, some of
them new, forming the pivot of an estate. Kenwood Park
at Sharrow and Broom Hall itself are the best examples
of houses still standing after their owners had sold
much of the surrounding estate. The new estates took the
form of great houses in new parks for the men of steel
who were no longer either parochial in outlook or pocket;
they established themselves with unparalleled grandeur
and for a generation or so the palaces at Endcliffe were
the scene of splendid occasions, the great of the world
were entertained, famous and influential people were
received in elegant Italianate drawing-rooms stuffed full
with the finest works of art that money could buy. Outside were vistas across splendid landscaped gardens to
the distant prospect of hills. When great men like John
Brown and Mark Firth died there were no giants of quite
the same order to succeed them. The glory was somewhat
short-lived and of all the houses associated with
Sheffield's suburban development these are now the most
melancholic.
    The three kinds of development were also to some extent
created in that order; furthermore, they represent a
radial expansion, each of the phases a little farther
from the centre of the town. The pattern thus distinguished
seems to have validity from several points of view. It
can be argued that this is in reality the predictable
pattern and timetable for the creation of the suburbs of
any great industrial town. In essence that is probably
true, but few towns managed to evolve so distinguished a
series of housing developments during the last century.
Furthermore, few are so little known and unsung and yet
none have matured so magnificently amidst their landscape,
making so bold a contrast with the industrial town to the
east. To drive along Fulwood Road today despite the
intrusion of great halls of residence for the university,
a towering hotel and several modern, miniature toy-like
houses, is still essentially to journey through a Victorian
suburb or, more accurately, through a Victorian landscape.
The trees are now mature, the larger buildings of the past
hidden discreetly so that you don't know that they are now
a school or a regimental headquarters, a prestige office
block or a Masonic lodge. In the distance the church of
St John, Ranmoor, can be seen, a great severe Gothic
Revival building with its tall spire beneath which, each
Sunday, the steel-men passed to prayer. The whole area

is evocative both of an era and of local history. It is
an interesting commentary upon local ideas and national
taste; it provides fine examples of nearly every aspect
of nineteenth-century housing history. But above all it
is a physical, sensory experience.

The initiation of nearly all the major developments can
all be traced back to the years around 1830. The Broom
Hall estate had belonged to James Wilkinson, Vicar of
Sheffield from 1754 until his death in 1805; he inherited
it from his mother who was a Jessop, the traditional owners
of the estate. (6) When he died it was bought by John
Watson, clearly with the intention of developing. The
first Endcliffe Hall was built on land purchased from the
Broom Hall estate. Then in 1829 Watson began to lease off
land immediately around the Hall itself. The estate which
he now created stretched from Eccleshall New Road (now
Eccleshall Road South) nearly to Clarkehouse Road, and
from the edge of the industrial and residential development which stopped just behind Broomhall Terrace to the
Broom Grove estate which was a thin wedge of land between
the Hall and the Botanical Gardens site. The 'Botanical
and Horticultural Gardens' were laid out in 1835-6 on an
18 acre site acquired in 1834, 'being a fertile and gently
broken acclivity, with a southern aspect, in a picturesque
vale of the river Porter, opposite the verdant and boldly
rising banks of Sharrow, which are occupied by the General
Cemetery, and many handsome villas'. (7) Exactly the same
might be said for the adjacent Broom Hall site. North-east
of the Broom Hall estate and across to Hanover Street,
which marked the boundary of the more mixed industrial town,
the Fairbank family, who had been the chief surveyors in
the town since the days of William Fairbank in the last
quarter of the eighteenth century, laid out the Spring
Lane estate belonging to Thomas Holly. (8) This consisted
of a considerable portion of land lying south of Wilkinson
Street and actually including the latter's south side.
Wilkinson Street itself lay just behind the main Glossop
Road. The work involved the laying out of several new
streets including New Porter Street, Havelock Street,
Havelock Square and Brunswick Street. As at Broom Hall
development went on for a long time, but the character
of each development was established differently and once
set out was adhered to in principle until all the land
was built over. Small plots with quite narrow frontages
and regular building lines were created on the Holly

Estate and although the houses varied from those for the well-to-do in Wilkinson Street to artisans' houses lower down the hill, the character of each was very similar. The Fairbanks's original plan, dated 1828, remained the clear guideline for development until the area was completed much later in the century. Plots were still being sold off in the 1860s. The buildings even in Wilkinson Street are simple and classical, relatively economically built in brick and all quite unpretentious. There were one or two other smaller schemes either executed or mooted at this time. One, dated 1832, for a development of villas further west at Endcliffe, on the south side of Endcliffe Vale Road, was not executed, but it showed the kind of ideas which were then current for a looser approach than on the Holly Estate. (9) The Broom Grove estate between Broom Hall and the Botanic Gardens was auctioned in 1830, leading to the construction of Broom Grove Road linking Clarkehouse Road and Eccleshall Road South. The most delightful of all the early developments was Endcliffe Crescent, acquired and laid out in 1830. (10) There are three plans in the Fairbank collection. The first, of 1830, is a 'Plan of the Land at Endcliffe Terrace belonging to the Building Company as now divided'. (11) It shows the four pairs of houses as built. One of the later plans shows the four pairs of semi-detached houses and nine other building plots, then a plan of 1855 shows allotment gardens against the garden wall of Endcliffe Vale House and a central open space, very much as it remained until quite recently, except for the steady encroachment from the east of the Victorian streets linking the area to Broomhill.

But if the fields between Endcliffe and Broomhill were to be developed fairly rapidly before the end of the century, the rest of the suburbs now familiar as part of modern Sheffield were still undeveloped. White's Directory of 1852 notes that 'many handsome stone houses have been erected during the last ten years'(12) on the Broomhall estate. It comments on the growth of Crookesmoor to the north, and elsewhere there are:

'many handsome villas and well built streets, which are amongst the best portions of the town and suburbs; especially on and near Glossop Road ... Upper Hallam is an extensive, wild and thinly populated township, forming the north western portion of the parish,

bounded on the north by the Rivelin and on the south
by the Porter, and containing 8836 acres, 1499
inhabitants and the scattered hamlets of Carsick
Hill, Crosspool, Fulwood, Nethergreen, Ran Moor,
Sandy Gate, Stephen Hill and Stumperlowe.' (13)

All these hamlets, of course, have been swallowed up in
the suburban expansion since the 1850s, most of the out-
lying parts only this century, but some were engulfed
rapidly in the wave of mansion building which took place
after 1860.

The Ordnance Survey map of 1853 (surveyed in 1851) gives
an interesting summary of building work up to that date
and shows how the future planning of the area was to a
large extent already pre-empted. Urban development, in
the sense of tightly built-up streets, still stopped short
at St George's Square to the north of Glossop Road and
along Gell Street to the south. The elegant brick villas
and disguised semi-villas with their three-storey flat
façades and slightly Grecian detailing which still line
the south side of Glossop Road, west of its junction with
Hanover Street, had been built in the 1820s, the first
attempt to provide Sheffielders with a middle-class
residential suburb on the outskirts of the town. Behind
them, in Wilkinson Street, parallel to Glossop Road, the
first and best stretch of housing, lying between Hanover
Street and Brunswick Street, was already laid out. These
houses exist today, all detached, but closely spaced, set
on the north side well back from the street itself, with
long front gardens facing south and setting off the
houses admirably. They give an open character to Wilkinson Street and when they were built established the
standard for future suburban amenity in that the spaciousness and softness created by their important gardens is
absent from other previous or contemporary classically
composed streets in the town. Most of the houses have
a Regency simplicity about their design, and some have
vestigial parapets. All are three bays wide, modified
later with occasional bay windows and, like those in
Glossop Road, have relatively flat façades with little
surface detail. But here in Wilkinson Street the houses
are only two floors in height, which changes the effective
scale considerably. All but one block of the land to the
south of Wilkinson Street was owned by Thomas Holly.
The Fairbanks parcelled it out for him in 1828 but little

building had taken place by 1851. When it did come it was less ambitious, as it was on the remaining Wilkinson Street sites, perhaps because the kind of people who lived in the area in 1830 were already moving further west to seek a more picturesque setting for their homes by 1850. The rest of Wilkinson Street is, then, more prosaic, with villas masquerading outwardly as detached houses but very often in fact a pair of houses with doors at either end rather than in the middle.

A number of other areas shown on the map as developed by 1851 have remained more or less recognisable until quite recently. On the whole such development followed the line of either Glossop Road or Western Bank, which is higher up the hill. Along Glossop Road near where it is joined by Wilkinson Street, Spring Field Place and Spring Terrace, both facing north, had been built, still using brick, but this time designed as continuous terraces. Their rather formidable appearance is not helped by the use once again of a very severe style. It is instructive to compare them with the much more mellow houses in Paradise Square. Opposite, Northumberland Road and Claremont Place were partly developed, this time with smaller, neater detached villas some in brick, others of stone. Further west there was a series of villas just below the site which would later be used for St Mark's church. Particularly fine and spaciously sited, they exist today facing south with long gardens running down the hill to Glossop Road. Opposite them, facing Glossop Road at its junction with Clarkehouse Road was, and still is, the smaller, less ostentatious, Stanton Broom terrace; which reinforces the theory that the best properties faced south, down the hill, and were so sited as to give them adequate gardens and privacy, while the cheaper properties faced north and were very often, in the 1850s, still built in terraces, although by then the terrace appears to have been largely given up as a favoured housing pattern. The distinction was no doubt primarily a commercial one, but the choice of sites for villas and terraces at this period does show basic justification for distinction in detail design as well as in the broader terms of land use. Western Bank was still dominated by Western Hall, (14) the home of the Misses Harrison, and west of it a little group of properties – Mushroom Hall, Goldthorp Place and Glen View – were wedged in between Mushroom Lane and the new dam. Opposite, on the south side facing north, Mushroom Villas and other

small detached properties stretched eastwards to where
the university now stands. Several of them still remain,
the rest have disappeared only recently to make way for
university expansion. They were a good group of well
designed, two-storey small villas, the later ones in stone,
contrasting well with the earlier brick façades lower
down nearer the town, and quite different in character
from the development on Glossop Road.

There was open country westwards up Whitham Road until
the rather dense little development behind The Mount at
Broomhill. The Mount, still in existence today, was once
a fine neo-classical terrace of houses, facing south,
built in the early 1830s. It masquerades as one building,
a nice conceit, perhaps explaining its construction when
the terrace on the whole seems to have been nearing the
end of its fashionable career. There was little else in
Broomhill except for the two groups of houses at either
end of what became the continuous Broomhill Terrace. If
you went west again along what was called Lower Randmoor
Road you would have passed the entrance lodge to Endcliffe
Crescent and another cottage further west. High up to the
north was Tapton Grove, perhaps the best sited of the
early houses. Then came two very stylish small houses
known as Endcliffe Terrace at the top of Endcliffe Vale
Road. Lower down that road, hidden in richly planted
grounds was the old Endcliffe Hall to the west and Endcliffe Grange and its cottage on the site of the university's
modern Earnshaw Hall to the east. Endcliffe House is now
part of another university hall of residence, Halifax Hall;
Ash Dell House and Oakholm (now part of Crewe Hall) were
isolated houses in virtually open country between Endcliffe
Vale Road and Broomhill. It is still possible to judge
the quality of the area at Oakholm where the house externally,
as well as the grounds and the entrance drive from Clarkehouse
Road are substantially as they appear on the 1851 survey.
The house is particularly severe, in the Barryesque early
Victorian classical style, built in ashlar with ample
proportioned windows and very little fuss; a winding drive
and picturesque miniature park in front of it complete
this civilised private world. Whilst no house is typical
of this group, all are characteristically four-square,
amply proportioned and relatively plain buildings, usually
with two main floors and a dominant roof. In style they
all owe more to the classical movement than to any other,
and nowhere is there the slightest trace of Gothic frills,

neither are there any other Victorian hints in detail or
massing. Much of this area remained little changed,
particularly to either side of Endcliffe Vale Road, for
some considerable time. Endcliffe Vale House was added
to the group of stately homes but has now been replaced
by the tower block of Sorby Hall. Its large stone stable-
block alone survives. Endcliffe Grange, bought by the
Jessops in 1867 and extended by them has disappeared too.
But a great deal of the landscape still remains and the
puny scale of much of the more recent housing does little
to affect the original picturesque park quality. Perhaps
this is one of the unique qualities of this beautiful road.

The gem of the whole area without any doubt is Endcliffe
Crescent - its lodge already mentioned in connection with
Lower Randmoor Road and its planning noted as part of the
wave of expansion around 1830. The site lies under the
lea of the hill and gently slopes down towards the big
houses in Endcliffe Vale Road. A steep approach road
from Lower Randmoor Road leads to a crescent which is
continued full circle around a central open space to meet
up again with the entrance road. Four pairs of rather
grand semi-detached houses were built on the choicest
site with long gardens in front to the south. These pairs
of houses are loosely related to one another echelon
fashion, but they have no firm relationship with the
crescent, indeed it is very difficult to see them, so
rural is the setting. They are all of two storeys,
finished in stucco without any decoration and capped with
slated roofs. Their proportions are generous. Each pair
has a four-bay façade with the entrances swept away to
the side and the whole effect is stately but deceptive,
giving no hint of the massive size of the rooms inside.
Until the construction of Endcliffe Avenue, the estate
remained a secluded oasis, the only piece of organised
development in the area for nearly a generation and, until
the construction of Sorby Hall looming up thirteen storeys,
the view from the houses must have been substantially
unchanged for about 125 years. Even now it is a quiet
retreat, rather like walking into a painting by Atkinson
Grimshaw. Paradoxically the whole concept of the area
is now seen best from the roof of Sorby Hall: from there
the careful siting and the relationship to the landscape,
is clearly visible. They are clearly a group - there is
not too much space between each pair - but care was taken
to achieve maximum sunlight and privacy. Endcliffe Crescent
is scenically perfect: all that is best in nineteenth-

century Sheffield is summed up in this little backwater.

The Broom Hall estate is different in character from either the Wilkinson Street development or that at Endcliffe, both of which adhered fairly closely to classical concepts of design if not always of planning. At Wilkinson Street and Glossop Road the layout of the late 1820s is clearly rectilinear and the houses heavily influenced by Regency and Greek Revival ideas of design, even though prone to provincial idiosyncracies and simplification. Endcliffe Crescent follows the same architectural style although the impact is different because of the dominant landscape which seems almost to have taken control of the physical characteristics of the development. At Broom Hall the layout is more deliberately romantic, the relationship of the houses to each other is less formalised and the houses were built after the strong classical influence upon design had weakened; there is more variety, more modelling of the mass of the house, so that the effect is very different from the earlier developments. Broom Hall Street leads from West Street across to the eastern approach to the old Hall. As already mentioned, the estate ran down to what is now Eccleshall Road South; to the north it was bounded by the gardens of the villas on Clarkehouse Road. The Broom Grove estate lay to its west and the Holly land being parcelled out south of Wilkinson Street came up to part of the north-eastern boundary. The main eastern edge was a continuation of Brunswick Street and here the urban town came abruptly to a halt. Beyond Hanover Street and Hanover Square, as yet not completely built up, were two of the town's rare neo-classical terraces – Sandon Place and Broom Hall Place. The first is routine work, but Broom Hall Place, with its elegant stone façades rising to three storeys and ornamented with Doric porches is outstanding, rivalling The Mount stylistically although less intentionally bombastic and much less sensationally sited. But, alas, it is in part ruinous and nearly entirely unloved. Opposite, a diminutive cottage marks the start of the Broom Hall estate and a complete change of scale. The contrast is dramatic after the formality of the Terraces and a wide well-wooded, street leads past the side of Broom Hall which is probably a late medieval house hidden behind seventeenth- and eighteenth-century façades. The final result is a building which is altogether surprisingly diminutive for so great an estate: a typical example of the Sheffield instinctive desire to underplay

183

its buildings before the Victorian era. Collegiate Crescent was laid out first, describing a great arc from the Eccleshall New Road, past the Collegiate School, which gave it its name, to meet Broomhall Road - the continuation of Broomhall Street within the estate - and then on behind it to join Brunswick Street on the estate's eastern edge. The first leases were granted in about 1829 and by the time of the 1851 survey there had been enough development to establish the character of the estate. Plots along Broomhall Road on either side of the Hall, ie as usual to the north of the road, facing south, were leased first. The same was true in the Crescent, the land between it and the back of Broom Hall and the new adjacent houses was already leased off in quite small plots which pre-empted later development. These, however, were not yet built upon. South of Broomhall Road there was as yet nothing. Victoria Road did not exist and there was little building facing on to Eccleshall New Road, except Collegiate House and Broom Parade - a terrace of six houses - at the Collegiate Crescent entrance to the estate and, at the east end, Clarendon Villas and Broom Mount. Opposite this stretch of road there were gardens leading down to the Porter Brook with its straggle of little industrial developments, then the General Cemetery occupying the north-facing slopes shunned by the living. The latter was laid out in the 1830s with suitable monumental Egyptian and Greek buildings. It is perhaps interesting that this classical and pre-classical architecture is paralleled in the housing of the town and so too is the shift to Gothic: the second Cemetery Chapel was built in 1848, by which time Gothic and Tudor houses were beginning to appear on the Broom Hall estate as they did just beyond the General Cemetery, a few years later, at Kenwood.

The houses already built at Broom Hall by 1851 show a different attitude in their relationship with the street and with each other. The larger ones entirely disregard the street and are set in miniature parks which deny any concept of a building line. It seems to have become the sensible custom to site a house to take the best possible advantage of prospect as well as aspect, and considerable attention seems to have been given to the garden with its sweeping drive and romantic layout. The houses are already more individual in style, more picturesquely detailed, and more distinctively modelled. They are Victorian, in fact; extrovert incidents in a rich masterful landscape. By the

time the next survey was carried out, in 1890, the ring
of villas to the north of Collegiate Crescent was complete.
These - Hillbrow, Belmont, Oakdale, Westbourne and Oak
Lodge - stretching from Oaklands just above the Collegiate
School and which was the only one built in 1851, to Park
Lane, which links the Crescent to Clarkehouse Road, are
the largest, on the finest sites with superb landscapes,
each sporting a Gothic bay or a similar ornamental detail.
Elsewhere the houses were smaller and the gardens less
ambitious although much of the spirit of the earlier work
remained. Victoria Road, on the lower, less scenic part
of the estate was constructed as a kind of response to
Collegiate Crescent. It extends from the eastern end of
Broomhall Road to the bottom (western) end of the Crescent.
The houses built on either side of it were of a different
order and they had to pay more attention to a building
line because they were closer together and more regimented.
Semi-villas dominated although still with an almost wilful
urge to maintain variety of form and avoid the monotony of
sameness. To help in this a number of detached houses
were sprinkled amongst them. Similar houses were built
on the Eccleshall New Road, backing on to Victoria Road,
and linking together the little pieces of earlier
development. One other planning device used on the estate
is worthy of note. At the east end of the Crescent on
the south side, the portion of land which appeared as gardens
in 1851 was developed by 1890 and, to overcome the
excessive depth of plots, two devices were worked out:
firstly, a private drive leading in between the houses
fronting the street to a pair of houses built at the rear
of the site and, secondly, two proper cul-de-sacs, Wilton
Place and Mackenzie Crescent, which contain quite modest
villas and, for this estate at any rate, are quite closely
packed together.

There is one other development in the town which should
be mentioned before this discussion of the Broom Hall
estate is concluded. This is the similar estate laid out
at Sharrow, across the Porter Brook on the southern slope
of the next hill. Kenwood Park estate was acquired by
George Wostenholm, a Sheffield cutler, in 1835. He built
a fine Gothic house for himself complete with a magnificent
rococo Gothic reception-room where great mirrors could be
wound up from the basement to cover the windows on winter
nights. (15) In summer there were views over the lawns
to the miniature lake, the rockeries and the young tree

plantations. The park has now matured and the rest of
the estate, which was laid out in 1853, might as well not
exist; the illusion of a silvan country estate is better
now perhaps than at any time in the past. Outside,
curving tree-lined roads were steadily filled with Victorian
villas which, as at Broom Hall, were slightly Gothic in
flavour with the same sense of the picturesque in part
attributable to the concept of the layout and in part to
the character of the houses.

West of the Broomhall Estate was the much smaller Broom
Grove estate. Broomgrove Road was constructed through it
in a perfectly straight line, between Clarkehouse Road
and the Eccleshall New Road. By 1851 the top part was
already built up with some grander-style houses, particularly the Grecian Broom Grove Lodge on the east side
which still survives in a setting which corresponds with
this early survey. There were smaller villas opposite,
but the later work lower down the hill was decidedly less
ambitious with many more semi-villas in the true Sheffield
Victorian manner. At the top of Broomgrove Road, again
going westwards, were Clark House and Clark Grove, the
Ball in Tree public house and a little group of cottages
around it. Then came the Botanical Gardens laid out on
another stretch of gentle south-sloping land between
Clarkehouse Road and the Eccleshall New Road; the last really
attractive piece of land before the two roads bend together
and join at Hunters Bar. The Gardens were laid out in the
1830s, the first 'amenity' in the area, and their architectural frontispiece, the Gatehouse, is another rather
severe classical essay built in 1836. Shortly afterwards
the pleasing array of greenhouses were added. But the
1851 survey shows little else by way of amenities: the
area was developing entirely as a housing suburb. Only
one other major building had appeared, taking full advantage of a fine site between Glossop Road and Clarkehouse
Road, very near to their junction, just above Broom Hall.
This was the Wesley Proprietary Grammar School, a magnificent and imperial building facing south across the valley,
with a great central portico and minor porticoes, one at
either end, all raised upon a podium. None of the churches
and chapels had yet been built. The traditional Anglicans
no doubt journeyed right down West Street to the parish
church of St James's; possibly they went to the Commissioners'
church, St George's, which was nearer but less genteel.
Their nonconformist friends likewise had to travel to

186

Carver Street or The Moor, Queen Street and Norfolk Street.
The first new Anglican church was St Mark's in Broomhill,
a little way downhill from The Mount. A temporary 'neat
wood and iron structure' (16) was built in 1859 then in
1871 the fine new Gothic Revival church was built. Its
spire alone survived the last war, the church was bombed
and rebuilt, but the tall robust tower with its spire
rising above the trees is in marked contrast to the
earlier Commissioners' churches. This was no mean parish
church, but the place where the new gentry of Sheffield
came to worship. St Silas, Hanover Square, on the edge
of Broom Hall was intended for the working population
to the east and therefore more suitably humble, while
the great church of the steel magnates, St John, Ranmoor,
was built in 1879 largely at the expense of J.N. Mappin,
the Sheffield cutler. Fire nearly completely destroyed
it, leaving only the tower and spire which form the
entrance to the reconstructed church built in 1887-8.
It is sumptuous and confident far beyond any other religious
building in the town, and it reflects the great days when
steel at last came into its own.
The Nonconformists were just as active both around Broom
Hall and across the valley at Sharrow. The Baptists and
the Congregationalists built in Cemetery Road in the late
fifties and near to Broom Hall, in Hanover Street, St
Andrew's Presbyterian Church was built in 1856. The great
United Methodist Free Church's Hanover Chapel lower down
the same street followed four years later in 1860. It
has gone, one of the giant chapels for which Sheffield
was once famous, and which punctuated the suburban streets
with buildings of an altogether different scale. Broom
Park Congregational Church, near the Grammar School in
Newbould Lane, and the Methodist New Connexion Chapel
opposite The Mount in Broomhill were both built in 1863,
the one tentative and Gothic, the other boldly and coldly
Classical. The expensive Wesley Chapel in Fulwood Road,
or Lower Randmoor Road as it was then called, on a plum
site just where Manchester Road comes down to join it,
was complete in 1867, resplendent with tower and spire.
(17) It alone remains but it is not long since all of
these were at least part of the physical fabric of the
area and, with the exception of the New Connexion, still
active for their proper purposes.
The spate of church and chapel building in the 1860s
corresponds with the growth of the steel industry and

with the consolidation of the western suburbs. As early
as the 1851 survey it was clear that the grand scale of
the best villas could not be sustained over large areas,
and nearly all the developments which took place before
the next survey in 1890, show a more middle-class scale
of house usually dominated by semi-villas, or the severe
curtailment of the individual house site. There were
several notable exceptions, especially the mansions west
of Endcliffe Vale Road described later. Elsewhere it
was different. Broom Hall we have already seen was
completed with the construction of Victoria Road and the
gradual development of the Collegiate Crescent sites.
If the houses are smaller, the character of the estate
was still maintained, although the chaste early Grecian
houses near the entrance lodge had long since given way
to the coarser Victorian designs. The only change now
was a gradual move away from the attractive slightly
effervescent Gothic to a plainer more sober version less
easily definable stylistically but characteristically
more flatulent. The same was true in Broomgrove Road
and the new streets Clarkegrove Road, Southgrove Road
and Eastgrove Road, that join it and fill up the remaining
space west of it before the Botanical Gardens.

Between Endcliffe Crescent and Broomhill a great deal of
development had taken place by 1890; semi-villas of a
much meaner sort in Endcliffe Avenue linked the Crescent
to Oakholme Road sweeping up to Ashdell Road and Broomhill.
The street names perpetuated the parks of the great houses
of an earlier generation, while the houses remained, bereft
of their rural setting and surrounding fields. Oakholme
Road, particularly, had some fine houses: the grander sort
of semi-villas were built here, for the sites were still
choice ones and the landscape helped to hold together the
character of the area. In fact it was probably the finest
of the new roads; it is particularly wide, with a generous
sweeping curve in its setting-out leading to the top of a
gently sloping hill. Carysbrook, a villa of the old
tradition sited independently of the road, was one of the
finer houses; the rest are more modest, following the line
of the road more closely and more are semi-detached. The
sort of smaller villa that was fairly typical can be seen
at the junction of Oakholme Road and Endcliffe Vale Road,
sturdy middle-class Victorian houses, amply proportioned
but tending to be plain in appearance. East of the junction
Westbourne Road was built to connect Clarkehouse Road to

Broomhill. Parts of it were not built up until the 1920s and 1930s but the rest has the typical semi-villa kind of development. There was also considerable building north of Clarkehouse Road itself; here Rutland Park was set out, but not as yet entirely developed. It was intended to be a simple crescent, not a park in the Broom Hill spirit. There was no land left in this area now which was not laid out. The nineties, in reality, show the whole area as it has remained in broad planning terms. The street pattern has changed very little, remaining plots have been filled, some buildings both large and small have given way to new blocks of flats and the intensive development of the eastern side of Endcliffe Vale Road for university residential purposes has brought about much new building, but at the same time it has encouraged the preservation of the landscape.

The major innovation of the years between 1851 and 1890 was the expansion westwards and northwards to Ranmoor. The older nucleus of Ran or Rand Moor remains, so too does the earlier building work at Fulwood, and Stumperlowe Hall stands in splendid isolation amidst a sea of inter-war housing, a clear reminder that Derbyshire manor houses were to be found on the outskirts of Sheffield itself. Nor did the population rise dramatically in the area; the 1861 census gives only 1,643 people and 364 houses in Upper Hallam. It might be more accurate to say that its 'wildness' as described by White's Directory in 1852 was cultivated by the gentry. Kelly's Directory in 1865 gives a more silvan view of the suburbs:

'The suburbs of Sheffield are very extensive and
picturesque, and the whole are studded with handsome
mansions, villas, and private residences, surrounded
by scenery far famed for its beauty; the towering
hills and frowning rocks embrace all the romantic
beauties of Wales and Switzerland, whilst the
sloping banks and verdant valleys intersect with
their rivers and tributary streams, give it all
the luxuriance of an Italian clime. There is
scarcely a street in the town from whence the
country cannot be seen, nor an eminance in the
vicinity that does not command a very beautiful
panoramic view of the town and pleasant suburbs.' (18)

Sir John Brown had two years previously completed the

189

rebuilding of Endcliffe Hall, the principal house west
of Endcliffe Vale Road up to this time. Originally part
of the Broom Hall estate, the land had been sold to
William Hodgson in 1818 and on this sublime site extending
to about 50 acres and running down towards Oak Brook he
built his house. Sir John had somewhat grandiose ideas
by Sheffield standards and his architects produced a house
in the Italian style on a new scale, a villa cum palace
as ornate as the homes of the first generation of Sheffield
gentry had been severe, complete with loggia and terraces,
pediment and cartouche. The style was described at the
time as 'Italian treated in the French manner' (19); to us
it is the epitome of High Victorian social and architectural
ideas.

'The house contains, among its many noble apartments,
a grand saloon for pictures and statuary, in which
there is an organ. Sir John has many valuable works
of art, with which the walls of his various rooms
are enriched, and abundant evidence of his sound
judgment and cultured taste are seen on every hand.
The buildings, furniture and decorations were all
designed in Sheffield, and almost entirely executed
by Sheffield workmen.' (20)

Its glory was but short-lived; before the end of the century
the grounds were for sale, now it stands surrounded by a
sea of tarmacadam parade ground, its grandeur depleted
on all sides, its interior empty of the great proud display
of wealth and taste. In one generation the Sheffield
steel-men achieved what had eluded their forefathers for
generations and they broke the barriers of sophisticated
respectability by the brute force of money. But the
illusion of a new landed aristocracy could not be sustained
for long: the cult of the great individual died with the
first generation and the scale of affluence immediately
began to ebb.

Mark Firth built next door across the Oak Brook, calling
his house by that name. The style is similar, the detail
different - doubtless it had to be. A great tower and
porte-cochère answer the loggia, the great stair and the
organ at Endcliffe Hall. Today it is a convent and modern
school buildings and a chapel eddy around the Victorian
shell. Firth was described as:

'the pioneer of Ranmoor', for he was practically
the first to open up this part of the town. At
the time Mr. Firth turned his attention to Ranmoor,
there were none of the many stately mansions
which now adorn the suburbs - the only residence
of any importance being the old Endcliffe Hall,
which Sir John Brown pulled down to erect on its
site the imposing pile which now bears his name.' (21)

Firth entertained the Prince and Princess of Wales at
Oakbrook and with this Sheffield must surely have 'come
out' socially.

Other houses sprang up across the Fulwood Road, around
Ranmoor church and along to Tapton; richly varied in
style, none were so grand as those of Brown and Firth,
not even Birch Lands, the home of J.N. Mappin, the other
great Sheffield name in cutlery and one of the town's
greatest benefactors. The head of Walker & Hall lived
in a sedate house which is now the Ranmoor vicarage.

So the Victorian suburbs were completed. It was
fortunate that the Victorians were able to match a superb
setting with such magnificent building and that the great
days of steel coincided with architectural talents well
able to respond to such a challenge. All that remained
was for the city to complete a new town hall during the
last decade of the century. Then Sheffield had all the
ingredients of a great industrial city; its industry,
its buildings, reflecting civic pride and its suburbs.
Natural factors had made Sheffield a centre of industry
and topographically unique. The Victorians had, at least
as far as the western suburbs were concerned, done the
rest, and the outcome was a most successful marriage of
talents.

Notes and References

Chapter 1

1 Long known as 'The Hotel' and becoming the Royal Clarence after entertaining the Duchess of Clarence in 1827.

2 Alexander Jenkins, <u>Civil</u> <u>and</u> <u>Ecclesiastical</u> <u>History</u> <u>of</u> <u>the</u> <u>City</u> <u>of</u> <u>Exeter</u> (Exeter, 1806), pp 212-13.

3 St Leonard's was absorbed by Exeter in 1877; Heavitree in 1913.

4 G. Oliver, <u>History</u> <u>of</u> <u>the</u> <u>City</u> <u>of</u> <u>Exeter</u> (Exeter, 1861), p 175.

5 Asa Briggs, <u>The</u> <u>Age</u> <u>of</u> <u>Improvement</u> (1964), pp 2-3.

6 D. Defoe, <u>A</u> <u>Tour</u> <u>through</u> <u>the</u> <u>Whole</u> <u>Island</u> <u>of</u> <u>Great</u> <u>Britain</u> 2 vols, ed G.D.H. Cole (London, 1927), I, p 222.

7 W.G. Hoskins, <u>Industry,</u> <u>Trade</u> <u>and</u> <u>People</u> <u>in</u> <u>Exeter,</u> <u>1688-1800</u> (Exeter, 1968), p 39.

8 Ibid pp 18-19.

9 The main areas of residential housing development were in the three wholly or mainly extra-mural parishes: St David, which lapped the city from north to east and south-east; St Sidwell, largely a working-class district, on the east; Holy Trinity from east to south; and also in the two rural parishes of Heavitree and St Leonard not then within the city. St Edmund's parish, on the east bank of the Exe, was also extra-mural, but was not a development area.

10 T. and H. Besley, <u>Exeter</u> <u>Itinerary</u> <u>and</u> <u>General</u> <u>Directory</u> (Exeter, 1828), p 27.

11 <u>Exeter</u> <u>Flying</u> <u>Post</u>, 16.10.1817.

12 W.G. Hoskins (ed), <u>Exeter</u> <u>Militia</u> <u>List</u> <u>1803</u> (Chichester, 1972).

13 Based on the census returns, 1841, <u>Parl</u> <u>Papers</u> <u>1844</u> <u>(587)</u> <u>xxvii</u>.

14 Flying Post, 6.6.1822; for the following two examples,
   ibid, 22.8.1822 and 8.6.1826.
15 Ibid, 14.10.1813.
16 Ibid, 27.7.1826.
17 H.E. Prothero, The Letters of Richard Ford 1797-1858
   (1905), p 135. The Devon and Exeter Institution had
   been founded in 1813 by and for local gentry.
18 H. Besley, Exeter Guide and Itinerary (Exeter, 1836),
   p 31.
19 Exeter Record Office, Diary of Margaret, Lady Paterson
   (MS, 1835).
20 For the occupants of houses, the main sources used are
   Besley's Exeter Directory, 1828, 1831, 1835; the
   Exeter Pocket Journal, 1797-1877; Pigot & Co, Royal
   National and Commercial Directory and Topography
   (1844); W. White, History, Gazetteer and Directory
   of Devonshire (Sheffield, 1850); Smith & Co,
   Devonshire Directory (1866). There is also much
   valuable information contained in the social columns
   and advertisements of the local papers.
21 Flying Post, 21.6.1832.
22 Exeter Record Office, Pearse Box 55/3/1, deed
   relating to certain buildings in Exeter, Thomas
   Dowell and John Gidley, 12.6.1829; Pearse Box 55/3/2,
   disclaimer of trusts by Mr John Dowell of Bristol,
   22.11.1830. For the subsequent history of the house,
   Pearse Box 55/3/3a-b, conveyance of 5 and 7.5.1822
   and 55/3/4 conveyance of 4.4.1842.
23 John Baring (1697-1748) emigrated from Bremen to
   Exeter in 1717. His eldest son, John, became MP for
   Exeter. His second son, Francis (1740-1810) founded
   the powerful financial house of Baring Brothers.
24 Flying Post, 8.10.1829 and 24.12.1846.
25 The Chamber comprised the mayor, eight aldermen and
   fifteen common councillors elected for life. Membership was severely restricted. The proceedings were
   held in secret.
26 G. Kitson Clark, The Critical Historian (1968), p 154.
27 The events of Jane Austen's Persuasion are set in
   1814-15; of Pride and Prejudice in 1811-12.
28 Flying Post, 10.7.1834. The advertisement and the
   social pretensions may not in fact be compatible.
29 The Times, 14.11.1857.
30 W.G. Hoskins, Industry, Trade and People in Exeter
   1688-1800, pp 19, 21.

31 Exeter Record Office, Diary of Margaret, Lady Paterson (MS, 1835); Exeter Probate Office, will 24.12.1870.

32 Flying Post, 17.7.1828; for the following two examples, ibid, 20.10.1830 and 9.9.1830.

33 Flying Post, 4.1.1816; for Stafford Terrace example below, 12.10.1826.

34 The earliest reference to the water-closet is in the Flying Post, 2.6.1780; for the following two examples, ibid, 12.10.1826 and 13.4.1815. I am indebted to Professor Hoskins for this reference.

35 Flying Post, 5.6.1823 and 1.7.1824. The houses were later known as Pennsylvania Terrace and finally as Pennsylvania Park.

36 A.E. Richardson and C. Lovett Gill, Regional Architecture of the West of England (1924), p 37.

37 Flying Post, 2.9.1819.

38 Exeter Record Office, Chamber Minute Book, 24.10.1774 and 23.11.1774.

39 Ibid, 3.12.1792.

40 Ibid, 11.4.1822; for Green and Kingdon examples below, 15.6.1822 and 11.12.1822.

41 Ibid, 21.8.1810.

42 Ibid, 3.1.1815.

43 Ibid, 8.2.1826 and 18.4.1826.

44 Ibid, 23.2.1816.

45 He advertised his Gandy Street house in Flying Post, 6.2.1827. His Southernhay address appears in the directory of 1828.

46 Flying Post, 2.7.1835.

47 Ibid, 2.9.1819.

48 Ibid, 14.7.1825.

49 Ibid, 8.5.1817.

50 Rowe, Cornish and Hooper, Valuation of the Houses and Lands in the City of Exeter (Exeter, 1838). A valuation carried out for the Guardians of the Poor and the Improvement Commissioners. This gives a brief description, situation, owner, occupier, gross and rateable value in respect of all properties in the city.

51 Flying Post, 23.10.1813; Western Luminary, 30.1.1827.

52 Flying Post, 5.7.1821.

53 Thomas Sharp, Exeter Phoenix (Exeter, 1946), p 28.

54 The houses were left as shells and could have been rebuilt as they were before.

55 Devon Record Office, Russell Estates, L 1258, 18th-19th centuries leases (1) Bedford Circus.

56 Ibid (2) building contracts, 1825; (6) (1) draft leases.
57 Flying Post, 26.7.1827.
58 Western Luminary, 30.1.1827.
59 Sharp, op cit, p 38. Barnfield Crescent was originally
   intended as a circus comparable to Bedford Circus.
60 Jenkins, op cit, p 357.
61 Flying Post, 27.5.1830 and 30.6.1825.
62 Flying Post, 7.5.1829; for the reference to Nosworthy,
   ibid, 28.4.1831.
63 Ibid, 1.11.1821.
64 Exeter Valuation 1838, p 10, records Brutton as owner.
65 Flying Post, 21.10.1819.
66 Exeter Record Office, Box 60/5/2, Colleton Estate,
   particulars of sale by auction, August 1827.
67 Exeter Valuation 1838, pp 94, 95.
68 Devon Record Office, Baring Papers, Box 116, indenture
   between John Baring and John Hooper, 7.8.1804.
69 Ibid, Box 113, indenture between John Baring and
   William Hooper, 15.2.1812.
70 Ibid, Box 115, building lease for an intended range
   of buildings to be called Baring Crescent, 9.4.1818.
71 Flying Post, 3.9.1818.
72 There were many Hoopers in Exeter and their relation-
   ships are difficult to establish. William Hooper sr
   (1757-1831) married at Heavitree in 1784 and had five
   children. William Hooper jr, who was in partnership
   with his father, disappears after the dissolution of
   the partnership in 1829. Henry Hooper (1794-1865) was
   his third child.
73 Flying Post, 6.3.1831.
74 Exeter Record Office, indenture of 25.8.1823 between
   Henry Baring, Sir Thomas Baring, William Hooper sr
   and William Hooper jr.
75 Flying Post, 13.10.1825.
76 Exeter Record Office, Box 67/9/1, abstract of title
   to a plot of land formerly parcel of the land ...
   called Larkbeare in the parish of St Leonard's.
   For subsequent transactions Pearse Box 52/2A,
   conveyances, indenture of 3.10.1829, sale to Samuel
   Haydon; Box 52/2B, lease of 5.9.1834 W.N. Nicholson
   to Edward Smalley; Box 52/3A, lease of 1.6.1838,
   W.N. Nicholson to James Bate, refers to Claremont
   Grove.
77 Exeter Record Office, survey of the Manors of Mount
   Radford and Heavitree, 1816; see also Fig 3.

78 Flying Post, 9.10.1828.
79 Ibid, 29.4.1830; 24.3.1831; 16.2.1831; 15.11.1832.
80 Ibid, 16.4.1829.
81 Exeter Record Office, Pearse Box 52/2B, lease of
   5.9.1834, W.N. Nicholson to Edward Smalley and 1.6.1838,
   Nicholson to J. Bate; Box 52/2b, inventory at Villa
   No 1 Claremont Grove, 1838. These houses were built
   on the field originally purchased from the Hoopers
   and known as the Grove.
82 Flying Post, 10.6.1830. For East Cottage below, ibid,
   17.11.1834; 5.7.1835; 29.6.1837. For Park Place below,
   ibid, 9.7.1840.
83 Flying Post, 26.4.1838.
84 Exeter and Plymouth Gazette, 17.7.1868.
85 Western Times, 21.8.1847 and 3.4.1858.
86 Exeter and Plymouth Gazette, 8.2.1851.
87 Exeter Record Office 53/6 Box 95, conveyance by
   Stribling and Painter to Edward Walker, 29.5.1795;
   for J.H. James, Exeter Record Office, 64/8/5/14
   agreement of 23.10.1824 between William Hooper,
   William Hooper the younger and John Haddy James.
88 Exeter Record Office, D7/594/4, King William Terrace,
   abstract of title; D7/596/2, mortgage of 31.5.1834.
89 Flying Post, 23.11.1831.
90 Western Times, 14.7.1868.
91 Sharp, op cit, pp 35-6.

Chapter 2

I would like to thank the following for their help in
this and other studies of Glasgow: Professor S.G.
Checkland, Dept of Economic History, University of
Glasgow, who inspired and directed my work, and his
colleagues, past and present, who gave constant and
critical encouragement; Mr R.F. Dell and the staff of
Glasgow City Archives; Mr J. Fisher and the staff of
the Glasgow Room, Mitchell Library; Drs J. Butt and
J.H. Treble, Dept of History, University of Strathclyde;
and Mr W. Cowie and a legion of friendly Glaswegians.

1 B.R. Mitchell and P. Deane, British Historical Statistics
  (1962), pp 24-7; H. Howells, Bide Me Fair (New York, 1968)
  p 16; W.J. Ecott, Second City (1912), passim.
2 Howells, p 141.

196

3 J. Butt, 'Working Class Housing in Glasgow, 1851-1914' in S.D. Chapman (ed), The History of Working Class Housing: A Symposium (Newton Abbot, 1971), pp 57-92.

4 A. Gomme and D. Walker, Architecture of Glasgow (1968), pp 12, 228-9, 255; A. McLaren Young and A.M. Doak (eds), Glasgow at a Glance (Glasgow, 1965, 2nd ed 1971), Introduction.

5 General Register Office, Census of 1961: Scotland (Edinburgh, 1966), Vol 6, Part 1, xv-xvi.

6 J. Pagan, Sketches of the History of Glasgow (Glasgow, 1847), p 105; S.G. Checkland, 'The British Industrial City as History: The Glasgow Case', Urban Studies, I (1964), p 43.

7 J. Cleland, Statistical Facts Descriptive of the Former and Present State of Glasgow (Glasgow, 1837), p 24; Checkland, p 44; J.F.S. Gordon, Glasghu Facies (Glasgow, 1872), II, pp 1127-8.

8 J.R. Kellett, 'Property Speculators and the Building of Glasgow, 1780-1830', Scottish Journal of Political Economy, VIII (1961), pp 211-32; G. McCrone, Wax Fruit (1947), p 22; G. Eyre-Todd, History of Glasgow (Glasgow, 1934), III, pp 466-7.

9 Kellett, 'Property Speculators', pp 217-20; Checkland, pp 43-5; Cleland, p 12; Eyre-Todd, III, pp 402-8, 461, 474; Pagan, p 184.

10 Kellett, 'Property Speculators', pp 217, 228; McCrone, Wax Fruit, pp 22, 35, 85-6, 126-31.

11 Gomme and Walker, pp 123-52; Checkland, pp 45, 48, 50; Anon, Memoirs and Portraits of One Hundred Glasgow Men (Glasgow, 1886), I, p 101 (Alexander Dennistoun).

12 Glasgow Herald, 2.8.1850 (Viewpark, Uddingston); 16.3. (Bothwell), 23.3. (Uddingston and Gairbraid), 1.6. (Killermont), 1860.

13 Glasgow Herald, 19.7.1830; 2.10.1840 (Kelvinside).

14 Kelvinside Estate Papers (KEP), Chartulary 1, Feu 21 (J. Christie, jr).

15 KEP, Chartulary 1, Feu 41; Chartulary 2, Feus 65, 67, 81; Chartulary 3, Feu 103; Chartulary 4, Feu 134; see also Hillhead Chartulary, Feu Contract, D. and J. Willkie with J. Monteath, 18.10.1844, T-MJ 134, Glasgow City Archives (GCA).

16 Glasgow Herald, 31.1. and 21.2.1870 (advertisements by D. Clow, builder); T.N. George, 'Geology and Geomorphology' in R. Miller and J. Tivy (eds), The Glasgow Region (Glasgow, 1958), pp 18, 20.

17 *Glasgow Herald*, 8.3.1850 (Supplement, 'A Sketch of the Progress of Building in Glasgow'); J. Nicol, *Vital, Social and Economic Statistics of the City of Glasgow, 1885-90* (Glasgow, 1891), pp 52-3.

18 J.J. Bell, *I Remember* (Edinburgh, 1932), pp 27-33; McCrone, *Wax Fruit*, p 158.

19 W. Simpson, *Glasgow in the Forties* (Glasgow, 1899), notes to Plate 43; Gordon, II, p 1141.

20 On the opening of the Yoker Turnpike, see *Papers of the Regality Club* (Glasgow, 1893), II, p 60.

21 Great Western Turnpike Road Trust, *Sederunt Book I*, pp 1-3, F8.3(1), GCA; M.A. Simpson, *Middle Class Housing and the Growth of Suburban Communities in the West End of Glasgow, 1830-1914*, Glasgow University, M.Litt. (1970), pp 230-49.

22 Mathew Montgomerie, quoted by J.R. Kellett, 'Urban and Transport History from Legal Records: An Example from a Glasgow Solicitor's Papers', *Journal of Transport History*, VI (1964), p 233.

23 J.B. Fleming, *Kelvinside* (Glasgow, 1894), p 4; M.A. Simpson, *Middle Class Housing,* etc, pp 249-85; M.A. Simpson, 'Urban Transport and the Development of Glasgow's West End', *Journal of Transport History*, N.S., 1 (1972), pp 146-60.

24 Checkland, p 49.

25 KEP, *Chartulary 1*, Feus 3 (Glasgow Royal Botanical Inst), and 4 (Glasgow Astronomical Inst); Glasgow Corporation, *Minute Book 60* (Parks Cttee), 8.3.1849; *Minute Book 61*, 30.1.1851, 10.2.1851; *Minute Book 68*, 8.1.1891;(GCA); D. McClelland, *Glasgow's Public Parks* (Glasgow, 1894), pp 41-9, 56, 103, 113, 153-5; J. Tweed, *Glasgow Handbook* (Glasgow, 1868), p 43; Howells, pp 5, 32, 69.

26 Tweed, p 41; M.A. Simpson, *Middle Class Housing*, etc, pp 301-11, 315-27.

27 M.A. Simpson, *Middle Class Housing*, etc, pp 294-333.

28 C. Kirkwood, *A Dictionary of Glasgow* (Glasgow, 1884), pp 77, 90; A. Aird, *Glimpses of Old Glasgow* (Glasgow, 1894), pp 96-7; J.H. Dawson, *An Abridged Statistical History of Scotland* (Edinburgh, 1853), p 661; A. Wallace, *A History of Glasgow*, (Glasgow, 1882), pp 184-5.

29 Anon, *The Old Country Houses of the Old Glasgow Gentry* (Glasgow, 1878), pp 143-4, 145-7, 149-50, 195-9; Gordon, II, pp 1129-46; W. Simpson, notes to Plate 41.

30 Glasgow Herald, 19.7.1830 (Kelvinside); 1.3. and
   23.4.1840 (Northpark); 6.3.1840 (North Woodside);
   28.1.1850 (Burnbank).
31 Anon, Old Country Houses, pp 195-9; Gordon, II,
   pp 1136, 1140-2, 1148-9; Glasgow Herald, 18.1.1830
   (Kelvingrove); 26.4.1850 (same); Glasgow Advertiser,
   31.7.1856 (same).
32 Glasgow Herald, 18.1.1830 (South Woodside).
33 Fleming, Kelvinside, pp 8-17; Anon, Memoirs and
   Portraits, I, pp 137-40 (J.P. Fleming), II, p 245
   (J.B. Neilson, FRS); KEP, Chartulary 2, Feu 25, Feu 71;
   KEP, Grand Annuals and Dispositions, Disp 1, Disp 2;
   The Bailie, 14.7.1880 and 11.3.1885 and 28.9.1881;
   Fairplay, 11.7.1884 and 19.9.1884.
34 Glasgow Advertiser, 24.1.1856 (Gilmourhill); Gordon,
   II, pp 1142-6; G. MacGregor, History of Glasgow
   (Glasgow, 1881), p 460.
35 Fleming, Kelvinside, p 4; Glasgow Herald, 18.3.1850
   (Open Letter, D. Bell to Lord Provost); J. Pagan,
   Glasgow Past and Present (Glasgow, 1884), I, xxxiv,
   p 234; McClelland, pp 41-56, 153-5; J.D. Marwick,
   Glasgow: The Water Supply of the City, etc (Glasgow,
   1901), pp 128-57, Appendix Z, p 66; Glasgow Corporation,
   Parks Committee minutes, eg 30.1.1851, 31.8.1854,
   14.5.1857, 27.6.1860, in Corporation Minute Books
   Nos 61-3; 'Proposed Plan of Ground to be Feued
   Immediately Adjoining Kelvingrove Park', (1853),
   T-MJ 494, GCA.
36 Fleming, Kelvinside, pp 1-2, 4, 20; Anon, Old Country
   Houses, pp 149-50; J. Cruickshank, A Sketch of the
   Incorporation of Masons, (Glasgow, 1879), p 317;
   KEP, Chartulary 1, Inventory of Title Deeds;
   Chartulary 2, Feu 56, Feu 57.
37 Glasgow Herald, 15.6.1840 (Montgomerie Fleming-Mowbray
   Howden Joint Stock Bank); A.W. Kerr, The History of
   Banking in Scotland (Glasgow, 1884), passim.
38 Kerr, pp 186-202, 216-7; Edinburgh Courant, 2.10.1878;
   Glasgow Herald, 19.10.1878 and 4.1.1879.
39 Great Western Road, Sederunt Book 1, p 46; Sederunt
   Book 2, pp 136-7, F8.3 (1-2), GCA; Burgh of Hillhead,
   Commissioners' Minute Book 1, 6.12.1870, 9.10.1871,
   14.11.1872; Minute Book 2, 9.8.1881; Minute Book 4,
   13.5.1889, H-HIL 1 (1-2, 4), GCA.
40 KEP, Standard Life Assurance Co Ltd, Bonds 1-10;
   Standard Life Assurance Co Ltd, Lists of Investments,

15.11.1870 and 15.11.1875 which show extensive lending
on landed security, totalling £2-3 millions.

41 E.J. Cleary, The Building Society Movement (1965), p 41
(quoting Royal Commission on Building Societies, 1871)
and conversations with the author.

42 Glasgow Herald, 17.9.1860, 16.12.1870, 4.2.1876,
7.4.1876, 4.1.1878 and 4.10.1878.

43 KEP, Chartulary 2, Feu 57; Kyle and Frew, surveyors,
Tracings, V (Victoria Park steadings, 18.5.1876,
15.5.1877, 14.1.1878), Scottish Business Archives,
Glasgow University; Glasgow Herald, 9.12.1870 and
3.3.1876.

44 For mortgage advertisements, see Glasgow Herald,
5.4.1830, 13.1.1840, 4.2.1850, 17.1.1870, 2.6.1879,
3.12.1900; Glasgow Advertiser, 24.1.1856 and 14.4.1860.
For sources of funds, see Glasgow Herald, 27.8.1830
(Directors of MacLachlan Free School), 13.11.1840
(friendly society), 25.11.1850 (Mr R.D., Helensburgh),
28.9.1860 ('Persons desirous of Borrowing Money on
Heritable Security, may hear of Lenders by addressing
6748, Herald Office'), 2.11.1860 (clothier), 29.7.1870
(W. Grahame, Firhill Foundry), and many others.

45 For Trust Fund advertisements, see Glasgow Herald,
18.1.1830, 29.5.1840, 26.7.1850, 3.2.1860, 1.7.1870,
21.1.1876, 8.3.1878, 3.1.1879, 10.9.1880, 3.10.1890,
2.2.1900, 6.3.1914; Glasgow Property Circular, 1.2.1893,
9.3.1897, and many others.

46 Pagan, Glasgow Past and Present, I, pp xxxvi, liii, liv,
77-80, 85; Anon, Memoirs and Portraits, I, pp 22-3
(John Baird I); Gomme and Walker, pp 87-9, 92; 'Plan of
the Lands of Claremont and South Woodside' (1830),
T-BK 157/11, GCA.

47 Fleming, Kelvinside, pp 1, 8, 17, 19; Anon, Memoirs and
Portraits, I, pp 137-40 (J.P. Fleming); The Bailie,
12.11.1884; Glasgow Herald, 8.3.1850 (Supplement,
'A Sketch of the Progress of Building in Glasgow');
R. Dutton, The English Interior (1948), p 161; 'Plan
of the Lands of Kelvinside and Gartnavel', (1867),
Glasgow Room, Mitchell Library; 'Sketch Feuing Plan
of Part of the Lands of Kelvinside', (1873), T-HB 227,
GCA; Decimus Burton, 'The Lands of Kelvinside and
Gartnavel', (1850), Maps, Vol I, no 46, Hill Collection,
Library of the Royal Faculty of Procurators, Glasgow.

48 Glasgow Herald, 27.5.1870; J.H. Muir, Glasgow in 1901
(Glasgow, 1901), pp 249-50; Gomme and Walker, pp 102, 242.

49 Glasgow Herald, 14.2.1840; 8.3.1850 (Supp); Gildard,
   p 116; G. McCrone, Aunt Bel (1949), p 37; Gomme and
   Walker, pp 89, 102.
50 Gildard, pp 108-9; Gomme and Walker, pp 92-9, 244-50;
   J.M. Reid, Glasgow (1956), pp 103-4. See also Note 35.
51 Glasgow Herald, 25.1.1850.
52 Fleming, Kelvinside, p 4; Great Western Road, Sed. Book
   2, p 46, F8.3 (2), GCA; The Bailie, 12.11.1884.
53 Glasgow Herald, 6.3.1840, 28.1.1850; Glasgow Advertiser,
   3.4.1856.
54 Glasgow Herald, 6.3.1840, 14.1.1850, 28.1.1850, 5.1.1870,
   4.3.1870, 9.9.1870, 1.1.1900; Glasgow Advertiser,
   24.4.1856, 10.7.1856, 22.1.1857, 21.4.1860.
55 Glasgow Herald, 16.1.1880.
56 For Christie, Young, Renwick and the Millers, see KEP,
   Chartularies 1-8.
57 Hillhead and Kelvinside (Annexation to Glasgow) Bill,
   1886, I, p 318, PP-Annex, GCA; Edinburgh Courant,
   8.10.1878; Glasgow Dean of Guild Court, Registers,
   1890-1914, GCA; Butt, pp 74-5.
58 Glasgow Herald, 14.2.1840, 5.4.1850, 31.8.1860,
   4.3.1870, and especially Supplement of 8.3.1850;
   Anon, Memoirs and Portraits, II, p 22 (J. Baird I);
   Glasgow Advertiser, 31.1.1856; Glasgow Boundaries
   Cmn, Report, II, p 71; M.A. Simpson, Middle Class
   Housing, etc, Map 11, 'The Growth of the West End by
   Decades', end pocket; Gomme and Walker, pp 87-102,
   284-98.
59 Kyle and Frew, Registers, No 9, pp 404, 424;
   M.A. Simpson, Middle Class Housing, etc, pp 37-83;
   Burgh of Hillhead, Dean of Guild Court, Lining
   Petitions, H-HIL 14 (4), GCA; Glasgow Boundaries Cmn,
   Report, II, pp 363-5, 782-3, 808-9.
60 Glasgow Herald, 21.1.1850, 27.5.1870, 16.1.1880,
   2.7.1900; Glasgow Property Circular, 1.2.1893.
61 Glasgow Herald, 11.1.1877.
62 Glasgow Herald, 9.7.1830, 27.7.1840, 6.11.1840,
   14.1.1850, 25.3.1850, 5.1.1870, 23.9.1870; Glasgow
   Advertiser, 21.4.1860.
63 Glasgow Herald, 8.3.1850 (Supp); KEP, Chartulary 1,
   Feus 3, 4, 25, 7-20, 21-4; Fleming, Kelvinside, pp 1,
   4, 7-9, 17, 18; Town Clerk on Legal Position of
   Corporation with Regard to Botanic Gardens, June 1890,
   Corporation Reports, C2.1 (4), GCA; Great Western
   Road, Sed. Book 1, pp 164, 221-4, 227; Sed. Book 2,

pp 42, 63-4, 95-6, 258.

64 KEP, Chartulary 2, Feus 25, 57, 70, 71; Grand Annuals and Dispositions, Disp 1, 2; See also note 33.

65 A.K. Cairncross, Home and Foreign Investment, 1870-1913 (1953), p 25; Mitchell and Deane, p 239.

66 Glasgow Herald, 14 and 28.1., 4.2., 22 and 25.3.1850.

67 KEP, Chartulary 2, Feu 71; GPO, Glasgow Post Office Directory (Glasgow, annually from 1826), 1847-1914, maps showing city's growth.

68 KEP, Chartulary 3, pp 97-100; Chartulary 5, pp 149-50; Chartulary 7, pp 199-200; Chartulary 8, pp 249-50; Chartulary 9, pp 300-1, and many other semi-detached pairs.

69 KEP, Chartularies 3-9: Feu contracts indicate sizes and minimum selling prices of all semi-detached pairs.

70 Burgh of Hillhead, Official Lists, 1872-91, H-HIL 15.1; Burgh of Partick, Official Lists, 1878-1911, H-PAR 48; Burgh of Maryhill, Official List, 1883-4, H-PAR 48, GCA; Hillhead and Kelvinside (Annexation to Glasgow) Bill, 1886, II, p 473, PP-Annex, GCA; J. Nicol, Vital Statistics, 1885-90, p 9.

71 Glasgow Herald, 27.4.1914.

72 Glasgow Herald, 5.3.1900, 5.1.1914, 2.2.1914; Glasgow Property Circular, 8.1.1893; Glasgow Property Index, 1900.

73 Glasgow Herald, 5.1.1914 (15 Westbourne Gardens, £750), 2.2.1914 (45 Westbourne Gardens, £850; 3 Bowmont Terrace, £250; 7 Cranbrook Drive, £250; 15 Westbourne Terrace, reduced to £650), 6.3.1914 (45 Westbourne Gardens, reduced to £700; 6 Belmont Crescent, reduced to £700), and others.

74 For prices in Pollokshields and other rival suburbs, see, for example, Glasgow Herald, 4.1.1878, 10.10.1890, 5.1. and 2.2.1900.

75 Burgh of Hillhead, Dean of Guild Court, Plans, H-HIL 14.6, GCA; York (now Novar) Drive plans, Glasgow Corporation, Dean of Guild Court, Plans, GCA.

76 Glasgow Property Circular, 10.1.1893 (19-20 Albion Crescent, £1,550), 5.1.1897 (Arlington Street, £20,190).

77 Glasgow Corporation, Valuation Rolls: Survey Books, 1913-14, for example, No 883.

78 Glasgow Herald, 7.10. and 11.11.1870.

79 Glasgow Herald, 7.10. and 25.11.1870.

80 Glasgow Herald, 4.2. and 7.4.1876.

81 Glasgow Herald, 8.3.1878, 7.2.1879, 5.1.1900.

82 Glasgow Boundaries Commission, Report, II, p 792.
83 Glasgow Herald, 2.2. and 6.3.1914 (Hyndland Road, Falkland Street: 5 rooms, kitchen, maid's room, electric, £46-50 pa; York Drive, 2 rooms, kitchen, electric, £19 19s-£23 pa).
84 Gomme and Walker, pp 11-12, 255; Young and Doak, Introduction; M.A. Simpson, 'Town Building, Town Design and Townscape in Victorian Glasgow', Fieldworker, I, Part 2 (1970), pp 56-61, 78.
85 Gomme and Walker, pp 122 (note 20), 242, 284-98.
86 Gomme and Walker, pp 87-102, 136-43, 191-230; Young and Doak, plates 36-7, 56-7, 69, 71-2, 74, 77, 79.
87 Gomme and Walker, pp 91-9; Fleming, Kelvinside, p 4.
88 Gomme and Walker, pp 91-2; Fleming, Kelvinside, pp 5, 20; McCrone, Wax Fruit, p 134; Young and Doak, plates 56, 59.
89 Glasgow Herald, 16.1.1880 (Dowanhill), 7.5.1900 (Redlands); Gomme and Walker, pp 102, 284-98; Young and Doak, plate 77.
90 Gomme and Walker, pp 123-52; Young and Doak, plates 60-74.
91 Gomme and Walker, pp 160-1; Young and Doak, plate 101.
92 Gomme and Walker, pp 228, 290-1, 297; Young and Doak, plates 151, 161, 165.
93 Details of furnishing in West End houses are taken from roup sale advertisements in the newspapers. See also Bell, pp 110-11; R. Edwards and L.G.G. Ramsay (eds), The Early Victorian Period (1958), passim; V. Wood, Victoriana: A Collector's Guide (1960), passim; Dutton, pp 169-76.
94 Glasgow Herald, 2.4.1860, 16.4.1860, 31.1.1870, 9.1.1880, 1.3.1880, 3.5.1880, 14.4.1890, 23.4.1890; M.A. Simpson, Middle Class Housing, etc, pp 346-52.
95 Glasgow Herald, 14.4.1890, 2.4.1900, 16.4.1900; Bell, pp 196-200.
96 Glasgow Herald, 1.3.1880, 14.5.1860, 14.4.1890; Fleming, Kelvinside, p 9; Bell, p 83; McCrone, Wax Fruit, pp 162-4.
97 P. Floud, 'Furniture', in Edwards and Ramsay, p 40.
98 J.B. Russell, Old Glasgow-Greater Glasgow (Glasgow, 1891), pp 14, 19, 22-6, 38; J.B. Russell (ed A.K. Chalmers), Public Health Administration in Glasgow (Glasgow, 1905), pp 19, 22, 54, 58, 503; A.K. Chalmers, The Health of Glasgow, 1818-1925 (Glasgow, 1930), p 193; Burgh of Hillhead, Medical Officer's Reports, Sanitary Inspector's Reports, 1869-91, Commissioners' General

Papers, H-HIL 15.5, GCA; M.A. Simpson, Middle Class
Housing, etc, pp 195-229.
99 Glasgow Herald, 21.1.1876, 2.1.1878, 3.1.1879,
5.1.1900, 3.1.1914; Burgh of Hillhead, Official Lists,
1890-1, p 21, H-HIL 15.1, GCA; Hillhead and Kelvinside (Annexation to Glasgow) Bill, 1886, II, p 473,
PP-Annex, GCA; Ecott, p 23; McCrone, Aunt Bel, p 1.
100 McCrone, Wax Fruit, pp 144, 162-4, 629; McCrone,
Aunt Bel, p 55; Bell, pp 83-107; Howells, p 21;
Ecott, pp 82, 205-6; F. Niven, The Rich Wife (1932),
passim; A.F. Blood, Kelvinside Days (Glasgow, 1929),
passim; Anon, 'A West End Dinner Party', Jeems Kaye
(Combined ed, Glasgow, ca 1886), pp 21-4.
101 Sir William Burrell's paintings and unique collection
of stained glass are now in the Glasgow City Art
Gallery. On MacFarlane, see Fairplay, 11.7.1884.
102 Hillhead and Kelvinside (Annexation to Glasgow) Bill,
1886, I, pp 257-8, 305-7, 333-4, 399; II, pp 442,
450, 455, 475-6; M.A. Simpson, Middle Class Housing,
etc, pp 145-194.
103 Post Office Directories, 1830-1914.

Chapter 3

1 Hampstead and Highgate Express, house and apartment
advertisements, 8.1.1910 and 7.5.1910; Charles Booth,
Life and Labour in London, 1st ser II (1902), p 424.
2 For the concentric theory of urban structure, see
F. Engels, The Condition of the Working Class in
England in 1844 (1950 ed), pp 45-6, and R.E. Park,
E.W. Burgess and R.D. McKenzie, The City (Chicago,
1925). For the sector theory, see H. Hoyt, The Structure
and Growth of Residential Neighbourhoods in American
Cities (Washington, 1939). The two ideas are combined
in P. Mann, An Approach to Urban Sociology (1965).
3 E. Walford, Old and New London (nd but 1877), V, pp 476-7.
4 Estates Gazette, LXXII, 14.11.1908, p 850.
5 Loc cit.
6 Greater London Record Office, Maryon Wilson Papers,
E/MW/H/III/38/17, House of Commons Committee on the
Marylebone and Hampstead Road Bill, 31.5.1820, evidence
of Peter Potter, p 33.
7 Ibid, petition of Sir T.M. Wilson against the Road Bill,
1820.
8 Ibid, statement of grounds of opposition to the Road

Bill, May 1820.

9 Ibid, resumé of evidence to be given, May 1820.

10 The elder Sir Thomas Maryon Wilson died in 1821, and his son, also Sir Thomas, was lord of the manor and owner (strictly, life-tenant) of the Maryon Wilson estate from then until 1869. For the saga of the Heath see F.M.L. Thompson, Hampstead: Building a Borough, 1650-1964 (1974), chaps 4 and 5.

11 E/MW/H/III/38/15, Statement of grounds for opposing the Road Bill, 1824. Finchley Road, Local and Personal Acts, 13 and 14 Vict c 103; Metropolis Roads Office, Metropolis Turnpike Roads North of the Thames, Accounts, Parl Papers, A & P, 1852, XVIII, p 579.

12 E/MW/H/III/38/15, Case of Sir T.M. Wilson against the Finchley Road Bill, May 1824. Thompson, op cit pp 210-4.

13 Eton College Papers, Eton College, Chalcots Box 1, Proposals for Building, 1.5.1829.

14 Loc cit.

15 Eton College Records, XLIX, No 48, John Shaw to G. Bethell, 23.4.1832, which shows the smallness of the early building applications, one from a plumber-builder and another from a shoemaker-builder; a stream of larger-scale applications began with No 79, Shaw to Bethell, reporting a request to take 10 or 12 plots in one lease.

16 Ibid, XLIX, No 114, Shaw to Bethell, 14.7.1845.

17 Ibid, XLIX, No 111, Agreement with Cuming for a Building Lease, 5.8.1844; No 112, Further Agreement with Cuming, 1.1.1845; No 114, Shaw to Bethell, 14.7.1845, further proposal by Cuming.

18 Ibid, No 114; and Chalcots Box 1, Capt Kelly Nazer, RN of 3 Chalcots Villas, Adelaide Road, to Provost of Eton, 13.12.1847.

19 Most of the original houses in Adelaide Road have now been, or are about to be, either destroyed or redeveloped. Sketch elevations of the houses are drawn on each individual building lease.

20 Private Acts, Upton Estate Act, 14 and 15 Vict c 7, p 197.

21 Under the directions of Greville Howard's will elevations of each house were drawn on each building lease. Bagot Papers, kept at Messrs Eland, Hore & Paterson, Lincoln's Inn Fields, Lease No 1, to John Wallace Duncan (George Duncan's son), 5.6.1856.

22 Bagot Papers, Lease No 183, to John Wallace Duncan,

5.6.1856, of 37 Priory Road, recording an insurance value of £750.

23 Details are in Thompson, op cit pp 91-100.

24 Church Commissioners Records (CC), File 7143, Heads of Proposed Agreement with Palmer, 17.1.1853.

25 Ibid, File 7141, Baxter, Rose & Norton (Davidson's solicitors), to J.J. Chalk, 25.5.1857; H. Davidson to Eccles. Comm. 9.1.1864.

26 Ibid, application by executors of C.H.L. Wood (Davidson's successor) for a 999-year lease, 4.6.1894; Hampstead Vestry Minutes, 28.3.1895, p 129.

27 CC File 7142, Proposals for a Building Lease to William Thomas Buller Lund, 14.11.1851. Dean and Chapter of Westminster Records, Westminster Abbey, Map 12534, the St John's Park estate, 1852. Hampstead Vestry Minutes, 14.3. and 6.6.1856 for early building applications by Richard Batterbury. Metropolitan Board of Works, Minutes, 15.5.1857, application by Batterbury to build with overhanging eaves for his houses in Park (Parkhill) Road; 17.12.1869, application for erection of 3 fever sheds at the Bartrams, Hampstead.

28 CC File 57425, assignments of deeds (on transfers), 1881-99, from which it is possible to extract information on the owner-occupiers, who formed a relatively high proportion - over one quarter - on this estate.

29 Dean and Chapter of Westminster Records, Map 12534.

30 CC File 7143, Plan No 215, Belsize Park estate, 1853. Hampstead and Highgate Directories, 1885-1914. Hampstead and Highgate Express, advertisement by the Lancaster Livery Stables (established 1876), 26.10.1895.

31 CC File 7141, H. Harris to Eccles. Comm. 23.2.1893, setting out his addition of a coachhouse and stables to a house in Rosslyn Terrace.

32 E/MW/H/III/26/54, F.J. Clark to W.W. Knocker, 30.11.1871.

33 E/MW/H/III/26/19, Clark to Bell & Steward, solicitors, 7.5.1872.

34 Ibid, Bell & Steward to Knocker & Wade, 26.2.1872.

35 Eton College Papers, Agreements with W. Willett, 27.7.1881, 18.12.1890, 14.12.1895. Dictionary of National Biography: Twentieth Century, 1912-21, sub Willett, William (1856-1915).

36 For example on the Kilburn Priory estate some of the early building leases, though prohibiting the carrying on of any trade or business, omitted any specification of the type and value of house which was to be erected: Bagot Papers, Lease No 6, 24.8.1824.

37 CC File 38689, Eccles. Comm. to Daniel Smith & Oakley, estate agents and surveyors, 23.5.1893, for the shops. File 33405, T. Matthews (owner of 8, England's Lane) to Eccles. Comm. 18.7.1895; Gush, Phillips, Walters & Williams (French's solicitors) to Eccles. Comm. 14.10. and 2.11.1895; Thomas French to Eccles. Comm. 6.5.1896 - all pleading on behalf of Messrs French & Co, licensed grocers.

38 CC File 7142, Proposals for a Building Lease to W.T.B. Lund, 14.11.1851. In the lease of the Rosslyn Park estate, File 7141, Proposals for a Building Lease to Davidson, 8.3.1853, the corresponding clause prohibited the use of any building 'for any chapel or meeting house or any collegiate or ecclesiastical purpose of persons dissenting from the Church of England'. In practice, however, Nonconformists were allowed a substantial foothold in the district in the shape of the 'Nonconformist cathedral', the Lyndhurst Road Congregational Church.

39 Bagot Papers, Lease No 1, Major General Upton to J.W. Duncan, 5.6.1856.

40 CC File 7141, Proposals for a Building Lease to Davidson, 1853.

41 Price information is scanty for Rosslyn Park, but this figure can be inferred from data on rental values and selling prices in the 1890s, by which time values had fallen somewhat in that district: File 7141, applications of 8.3.1893 and 4.6.1894 for 999-year leases.

42 CC File 38689, Proposals for a Building Agreement, 11.12.1867; assignments of building leases on separate houses, 29.2., 16.3. and 2.10.1876; 15.3., 1.4., 11.5. and 1.9.1877. One purchaser insured his house for £3,500.

43 CC File 33405, Messrs Cluttons to Eccles. Comm. 7.7.1875. William Willett indeed seems, quite simply, to have been trusted to build good and fitting houses, since his building agreements with Eton College do not specify any conditions on house types or values.

44 CC File 33405, Messrs Cluttons to Eccles. Comm. 4.8.1871, reporting on Tidey's bankruptcy and on the existence of many of his houses which had never been let; same to same, 9.6.1884, on demolition of 48 Belsize Park Gardens and replacement by Manor Mansion flats.

45 CC File 7141, Messrs Cluttons to Eccles. Comm.
7.8.1891, 13.8.1895, 23.11.1897, 27.6.1898, all
relating to ladies' schools on Rosslyn Park estate.
46 CC File 38689, Messrs Cluttons to Eccles. Comm.
3.8.1905, reporting an application to use 13 Belsize
Avenue as a boarding house. The owner's solicitors
claimed 'that many houses in the neighbourhood are
used for a similar purpose'.
47 Hampstead and Highgate Express, Jan and May 1895 and
1910.

Chapter 4

1 Nathaniel Hawthorne, The English Notebooks (New York,
1962), p 566.
2 Ibid, p 568.
3 Ibid, p 565.
4 Ibid, p 565.
5 Nathaniel Hawthorne, Our Old Home (London, 1883), p 64.
6 H.B. Granville, The Spas of England and Principal Sea
Bathing Places (London, 1841), II, p 250.
7 Leamington Spa Courier, 3.9.1831.
8 Granville, op cit, p 223.
9 Hawthorne, The English Notebooks, p 121.
10 Warwick Advertiser, 6.1.1810.
11 T.B. Dudley, A Complete History of Royal Leamington
Spa (Leamington, 1896), p 67.
12 Warwick County Record Office (WCRO), DR 514.
13 J. Gibbs, Notes ... on Leamington (1873), p 9.
14 WCRO, CR 1235/3.
15 Leamington Spa Public Library, L 808, Notes of James
Bissett (MSS unpaginated) Books 9, 10.
16 Leamington Spa Courier, 13.6.1848.
17 R. Chaplin, 'The Rise of Leamington Spa', Warwickshire
History, II, 2, winter 1972/3. It is true that the
Duke of Bedford was an early visitor to the town and
that several streets were named after the family.
However, Mr Chaplin does not quote any instance of
Bedford investment or offer any proof of his contention
that the various Russells living in Leamington were
scions of the ducal family.
18 W. Field, History of Warwick, (new ed Wakefield, 1969),
p 78.
19 WCRO, CR 611, Box 54.
20 Parliamentary Papers (1837), XXVIII, p 215.

21 Examined by kind permission of Midland Bank Ltd.
22 T.E. Gregory, The Westminster Bank Through a Century
   (Oxford, 1936), p 248.
23 WCRO, Auction Catalogue, CR 612.
24 The statements about land and houses are based
   chiefly on deeds and abstracts of title deposited in
   Warwick County Record Office. Other material has
   been derived from contemporary newspaper advertisements.
25 WCRO, CR 611, Box 54.
26 WCRO, CR 1247/14.
27 WCRO, CR 1247/11.
28 WCRO, CR 1247/12.
29 WCRO, CR 1247/13.
30 WCRO, CR 1247/23
31 P.F. Robinson, A New Series of Designs for Ornamental
   Cottages and Villas, Design No 1.
32 WCRO, CR 1247/24.
33 WCRO, CR 1247/17.
34 WCRO, CR 1247/2, 3, 4.
35 WCRO, CR 1247/8.
36 WCRO, DR 514.
37 Warwick Advertiser, 24.5.1834.
38 Extracts from the Journals and Correspondence of
   Miss Berry ed T. Lewis (London, 1866)II, p 432.

Chapter 5

The author wishes to express his gratitude to Mr G.E.
Cole, manager and Secretary to The Park Estate,
Nottingham, for his unstinted help in the preparation
of this chapter.

1 R Lawton, 'An Age of Great Cities', Town Planning
  Review, Vol 43, No 3, July 1972.
2 A. Briggs, foreword to H.E. Meller, Nottingham in
  the Eighteen Eighties (Nottingham, 1971).
3 A. Briggs, Victorian Cities (London, 1963).
4 K.C. Edwards, 'The Geographical Development of
  Nottingham', pp 363-80, from Nottingham and its
  Region, ed K.C. Edwards, British Association for
  the Advancement of Science (1966).
5 D. Gray, Nottingham, Settlement to City (Nottingham,
  1953), p 68.
6 S.D. Chapman (ed), The History of Working-Class
  Housing: A Symposium (Newton Abbot, 1971), pp 158-9.

7 J.D. Chambers, <u>Modern Nottingham in the Making</u>
(Nottingham, 1945), p 10.

8 <u>The Nottingham & Derby Railway Companion</u> (1839),
pp 13-14.

9 M.I. Thomas, <u>Old Nottingham</u> (Newton Abbot, 1968),
pp 27-37.

10 A.N. Newman, 'The Evolution of Leicester 1066-1835',
p 283, and R.H. Evans, 'Leicester and Leicestershire
1835-1971', p 291, from <u>Leicester and its Region</u>,
ed N. Pye, British Association for the Advancement
of Science (1972).

11 W.A. Richardson, <u>Citizen's Derby</u> (1949), pp 149, 178.

12 Edwards, op cit, pp 363-80.

13 R. Mellors, <u>Men of Nottingham and Nottinghamshire</u>
(Nottingham, 1924), p 34.

14 During the present century a number of keys were given
to householders which unlocked a doorway at the Derby
Road end of the tunnel. With the closing of the
pathway these keys were surrendered. Further south
another pedestrian outlet led to the Ropewalk.
This consisted of a steep pathway which terminated in
a flight of steps leading up from Park Valley, and
though it reaches the heart of the extended hospital
area, it is still used to a limited extent.

15 N. Pevsner, <u>The Buildings of England: Nottinghamshire</u>
(1951), p 142.

16 An earlier map, dated 1827, was drawn by an architect,
P.F. Robinson, for the fourth Duke of Newcastle to
show how The Park could be laid out. This was also
a geometric plan, giving a rectangular grid with two
ornamental squares, one east and the other west.
The south limit was Lenton Road, which was to be
completed the following year.

17 R. Iliffe and W. Baguley, <u>Victorian Nottingham</u> (1972),
Vol 8, p 56.

18 Mellors, op cit, p 71.

19 H.E. Meller (ed), <u>Nottingham in the Eighteen Eighties</u>
(Nottingham, 1971), p 44.

20 Ibid, p 58. Tarbotton's name is commemorated in Ogle
Drive, an extension of Huntingdon Drive which leads
into Peveril Drive.

21 Ibid, p 54.

22 Mellors, op cit, pp 226-9.

23 Meller, op cit, p 58.

24 Ibid, pp 48-9.

25 Cecil Roberts, The Growing Boy, Being the First Book
   of an Autobiography, 1892-1908 (1967), p 95.
26 The university lies 2 miles south-west of The Park.
   It was founded as a university college in 1881 and
   until 1928 existed in the centre of the town, but
   through the benevolence of Sir Jesse Boot, moved out
   to its present large-scale campus.

Chapter 6

1 The topographical engraving by the Bucks, c 1740;
  Ralph Gosling's plan of 1736, the Ordnance Surveys of
  1853 and 1890, together with various plans of estates
  proposed and executed, chiefly from the Fairbanks
  collection in the City Library, Sheffield, provide
  the main source of planning information for this paper.
  The information is scanty and requires detail knowledge
  of the area now to make it meaningful to the historian.
2 I have drawn upon two works here and in the next few
  pages. For the general background Mary Walton,
  Sheffield: Its Story and Its Achievements (Sheffield,
  4th ed, 1968); and for industrial matters specifically,
  Sidney Pollard, A History of Labour in Sheffield
  (Liverpool, 1959).
3 For the problems of other industrial cities see
  J.N. Tarn, Five Per Cent Philanthropy (1973).
4 My attention was first drawn to the importance of the
  south-facing slopes by John K. Page, Professor of
  Building Science at Sheffield University.
5 The information here is extrapolated from the various
  nineteenth-century directories and the 1853 Ordnance
  Survey.
6 Walton, op cit, pp 136-7.
7 White, West Riding Directory (1837), p 85.
8 There are three relevant plans of the Holly Estate
  in the Fairbanks collection.
9 The plan is in the local collection at the Sheffield
  City Library.
10 This is the area described by Sir John Betjeman in a
   reference which I cannot trace as 'the most beautiful
   suburb in England' - the judgement of a national critic
   rather than one of local civic pride.
11 This also is in the local collection at the Sheffield
   City Library.
12 White, West Riding Directory (1852), p 35.

211

13 Ibid.

14 Subsequently bought by the corporation and made the nucleus of the Western Park Museum (now part of the Mappin Art Gallery).

15 Altered and added to later, it is now a hotel.

16 White, West Riding Directory (1860), p 6.

17 White, West Riding Directory, 1868, considers it worth-while to summarise the church and chapel building to date.

18 Kelly, Directory (1865), p 738.

19 Sheffield Illustrated. Views and portraits which appeared in the Sheffield Weekly Telegraph during the year 1884.

20 Ibid.

21 Sheffield Illustrated. Views and portraits which appeared in the Sheffield Weekly Telegraph during the year 1885.

Index

amenities and services, 13, 23, 24, 27, 31, 32, 39, 40, 44, 49-51, 53, 54, 61, 66, 68, 88-90, 92, 99, 109, 114, 116, 119, 127, 136, 138, 151, 162, 164, 167, 177, 186, 187

architects, 13, 17, 26, 32, 38, 39, 41, 59-63, 66, 77-81, 95, 107, 134-8, 141-3, 145, 151, 157, 159, 161

architectural styles, 12, 13, 24, 29, 31, 33, 34, 36, 40, 41, 43, 46, 60, 77-81, 92, 98, 108, 136, 159, 161, 166, 169, 172, 175, 176, 179, 181, 183-6, 188, 190

Booth, Charles, 87

builders, see developers

building covenants and leases, 25-27, 29, 31, 34-36, 49, 50, 62, 94, 96, 97, 99, 104, 108-111, 134, 139, 167, 168, 184

building industry, 14, 17, 63, 118, 119, 121, 124, 137

building materials, 13, 24, 28, 29, 31-35, 49, 62, 63, 78, 98-9, 157, 161, 178-9, 181-2

building societies, 58, 130

Buck, Nathaniel and Samuel, engravers, 170

climate, 17, 19, 23, 51-2

developers (builders, landowners, speculators), 13, 17, 23-6, 28, 29, 31-6, 38-43, 45, 49-51, 55-67, 71, 76, 79, 86, 90, 92-109, 111, 116, 117, 120, 124-5, 127-44, 149, 154-7, 159, 161, 165-7, 177, 179, 190

domestic servants, 23, 27, 83, 87, 98, 147-9

estate agents and surveyors, 17, 50, 59, 64, 87, 90, 174, 177

Exeter, architects, 17, 26, 32, 38-9, 41; Chamber, the, 20-2, 24-7; developers, 23-6, 28, 29, 31-6, 38-43; estate agents and surveyors, 17; principal locations: Baring Crescent, 26, 35, 36, Baring Place, 23, 34, Barnfield Crescent, 31-2, Bedford Circus, 29, 39, 42, Blackboy Road, 24, Claremont Grove, 36, 38, Colleton Crescent, 28, 33, Heavitree, 12, 14, 19, 20, 23, Heavitree Road, 34, 36, Holloway Street, 33, Howell Road, 41, Longbrook Street, 23, Magdalen Road, 34, 38, Mount Radford House, 19,

34, 36, 38-9, Mount
Radford Gardens, 36, 38,
Mount Radford Terrace,
36, 38-9, Northernhay
Terrace, 26, 32-3,
Pennsylvania Buildings,
24, 26, Queen Street,
40-1, Radford Crescent,
19, 38, St David's, 12,
14, 28, 40-1, St Leonard's,
12, 14, 17, 19, 34, 36,
39, 40, St Leonard's Road,
38, St Sidwell's, 14, 43,
Southernhay, 19, 24-8,
31, 39, 41, Wonford Road,
38

finance, 19, 42, 54, 56-9,
62, 63, 68, 76, 120,
129-32, 139, 144

Glasgow, architects, 59-62,
66, 78-81; developers,
49-51, 55-8, 60-4, 66-7,
71, 76, 79; principal
locations: Argyle Street,
52, Blythswood, 46-8,
54-5, 57, Byres Road, 65,
Charing Cross, 68,
Claremont, 54-6, 59-60,
65, 68, 78, Crown Circus,
65, 79, Dowanhill, 54,
60-1, 63-5, 69, 71, 73,
77, 79, Dumbarton Road,
49, 52, 61, Gilmourhill,
54, 56, Great Western
Road, 49-53, 60, 62-3,
65-6, 68-9, 79, 80, 84,
Great Western Terrace, 80,
Grosvenor Terrace, 79,
Hillhead, 54, 60, 64-6,
68-9, 71, 73, 76-7, 80,
84, Hyndland, 54, 60,
65-6, 77, Hyndland Road,
80, Kelvinside, 47,

49-50, 54, 56-8, 60, 62-7,
69, 71, 73, 77-9, 84, Kew
Terrace, 49, 63, 66, 79,
Kirklee Road, 81, Kirklee
(formerly Windsor) Terrace,
66, 78-9, Maryhill, 65, 67,
71, North Woodside, 54-6,
62, Park Circus, 69, 77,
79, Partick, 49, 60, 61,
71, Partickhill, 60, 61,
65, 69, Pollokshields,
46-7, 74, 80, Sauchiehall
Street, 49, 53, 55, 61, 65,
68, 76, South Woodside,
55-6, 59-60, 65, 68, 78,
Westbourne Terrace, 51,
80, Woodlands Hill, 60-2,
65-6, 79

Gosling, Ralph, writer, 171
Granville, A.B., writer,
116-7

Hampstead, architects, 95,
107; developers, 90, 92-4,
97-9, 101-7, 110; estate
agents and surveyors, 90;
principal locations:
Adelaide Road, 97-9, 108,
Avenue Road, 94, 97, 108,
Belsize estate, 99-101,
105, Belsize Park estate,
104, 110, 112-3, Boundary
Road, 86, 108, Chalcots
estate, 95, 99, 103, 110,
Chalk Farm, 87, Edgware
Road, 86, Finchley, 93,
96, Finchley Road, 86-7,
92-5, 97, 99, 106, Fitz-
john's Avenue, 98, 105-8,
Fleet Road, 100, 102-3,
108, Hampstead Garden
Suburb, 86, Hampstead
Heath, 86, 93-4, 102, 105,
Hampstead Road, 95-6,
Haverstock Hill, 87, 89-90,

96, 100, 109, Kilburn
Priory Estate, 95, 99,
110, Lyndhurst Road, 102,
108, 111, Parliament Hill,
100, 102-3, 108, 110, 113,
Primrose Hill, 96, 108,
Priory Road, 99, 106,
Rosslyn Hill, 87, Rosslyn
Park estate, 102, 104,
107, 110-2, Redington Road,
107-8, St John's Park
estate, 102, 110, St John's
Wood, 90, 93-5, 97, South
End Farm estate, 103,
South Hill Park, 103, 113,
Swiss Cottage, 86, 90,
97-8, 100, 105, Wadham
Gardens, 107-8, West End,
92-3, West End Lane, 89-90
Hawthorne, Nathaniel,
writer, 114-5, 117
hotels, 12, 17, 88, 117-9
houses, interiors and
domestic offices, 19,
22-4, 28-33, 35, 39, 41,
69, 74, 81-3, 103-4, 107-8,
115, 148-50, 161-2;
occupiers of, 12, 19-21,
23, 24, 27-9, 31-6, 39-42,
44-5, 85, 87, 103, 112,
147-50, 156-7, 162, 164-6,
185, 187, 189-91; prices
of, 19, 27, 34, 35, 38,
39, 42, 67-9, 70-1, 73,
99, 108, 111, 139, 144-5,
147-8; rents of, 29, 31,
35, 38, 39, 41, 67-9, 74,
76, 115, 125, 146, 148-51

Jephson, Henry, physician,
141

land prices, 29, 36, 42,
56-7, 68, 105, 119, 127,
129, 133-40, 142, 143

landowners, see developers
landscapes and views, 13,
14, 19, 20, 22, 24, 28, 29,
46, 50-1, 54, 61-2, 81,
92-3, 170, 176-7, 181-2,
184, 186, 188-9, 191
Leamington, architects,
135-8, 141-3, 145, 151;
developers, 125, 127-44,
147, 149; principal locations:
Bath Street, 144, Binswood
Avenue, 144, Beauchamp
Square, 137, 141-2, 152,
Bedford Street (see Frost
Street), Brook Street, 141,
Brunswick Street, 125,
Clarendon Square, 137, 143,
147-8, Clarendon Crescent,
143, Clemens Street, 134,
Cross Street (later Regent
Street), 119, 133, Eastnor
Terrace, 139, Frost Street
(later Bedford Street),
134, Lansdowne Circus, 115,
144, Lansdowne Crescent,
144, Lansdowne Place, 148,
151, Portland Street, 148-
50, Quarry Fields, 127,
135-7, 141, Ranelagh Terrace,
125, Regent Street (see
Frost Street), Union Parade,
119, 125, 129, 133, Victoria
Terrace, 144, York Terrace,
148
local government, 13, 20, 21-2,
24-5, 56, 61, 154-5, 165, 167
lodging houses, 25, 41

Metropolitan Board of Works,
105
Metropolitan Road Commissioners,
94
middle classes, 20-1, 27, 44-5,
87